THE MIST
OF
DRAGON LORE

THÉUN MARES

About the Author

Théun Mares was born in Zimbabwe, of a father who was a gold miner, and a mother who was a natural seer. Raised in the heart of nature, his current training started when he was only five years old. His teacher, a formidable Warrior called the Nagal J, taught Théun that his tradition was not a spiritual practice, but a practical and universal pathway to true knowledge. Thus he learned from an early age that the aim of all true warriors was to become Toltecs, meaning "men and women of knowledge", and that true knowledge was only earned the hard way, through practical experience in life.

Since 1992 Théun has devoted himself full-time to his role as nagal (or leader of warriors), teaching his own apprentices, and carrying out his assignment of committing to writing the true nature and extent of the Toltec tradition through this series of books. Assisting Théun in his task is Marianne, the nagal woman, who is providing the guidance for the necessary balance to emerge between the male and the true female.

Théuns 40-year training has left him a strong optimist. In his view, the current challenges facing humanity provide a wealth of opportunity for men and women who are willing to try, to really take charge of their lives and to achieve an unparalleled measure of freedom and self-determination.

He and Marianne reside in Cape Town, South Africa, where, in addition to writing, he teaches his personal apprentices, as well as finding time to be available to meet with individuals seeking his guidance and running the courses and festivals described at the end of this book.

THE MISTS OF DRAGON LORE

THÉUN MARES

THE TOLTEC TEACHINGS
VOLUME THREE

lionheart
PUBLISHING

ISBN 1 919792 01 5 (Hardcover)
ISBN 1 919792 02 3 (Paperback)

Cover and text illustrations by Tony Butler
Constantia Cottage, Firgrove Way, Constantia,
Cape, South Africa

Printed and bound by
Cape & Transvaal Book Printers, Parow, Cape

lionheart
PUBLISHING
Private Bag X5
Constantia, 7848
Cape Town
Republic of South Africa
e-mail: cajmi@iafrica.com
www.toltec-foundation.org

to all those dedicated to the Path of Freedom,
past, present, and yet to come . . .

OTHER BOOKS BY THÉUN MARES

The Toltec Teachings series
RETURN OF THE WARRIORS
CRY OF THE EAGLE

CONTENTS

LIST OF ILLUSTRATIONS

TABLE OF DIAGRAMS

PREFACE

As a result of feedback received from the readers of the first two books, it is necessary to point out that not all Toltecs are the same, nor is every person who is apprenticed to the Warrior's Path necessarily Toltec. However, considering the fact that Toltecs have been solitary birds for an awfully long time, it is hardly surprising that the world at large knows very little, if anything at all, about us and our activities. In fact, some of those few who have heard of us have more or less come to think of us as nothing more than a myth, whilst some others, that is, those who have come to know about us through the books written by Carlos Castaneda, tend to look upon us as being sorcerers. It is indeed undeniably true that Carlos Castaneda, as well as the other current writers who claim to be associated with the content of the Castaneda books, all portray the Toltec tradition in terms of the practices of sorcery. And yet, the true Toltec is not a man or a woman who indulges in those pursuits of sorcery that are today engendering so much curiosity.

Toltecs are *men and women of knowledge*, and although our knowledge would not be complete if we did not also have a knowledge of sorcery, I must stress that the practices of sorcery form only a tiny fragment of the full extent of our knowledge. Furthermore, true toltecs know that sorcery does not lead people to freedom, but instead leads to their continuing enslavement.

Ever since the destruction of Atlantis the Toltec brotherhood has stood divided into two major groups: one, those who are exclusively dedicated to the empowerment, and consequently the freedom of the individual; and two, those who are only interested in the evolution of awareness for their own selfish gain. The first group are those of us who walk what is known as the Path of Freedom. The second group are those of the brotherhood who walk what is termed the Path of High Adventure. These two groups both consist of various ranks, or degrees of proficiency and skill which, for the sake of convenience, are listed in the Appendix.

Broadly speaking, there are really only two degrees open to those who walk the Path of High Adventure; namely, Warriors of the First Attention and Warriors of the Second Attention. To put this in a nutshell, the First Attention is the full potential of what may be termed rational, or normal awareness – a potential which average men and women have not yet begun to explore fully. The Second Attention, on the other hand, is a level of awareness which is completely irrational and, generally speaking, not even vaguely understood by average men and women, let alone explored. This is a truly vast area of awareness which completely transcends the relatively small and rather limited scope of the rational mind of man.

It is the Second Attention which is the forté of those of our brothers who tread the Path of High Adventure. Upon this path are to be found all those glamorous aspects of the Toltec tradition which do not lead to freedom, and which pertain to what might best be described as phenomena of every description – the weird and the wonderful – sorcery and magic as most understand it. Those Toltecs who have chosen this path have developed their skills solely within the confines of the First and the Second Attention, and it is their proficiency in these two areas of awareness that are termed the *First Ring of Power* and the *Second Ring of Power*, respectively.

However, very few of those who are interested in the ancient practices of the Toltec tradition and who are in some way trying to put these teachings into practice have paused to consider the fact that a little knowledge is invariably a dangerous knowledge. This is especially true in connection with the practices of sorcery, for very few indeed of those who feel drawn to that particular pursuit of knowledge have ever questioned the efficacy of practices which, by their very nature, encourage the practitioner to hand his or her *power* over to some other person or being.

How can any such practice possibly lead to freedom? And yet it is truly amazing to note how many misguided souls still persist in adhering to thoroughly outdated practices, such as, for example, enlisting the aid of inorganic beings, the evocation of energy through the use of ritual and the use of hallucinogenic drugs. Believing that such practices will enhance their *power* or, more precisely, enhance their power *over* their fellow men, these practitioners are wholly unaware that both the *First* and the *Seconds Rings of Power* are not goals in themselves, but are merely necessary stepping stones leading man into the unfoldment of his full potential, namely, the Third Attention, a form of awareness which transcends the Second Attention, and which is not accessible to any other than those trained upon the Path of Freedom.

To try to explain the Third Attention in just a few words is well-nigh impossible, but let it suffice for now to say that the Third Attention is that point in the manifested universe, that level of awareness, where the awareness of both the unmanifest and the manifest is assembled in a mutual and fully intelligent act of co-operation. In this respect it is the ultimate paradox, but a paradox which grants access to the blueprint of the universe, and which is therefore termed the *Third Ring of Power* – a type of *power* that is completely unknown to those trained only in the arts of sorcery.

Whoever has access to the *Third Ring of Power* does not have to resort to the rather petty practices of sorcery, and not even to the glamorous powers offered upon the Path of High Adventure, for such a person quite literally holds within his or her grasp the ultimate keys to both creation and destruction. Clearly, there is no magic higher than this. Consequently a Warrior of the Third Attention does not have to hurl thunderbolts at his enemy, nor is there any need for him to enlist the aid of inorganic beings, for a mere focused thought directed along the hidden paths of human awareness is, generally speaking, all that is needed. It is exactly for this reason that this type of *power* is not available to those who have not yet acquired the necessary all-encompassing vision that is needed so as not to use such *power* for selfish gain.

The task of the Warriors of the Third Attention is to use their *power* for destroying those *forms* which imprison and disempower, and to provide humanity with the necessary knowledge so that each individual can uplift him or herself, and by so doing also uplift all those around him or her, for it must be realised that all of life is thoroughly and completely interrelated, and therefore also interactive and interdependent. Therefore, Warriors of the Third Attention are capable and willing to challenge anyone and anything that stands in the way of the individual being able to claim his or her *power* and consequent freedom.

In relation to the above, realise that if you as the reader are serious in wanting to tread the Warrior's Path, then it is imperative for you to discriminate between the Path of Freedom and the Path of High Adventure. The question that is often asked here is, freedom from what? Once again this is no easy question to answer within the context of a preface such as this, for the implications of freedom are vast indeed. But let it suffice for now to say, freedom from the great many illusions born of man's lack of knowledge, his social conditioning and ignorance of his own divine nature. Apropos this, few people as yet realise that man is not a physical creature confined to the physical plane, but is instead a stupendous being of the universe that has both magic and *power*. Therefore in leading others to freedom, Warriors of the Third Attention work in close collaboration with their presiding nagal in leading people into a realisation of their true potential, and indeed, their true heritage as magical beings of the universe.

I personally am Toltec of the Third Attention, and my official mandate amongst Toltecs is an office that I have filled periodically over many, although not consecutive lifetimes, an office known as the Dragon Wolf. Very briefly, the purpose of the Dragon Wolf is to bring into the world the forces of discrimination so that the light of sobriety may illumine the way forward in the evolution of awareness. Therefore, the work of the Dragon Wolf is to separate light from darkness, to separate that which uplifts from that which suppresses, that which has substance from that which is void of meaning, that which nurtures from that which destroys and, in short, to separate that which leads to freedom from that which leads to bondage and slavery – to separate that which is life-supporting from that which is life-destructive.

However, *power*, peace and freedom cannot be given, nor can they be bestowed. *Power*, and peace and freedom, have to be fought for, and claimed. As a result, the Dragon Wolf is a being that teaches people, firstly, how they are being held in bondage; secondly, that no man can be trapped without his consent; and thirdly, that men and women can claim their *power* by fighting for their freedom. Consequently, in the wake of the Dragon Wolf there is always a wide trail of separation and struggle, but also an equally wide trail of hope, and of renewed courage born of self-respect.

The reason I once again hold the office of the Dragon Wolf in this lifetime is because of the dire need to point out to humanity the huge opportunities for change and freedom that are inherent in the present world situation. In this respect, realise that men and women everywhere are beginning to despair as their old and comfortably-familiar world is continuing to fall apart. The escalating violence and crime in the world in general; the insecure economic situation; the deterioration of ethical standards; the deterioration of relationships in general, but within the family unit in particular; the twisting of truth for selfish gain; the gross manipulation of awareness through the unscrupulous actions of not only the likes of politicians and the news media, but also of self-styled healers, prophets and truthsayers, are all forcing humanity into a desperate corner in which man has his back firmly up against the wall. Finally, no longer knowing whom to trust and who to listen to, men and women everywhere are becoming desperate enough to fight for their freedom.

In fact, there are in the world today a great many men and women who are extremely anxious to flex their psychic muscles and to make their mark upon the world, but what holds them back is their lack of vision, their lack of the much-needed knowledge on what constitutes the true nature of life and the world, and ignorance of their own magical heritage. Add to all of this the debilitating restraints of social conditioning and it is hardly surprising that there are so many frustrated people in the world today – people who would dearly love to bring change into their lives and into the world around them, if only they knew how, and if only they did not feel so powerless.

As far as the Toltecs are concerned, this is a very fine state of affairs indeed, for it is only when man has his back firmly up against the wall that he is ever willing to consider that maybe, just maybe, there is a different way of thinking, of feeling, and of doing things. Only then does man become charged with enough emotion to start fighting for what he himself believes in and what he himself longs for. It is primarily for this reason that the Warriors of Freedom have once again chosen to take their rightful place in the world as Toltecs. Furthermore, we who are dedicated to the Path of Freedom are fully prepared, and indeed ready, to cash in on man's desire for change, his deep wish for peace, his intense search for prosperity, and above all, his growing desire for finding that knowledge which will enable him to claim his *power* as an individual who has the right to think and to act by himself, and for himself. But in order to do so, man will have to face and dismantle his past, which includes fighting to free himself from the disempowering restraints of his social conditioning.

Today there is a great deal of speculation concerning the end of the world and also the coming of the new age. From a Toltec perspective the end of the present known world is inevitable, simply because man has come of age, and therefore instead of continuously building sand castles and then destroying them with childish abandon, man must now take responsibility as an adult and begin to play a really meaningful part within the broader implications inherent within the evolution of awareness, and in this respect also take responsibility for the fact that he is essentially a magical being that has the *power* both to create and to destroy. Once man has taken responsibility for his heritage, then we will indeed see coming into existence a totally new age, and a completely new world – a new age and a new world which is not just going to descend from out of heaven, but a new age based upon man's responsible acceptance of his true role within the universe.

Therefore, as far as the Warriors of Freedom are concerned, realise that unlike our brothers who tread the Path of High Adventure, and who devote their time to the practices of sorcery, we are fully committed to freedom, and in this respect intend to use this time, and the present world situation, to the full advantage of all of life. Therefore our commitment is to the freedom, to the self-empowerment, to the self-respect, and to the well-being of every individual, human and otherwise. It is to this end that I too am playing my part in imparting to humanity its Toltec legacy.

INTRODUCTION

The Great Chief in Washington sends word that he wishes to buy our land. The Great Chief also sends us words of friendship and good will.

This is kind of him, since we know he has little need of our friendship in return. But we will consider your offer. For we know that if we do not sell, the white man may come with guns and take our land.

How can you buy or sell the sky, the warmth of the land? The idea is strange to us. If we do not own the freshness of the air and the sparkle of the water, how can you buy them?

Every part of this earth is sacred to my people. Every shining pine needle, every sandy shore, every mist in the dark woods, every clearing, and humming insect is holy in the memory and experience of my people. The sap which courses through the trees carries the memories of the red man.

The white man's dead forget the country of their birth when they go to walk among the stars. Our dead never forget this beautiful earth, for it is the mother of the red man. We are part of the earth and it is part of us. The perfumed flowers are our sisters; the deer, the horse, the great eagle, these are our brothers. The rocky crests, the juices in the meadows, the body heat of the pony, and man — all belong to the same family.

So, when the Great Chief in Washington sends word that he wishes to buy our land, he asks much of us. The Great Chief sends word he will reserve us a place so that we can live comfortably to ourselves. He will be our father and we will be his children. So we will consider your offer to buy our land. But it will not be easy. For this land is sacred to us.

This shining water that moves in the streams and rivers is not just water but the blood of our ancestors. If we sell you our land, you must remember that it is sacred, and you must teach your children that it is sacred and that each ghostly reflection in the clear water of the lakes tells of events and memories in the life of my people. The water's murmur is the voice of my father's father. The rivers are our brothers, they quench our thirst. The rivers carry our canoes, and feed our children. If we sell you our land, you must remember, and teach your children that the rivers are our brothers, and yours, and you must henceforth give the rivers the kindness you would give any brother.

The red man has always retreated before the advancing white man, as the mist of the mountain

runs before the morning sun. But the ashes of our
fathers are sacred. Their graves are holy ground, and
so these hills, these trees, this portion of the earth is
consecrated to us. We know that the white man does
not understand our ways. One portion of land is
much the same to him as the next, for he is a
stranger who comes in the night and takes from the
land whatever he needs. The earth is not his brother,
but his enemy, and when he has conquered it, he
moves on. He leaves his fathers' graves behind, and
he does not care. He kidnaps the earth from his
children. He does not care. His fathers' graves and his
children's birthright are forgotten. He treats his
mother, the earth, and his brother, the sky as things
to be bought, plundered, sold like sheep or bright
beads. His appetite will devour the earth and leave
behind only a desert.

I do not know. Our ways are different from your ways.
The sight of your cities pains the eyes of the red man.
But perhaps it is because the red man is a savage and
does not understand. There is no quiet place in the
white man's cities. No place to hear the unfurling of
leaves in spring or the rustle of insects' wings. But
perhaps it is because I am a savage and do not
understand. The clatter only seems to insult the ears.
And what is there to life if a man cannot hear the
lonely cry of the whippoo will or the arguments of the
frogs around a pond at night? I am a red man and do
not understand. The Indian prefers the soft sound of

the wind darting over the face of a pond, and the smell of the wind itself, cleansed by a midday rain, or scented with the pinon pine.

The air is precious to the red man, for all things share the same breath – the beast, the tree, the man, they all share the same breath. The white man does not seem to notice the air he breathes. Like a man dying for many days, he is numb to the stench. But if we sell you our land, you must remember that the air is precious to us, that the air shares its spirit with all the life it supports. The wind that gave our grandfather his first breath also receives his last sigh. And the wind must also give our children the spirit of life. And if we sell you our land, you must keep it apart and sacred, as a place where even the white man can go to taste the wind that is sweetened by the meadow's flowers.

So we will consider your offer to buy our land. If we decide to accept, I will make one condition: The white man must treat the beasts of this land as his brothers. I am a savage and I do not understand any other way. I have seen a thousand rotting buffaloes on the prairie, left by the white man who shot them from a passing train. I am a savage and I do not understand how the smoking iron horse can be more important than the buffalo that we kill only to stay alive. What is man without the beasts? If all the beasts were gone, men would die from a great loneliness of spirit. For whatever happens to the beasts, soon happens to man. All things are connected.

You must teach your children that the ground beneath their feet is the ashes of our grandfathers. So that they will respect the land, tell your children that the earth is rich with the lives of our kin. Teach your children what we have taught our children, that the earth is our mother. Whatever befalls the earth, befalls the sons of the earth. If men spit on the ground, they spit upon themselves.

This we know. The earth does not belong to man; man belongs to the earth. This we know. All things are connected like the blood which unites one family. All things are connected. Whatever befalls the earth befalls the sons of the earth. Man did not weave the web of life; he is merely a strand in it. Whatever he does to the web, he does to himself.

But we will consider your offer to go to the reservation you have for my people. We will live apart and in peace. It matters little where we spend the rest of our days. Our children have seen their fathers humbled in defeat. Our warriors have felt shame, and after defeat they turn their days in idleness and contaminate their bodies with sweet foods and strong drink. It matters little where we pass the rest of our days. They are not many. A few more hours, a few more winters, and none of the children of the great tribes that once

loved this earth or that roam now in small bands in
the woods, will be left to mourn the graves of a people
once as powerful and hopeful as yours. But why
should I mourn the passing of my people? Tribes are
made of men, nothing more. Men come and go, like the
waves of the sea.

Even the white man, whose God walks and talks with
him as friend to friend, cannot be exempt from the
common destiny. We may be brothers after all; we
shall see. One thing we know, which the white man
may one day discover – our God is the same God. You
may think now that you own Him as you wish to
own our land; but you cannot. He is the God of man,
and His compassion is equal for the red man and the
white. This earth is precious to Him, and to harm the
earth is to heap contempt on its Creator. The whites
too shall pass; perhaps sooner than all other tribes.
Continue to contaminate your bed, and you will one
night suffocate in your own waste. But in your
perishing you will shine brightly, fired by the
strength of the God who brought you to this land and
for some special purpose gave you dominion over this
land and over the red man.

That destiny is a mystery to us, for we do not
understand when the buffalo are all slaughtered, the
wild horses are tamed, the secret concern of the forest
heavy with the scent of many men, and the view of
the ripe hills blotted by talking wires.

Where is the thicket? Gone. Where is the eagle? Gone.
And what is it to say goodbye to the swift pony and
the hunt? The end of living and the beginning of
survival.

So we will consider your offer to buy our land. If we
agree, it will be to secure the reservation you have
promised. There, perhaps we may live out our brief
days as we wish. When the last red man has vanished
from this earth, and his memory is only the shadow of
a cloud moving across the prairie, these shores and
forests will still hold the spirits of my people. For they
love this earth as the new-born loves its mother's
heartbeat. So if we sell our land, love it as we've loved
it. Care for it as we've cared for it. Hold in your mind
the memory of the land as it is when you take it. And
with all your strength, with all your mind, with all
your heart, preserve it for your children, and love
it.......as God loves us all.

One thing we know. Our God is the same God. This earth
is precious to Him. Even the white man cannot be
exempt from the common destiny. We may be brothers
after all. We shall see.

The speech above was delivered in 1854 by the Red Indian
chief, Seattle. It was not an attempt to reverse the irrevocable,
for Seattle understood full well that it was too late for that.

Instead, Seattle offered this speech as a poignant warning against the dangers of humanity's ignorance and its total disrespect for anything other than its self-centred greed.

However, the deeper motive for quoting this speech here is not just to draw the reader's attention to man's insatiable greed, but to illustrate that where there is a true understanding of the interrelationship of life, there can be no blame, for the simple reason that there are no real victims or victors in this world. Seattle made this very clear in his speech, for he understood and practised the interrelationship of life. Therefore, whilst he neither condoned nor grasped the actions of his conquerors, he did not stand back in self-righteousness to cast judgement upon the white Americans. Instead he repeatedly pointed out that there is but one life and one truth, and that the only cause of separation and division is behaviour. Thus Seattle did not condemn the white Americans, but he did speak up for what it is he and his people stood for, and in doing so made clear to the white Americans that their behaviour is wrong, for it does not take into account the fact that all of life is interrelated.

Seattle knew that he and his people were not victims, even though destiny had decreed a fate other than what he would have preferred. Through this approach he demonstrated the spirit of the impeccable warrior, for although it would have been easy for him to fall into the trap of believing that the red man had been victimised, he chose to acknowledge that his people had lost the battle and, true to the rule of the hunt, the winner takes all. Therefore Seattle accepted the challenges posed by fate with utter impeccability and with all the dignity and grace of the true warrior who believes in the invincibility of his spirit. Seattle's only regret was that some of his warriors apparently did not have that same measure of honour, and so allowed themselves to indulge in a sense of shame and self-pity.

It is also clear from Seattle's speech that he did not see the white Americans as victors, for he knew that their wrong actions had already started to undermine their temporary triumph. Here Seattle again pointed out the importance of behaviour, for unless we are total bigots, none of us can deny that we, and the world we live in, are but the products of our actions. If we are victimised, then it is only because we have become the victims of our own actions, physical, emotional or mental. In this respect, realise that Seattle and his people had merely lost a battle, but in that struggle the white Americans had become the victims of their own sense of superiority, greed and disrespect for life, for although it is true that Seattle and his people had to relinquish everything that was dear to them, it is also true that the white American people have never stopped paying the price for having been the so-called victors. Therefore the real victim on that day was not the red man, but the white man.

NOTHING IN THIS UNIVERSE IS FOR NOTHING; EVERYTHING HAS A PRICE ATTACHED TO IT.

Losing a battle has a price. Winning a battle has a price. It is therefore quite ridiculous to believe that we are being victimised when we are called upon to pay the price for having lost a battle. As has already been pointed out, to the true warrior, who recognises and practises the interrelationship of life, the concept of victor versus victim makes little sense. The only thing that does make sense to the warrior is the fact that we can either act impeccably or unimpeccably. This is the warrior's only concern, and therefore also his only battle.

The warrior sees every battle as a battle to be impeccable, and provided that he always does remain impeccable, he can never possibly be defeated, even if he does lose some of his battles. Therefore the warrior cannot see himself as being victimised by his oppressors, for he understands full well that he can only be victimised if he chooses to believe and to behave as if the actions of his fellow man have the power to make him a victim. But to entertain such a belief, and to indulge in such behaviour, is totally unacceptable to the warrior. Instead the warrior chooses to look upon the actions of his fellow men as being so many opportunities to practise being impeccable.

This is an enormously important point which must be grasped fully if the reader is going to draw any real benefit from what is to follow here. It is true that a great many individuals, as well as whole races of people throughout the ages, have had to suffer all sorts of atrocities inflicted upon them by others. And yet, as we have seen from the example of Seattle and his people, we always have a choice as to where we place the focus. We can place the focus on being a victim; or we can place the focus on the impeccability of the warrior's spirit. However, we cannot learn the way of the warrior if we insist on seeing ourselves as victims, or if we continue to believe that we are powerless in the face of the odds against us. All our challenges in life are there so that we may learn the true value of the priceless gift of life and, in doing so, also learn what it is to take charge of the huge responsibility inherent within knowledge. This is true no matter whether we are the so-called victors or victims. Therefore, if we wish to acquire the impeccability of the warrior's spirit, we cannot afford to take our circumstances in life at face value, but must strive instead to find the *gifts of power* they bring us.

Today, one hundred and forty years after Seattle delivered his moving speech, it appears that not much has changed, or at least, not at face value. Man is still totally self-centred, and his greed is as insatiable as ever before. Driven by this greed man continues to plunder the natural resources of the planet, and continues to exploit his fellow men and creatures with absolutely no regard for the consequences. Yet consequences there are, and not only are these mounting up rapidly, but they are also dire and close to the point of becoming critical. Once a certain critical point has been reached, these consequences will rebound upon man in no uncertain terms, for, as Seattle warned, *"continue to contaminate your bed, and you will one night suffocate in your own waste"*.

It is simply not possible to keep upsetting the delicate balance of life without having to bear the consequences. This is something every Toltec remembers only too well from the times of Atlantis. In that forgotten era the Atlanteans unbalanced the forces of *nature* to such an extent that natural cataclysms ultimately destroyed Atlantis. Today, modern man is unbalancing the forces of *life* to the extent that major cataclysms within the interrelationship of life are imminent and irrevocable. Man has indeed come a full circle, and therefore what was initiated in the times of Atlantis must and will now be brought to a conclusion.

However, in spite of the face value of the statements above, I am not a prophet of doom. On the contrary, I look upon this time as presenting the most exciting challenge humanity has yet had to face. Had humanity not walked this sad path of self-destruction, and had it not worked itself into this utterly uncompromising corner, the awesome opportunities which are present today would not have come about.

Man's nature is such that he will never veer from his mindset unless his survival is threatened in some way. This human trait is but one of the results of the very necessary development of the rational mind, a development that also led man into the gradual recognition of his godlike potential for both creation and destruction, and the consequent temptation to try his hand at both. And yet, realise that there is not much that can be done about this, for just as a tiny infant falls and hurts itself many times over as it attempts to walk, so too was it necessary for humanity to bring about the many sad events that have culminated in the present world situation. This was the price that had to be paid in order for man to learn to think for himself, and to come to grips with his potential. Thus the crippling of the planet, the terrible devastation of the planet's natural resources, the cruel exploitation of animals, and man's inhumanity to man, are all the results of man's progress upon the path of evolution, as was the destruction wrought by the two world wars.

Although the Guardians of the Race have always had the *power* and the ability to prevent these atrocities, They chose instead not to interfere, but to stand back and allow infant humanity to grow up. In this respect Toltecs have always known that although none of us, including the Guardians of the Race, can ever possibly justify our actions, yet we can also be at peace in the knowledge that this was the only viable course open to us. Although every Toltec knew full well that the consequences of the decision taken by the Guardians would be horrendous, we also knew that the consequences of the alternative would have been far worse. It was quite literally a case of having to choose between the devil and the deep blue sea, and from our own personal experience, we have never doubted the wisdom of the decision taken by the Guardians.

Realise that the evolution of awareness had reached a point at which man was beginning to learn to think for himself and, as a result, was also starting to uncover his true potential. Once this happened, the evolution of awareness was speeded up beyond all expectation, and suddenly both the Guardians and the Toltecs found themselves facing the challenges posed by the implications inherent within man's coming of age. The greatest challenge of all was the question of how best to prepare humanity to take charge of its awesome heritage once the time came for it to do so. Obviously in taking charge of his heritage, man would also have to take charge of the huge responsibility of his innate capacity for both creation and destruction, for this is the essence of his instinctive nature. It was because the Guardians have always fully acknowledged this fact that They knew that They did not really have a viable alternative other than the course They chose.

As terrible as the consequences of this decision were, it must be understood that not even the Guardians of the Race have the ability to change man's instinctive nature. But even if They did possess such powers, the Guardians would still not have considered aspiring to such arrogant interference, or to such a gross infringement of human rights, for each and every one of Them is dedicated to the Path of Freedom. All the Guardians could do in the face of this inevitable outcome of man's evolution was to make the decision to step back and allow evolution to take its natural course.

The wisdom of the decision taken by the Guardians is now very clear to see from the effect it has had upon the evolution of awareness in general. Today, with the world situation being what it is, men and women everywhere are beginning to question everything which they had previously taken at face value, or else had just accepted without question. Slowly but surely the average man and woman are starting to wake up to the fact that man has been avoiding taking responsibility for his life, and in this has always been far too happy to hand his power over to some Big Brother who clearly does not have the interests of the people at heart. In every department of human endeavour corruption has become so common that people have begun to look upon it as being normal. The political systems of this world are quite infamous for the gross abuse of power and finances which do not belong to them. The judicial systems of the world have long ago already abandoned all sense of true justice in their over-inflated sense of self-importance and supreme power. The educational authorities today are more concerned with the reputations of their schools and teachers than with the true education and well-being of pupils. Religious leaders too, have a great deal to answer for in pushing interpretations and philosophies that seem to infer that all people are naturally born idiots. Even in the departments of science and medicine there are far too many practitioners who have allowed their sense of ambition to dictate their practices.

In all of this, average men and women are beginning to realise that Big Brother is more of an oppressor than a true guardian. But what, if anything, can be done? The answer to this question is really quite simple and straightforward. We as individuals, as well as the world we live in, are but the products of our actions, and if we are being victimised, then this is only because we have become the victims of our own actions. Therefore, if we do not like what is happening to us, then we must change our actions – something which every man and woman can do very easily.

It is important to realise that although the lone individual may generally speaking seem powerless to change the government or, for that matter, the judicial system of a country, yet even as a lone individual he or she is powerful beyond imagination. The only thing that renders an individual powerless, is his *belief* that he is powerless. What always incapacitates people is that they insist on believing that they are powerless to fight a system which is simply a manifestation of their own actions. As a result, average men and women are all too prone to indulging in a sense of apathy, and by doing so, continue to empower their oppressors. If the individual would stop believing that he is powerless, and instead start taking charge of his life by claiming back his *power*, the world situation today could be changed almost overnight.

Let me use an analogy to clarify this point. Think of the *power* of an individual as being like the flame of a candle. It is very easy to argue that the little flame of a candle is pathetically small when measured against the power of, say, the judicial systems of the world. However, if all individuals in this world who feel that the judicial systems are unfair should stand together, there would be millions upon millions of candles, and the sum total of that combined *power* would be astronomical. But, as we all know, people never do stand together in this way, and therefore they indirectly continue to support the very thing that grieves them the most. Why should this be so? Simply because man thinks, feels and acts in terms of separativeness, and where there is separativeness there can be no unity, no standing together. Thus we see once again that it is the individual's own actions which render him powerless and lay him open to being victimised.

This is a point of enormous implications, especially at this time when humanity as a whole has come of age, because of the individual today having the ability to think for him or herself. This is, of course, thanks to the development of the rational mind, for had it not been for the development of the rational mind, individuals would still not be able to think for themselves. However, now that the individual does have this ability, the separative quality of the mind must be transmuted into discrimination. Realise, though, that true discrimination has nothing at all to do with any of the unjust practices based upon prejudice with which the term has become associated, but is instead the ability of man to distinguish with clarity between different values. What man has hitherto called discrimination is not really discrimination at all, but rather the effects of separativeness.

The transmutation of separativeness into discrimination is vital if humanity is going to be able to handle the challenge of receiving its heritage. Unless man starts to discriminate wisely, so as to sift the real from the unreal, the truth from falsehood, and that which empowers from that which oppresses, man's heritage will without a doubt fall into the hands of Big Brother. If this does happen, the world will see an abuse of *power* and an oppression like never before, for the Toltec teachings are a truly vast and mighty system which, like anything else, can be horrendously twisted to serve evil needs. If man, now that the teachings are being revealed, continues to indulge in his sense of apathy and powerlessness, his own heritage will be used against him as a weapon by the very institutions which are supposed to be his protectors.

Apropos the above, the reader should not be lulled into a false sense of security by thinking that the major institutions of man will scoff at the Toltec teachings as being so much spiritual hocus-pocus. On the contrary, the wise reader will be quick to realise that institutions are made up of individuals – individuals who not only have their own particular belief systems, but also their own ambitions and hidden agendas for which their particular institution merely provides the means to an end. It should also not be forgotten that many an orthodox institution has in the past been guilty of overtly denying any interest in a particular field, but at some later date has had to admit that such denial had only been an attempt to cover for its own secret missions and experimentation in that area.

In all of this, Toltecs will, as much as is within their power to do so, try to ensure that man's heritage does not fall into the wrong hands, and that it will always remain the divine birthright of every man and woman. This we can do by the manner in which the teachings are imparted, but there is a limit to how much we can do. Toltecs cannot be held responsible for man's sense of apathy, and unless the individual is willing to start believing in himself, and is willing to stand up and be counted, there is nothing we can do to force the individual to claim his *power*. Much of what could be done in this respect has already been achieved by man himself when the Guardians of the Race took the momentous decision to step back, so as to allow man to grow up, and in the process to precipitate a world situation which constitutes the proverbial sword dangling overhead.

The stage is set, and the only thing that is required now, is for individuals all over the world to become desperate enough to start believing that they can claim their *power* and to do so. If the individual can rise to this challenge, political, religious and racial barriers will collapse overnight as men and women everywhere start to stand together in the true spirit of democracy to say, "Enough is enough! We are now taking back our *power* and will determine for ourselves the course to be followed in setting up a new world and a new life". This is the crossroad which was mentioned in *Return of the Warriors* – a truly breathtaking opportunity for all men and women to claim their *power*, their freedom, and their divine birthright.

Both the Guardians of the Race and we as Toltecs firmly believe that average men and women are ready to receive their heritage and to claim their *power*. This is the moment the Warriors of Freedom have hoped for, prayed for, and worked for, for as long as any of us can remember, and the Guardians for even longer. This is humanity's *hour of power*, this is the *Cry of the Eagle* – a fleeting moment of chance that man cannot afford to miss.

Toltecs stand ready to play their part in giving any assistance that they are capable of, but my challenge to you as the reader is, are you prepared to take what we are offering you and to use it? Are you prepared to forego a life of bondage and claim your freedom? Are you willing to exchange powerlessness for *power*? Are you willing to be a victor instead of a victim? Are you willing to exchange a life of dull routine for a bright adventure of hope? Are you willing to stand up and be counted instead of being only a number? Are you willing to live instead of merely existing? Are you willing to take charge of your own life, or would you prefer to keep handing your *power* over to someone else? Are you willing to believe in yourself? Are you willing to believe that you as an individual do have the *power* which is your birthright? And above all, are you willing to change your actions, to stop practising separativeness and to join hands with those who strive for the freedom of all?

If you feel that you have what it takes, then stand up and be counted. Stop indulging in feelings of helplessness and apathy. Each and every person has something to offer, no matter how small or little it may be, and at this time of dire need, I can assure you every little bit counts and is of enormous value. In the challenge facing humanity every man and woman is needed, irrespective of talent or ability, and therefore the opportunity for all is also quite obviously unprecedented. In this respect it is not the sky that is the limit, but your belief in yourself.

We are not challenging you to become anti-establishment, or to take up military arms, but we are challenging you to become anti-social-conditioning, and to arm yourself with the sobriety, the courage, and the spirit of the warrior. It is not another world war that is needed, but a world revolution in terms of man's way of thinking and his belief systems. It is not that governments have to be overturned, but rather that people everywhere must claim back their *power*, and stop handing it over to unscrupulous men and women who are only interested in promoting their own personal ambitions in the name of democracy. It is not that the judicial systems of this world have to be crippled, for then we will see anarchy like never before, but what is needed is for men and women to start questioning the horribly outdated legal tenets which are based upon man's social conditioning. We all need to acknowledge and to adhere to universal law, but there is no need for any person be subjected to the gross injustices and humiliation of man-made laws based upon ignorance and prejudice, and most especially not where so-called common law violates the constitution of a country and its bill of human rights. This same yardstick should also be applied to every other department of human endeavour; religious, scientific, educational and medical, for political and judicial practices are but a reflection of all these. It is time for men and women everywhere to stop leaving their lives and their future in the hands of the so-called experts, and to start using their own ability to think and to discriminate for themselves.

All of this is something that is one hundred percent the responsibility of every individual, for only the individual can claim his *power* by himself, for himself. No-one can claim our *power* for us, or on our behalf. If individuals the world over do respond to the opportunity presented by this crossroad, then we will see coming into being what Toltecs refer to as *Dragon Lore*.

Dragon Lore is not at all easy to explain in rational terms, but let it suffice for now to say that Dragon Lore is the product of having initiated that aspect of awareness termed *discrimination*. Dragon Lore starts with *sobriety* but ends in what can only be termed a true expression of man's godlike potential as a magical creature of the universe. Superstition and old wives' tales have led people to believe that magic is acquired through some supernatural process, but this is not true. The magic of man is acquired through an act of sobriety, which ultimately leads to an act of *intent*. Therefore what appears to be magic to the uniniti-ated, is purely an act of *intent*, a potential which is common to every man, woman and child. In this respect, realise that only fools stand in awe to gape at another who is exhibiting this potential. No-one in his right mind would even think of gawking like a village idiot at a professional tennis player, and of whispering non-sensical words like "supernatural". We may well admire and applaud with enthusiasm the skill and the expertise of the tennis player, but to look upon these as being super-natural is just plain ignorance.

Dragon Lore is an expression of the true nature of man. However, just as it takes a great many years of hard training in order to become a really accomplished tennis player, so too does it take many lifetimes of an even harder training to start bringing out our true nature as man. But realise too, that we can only start wherever we are at, and unless we make a start, we will never get there. Therefore, although the true nature of man might at this moment appear to be a vague nebulous "something out there", it is nonetheless the beginning of true man, just as it is also the beginning of a star.

Those great intelligences which periodically manifest by indwelling what we call a star, start their physical existence by using their *intent* to gather around themselves cold and insubstantial gasses. Then by an act of their focused *intent*, an aspect of which is recognised by science as gravity, these beings begin to materialise from out of these gasses the body of what is to become a star. True man, the microcosm of the macrocosm, is in truth a solar being, and therefore, when finally the human being has reached a point in its evolution where its own true inner nature can begin to manifest itself within life upon the dense physical plane, then just like its progenitor, the inner core of the human being begins to focus its *intent*, and starts to gather around itself what are termed the *Mists of Dragon Lore*. This is the beginning of true man, that magical creature which has all the potential and the *power* of a true star.

As has already been mentioned, the stage is set, and men and women on average are ready to commence their careers, no longer as human beings, but as true man, as stars of the universe. The mists have already started to coalesce in response to humanity's *intent*, and in this respect the tide of evolution cannot be stemmed, but just as the birth of a star is a thoroughly unstable and therefore potentially dangerous occurrence, so too does the present moment in the history of humanity mark a crisis point. It is for this reason that discrimination is so vitally important now, for the success of this birth depends entirely upon the individual human being.

In order to grasp the above point fully, it must never be forgotten that there is only one life and one awareness. Every individual is a unit of this one life and this one awareness. In other words, every individual is like a particle of gas. However, one particle of gas cannot become a star, for the simple reason that the mechanics involved in the formation of a star require the interaction between an untold number of particles. This is true also of man, and it is for this reason that the dreamers of mankind are completely *group-conscious*.

True group-consciousness has absolutely nothing to do with any of the moral issues with which most people have come to associate it, but instead it has its basis in intelligent co-operation, based upon the interdependence, the interaction, and therefore the interrelationship of all life. This does not imply that the individual can never become true man in his or her own right, but it does imply that in order to do so the individual must cease being separative and must become group-conscious. Therefore the accent throughout this book will be on the preliminary steps which lead to group-consciousness, the prerequisite for becoming man, and therefore also the prerequisite for all forms of true *magic*.

Having explained this much, I am now in a position to clarify what I really meant when I made the statement that Toltecs will do what they can to ensure that the Toltec teachings will never be used as a weapon against anyone or any group of people, but will instead remain the property of every man and every woman. From what has been explained so far, realise that it is perfectly possible for any individual to unleash his or her true potential, but whenever this is done in an individual capacity there is always the temptation to abuse the *power* acquired. Whilst it is true that in order to acquire this *power* group-consciousness of one kind or another is required, realise that there is more than just one form of group-consciousness, just as there is more than just one motive for wanting to have *power*. In other words, group-consciousness in itself does not ensure selflessness, nor does it automatically confer harmlessness.

The only form of group-consciousness which does ensure harmlessness and selflessness, is that group-consciousness which comes from at-one-ment with one's own inner being, for the dreamers of mankind are all fully aware of the dangers inherent within *egotism*. It is in recognition of this that all Warriors of Freedom today spurn any aspects of their vast heritage of practices which uphold, or even just imply, a sense of separativeness. Therefore the manner in which I am imparting the teachings is one which ensures that if the reader is to derive any benefit, then he or she will be forced into having to strive for the group-consciousness of the dreamers of mankind. To impart the teachings in any other way would be as stupid as to give a group of children an atom bomb with which to play fireworks.

The *Cry of the Eagle* has already been sounded, and consequently the opportunities for every individual at this time are unlimited. The *Mists of Dragon Lore* have begun to coalesce, and in this book I will show you the preliminary steps to be taken in starting to unlock your true potential. But in order to make use of these teachings, you will have to be willing at least to *try* to fulfil three requirements. The first is that you must start believing in yourself; the second is that you must try to drop your sense of separativeness; and the third is that you must be willing to take heart, to take courage, and to take hands in an honest gesture of true democracy based upon the group-consciousness born of intelligent co-operation, the basis of which is the interrelationship of all life.

If you are able to fulfil these three requirements, even if only partially, but with the heartfelt intention that you do want to master them impeccably, then these teachings will work for you in ways that you do not now even dare to hope for. That you may find the courage to dare, and that you may find it within your heart to believe in your own godlike potential, is my most sincere wish for you.

PART ONE

THE DREAM

THE DREAM

Mixed Media: Tony Butler

THE SONS OF MAN WILL DRIFT IN DEEP SLEEP, SOMETIMES TOUCHING BRIEFLY THE ONE POWER, SOMETIMES BRUSHING PAST THE SPEAR, BUT MOSTLY NEVER KNOWING WHAT IT WAS THAT THESE BRIEF ENCOUNTERS SPARKED OFF WITHIN THEIR INNERMOST CORE. HAVING NO MEMORY OF WHAT IT IS TO BE MAN, THESE SONS OF MAN MUST BUILD ANEW THE ABILITY TO CONJURE.

FOR AEONS UPON AEONS THE SKIES ABOUT THE SONS OF MAN SHALL REMAIN CLEAR AND COLD, THE FORM OF THE DREAM A DULL OPAQUE GREY, SHOWING ONLY HERE AND THERE A TINY SPARK OF LIGHT EVERY TIME A LONE INDIVIDUAL WAKES SUFFICIENTLY TO RECALL THE MADNESS OF THE DREAM.

BUT ... IN RECALLING THE MADNESS, THE LITTLE LIGHT WAXES STRONGER ... SUDDENLY FLARES FIERCELY ... A TINY FLAME ... YES ... TINY ... MINUTE ... BUT STILL A FLAME ... A TINY HOPE THAT THE DREAM WILL NOT BE ALL-ABSORBING FOR EVER.

SLOWLY ... SLOWLY ... WITH EVERY TINY SPARK WHICH FLARES, TINY SPECKS OF MIST BEGIN TO FORM ... AND SEE! ... THE DREAMERS ARE BECOMING RESTLESS IN RESPONSE TO THOSE TINY SPECKS OF MIST!

From the prophecies of The Nameless One

CHAPTER ONE

THE FOUR POSTULATES OF STALKING

*IT IS THE BANE OF MAN'S EXISTENCE THAT THE LIMITATIONS OF
HIS FINITE MIND FORCE HIM TO LOOK UPON THE MYSTERY OF
BEINGNESS AS A DULL MUNDANE OCCURRENCE WITH NO
PARTICULAR SIGNIFICANCE.*

The fact that the *Mists of Dragon Lore* have begun to coalesce is
proof that men and women are becoming aware of their true
potential, albeit as yet at a most fundamental level of cognisance,
rather than consciously. However, if man is to unfold his full
potential, it is imperative for men and women to start acknowledging these deep inner drives consciously, for by doing this it
becomes possible to see that we are meant to use every
challenge, including current world events, to aid us in bringing
out our hidden potential.

Having laid the necessary foundations in the two previous
volumes for the more advanced concepts of the Toltec teachings,
it is now possible to start revealing these practices. In doing so
we must return to the techniques already imparted, so as to look
at their deeper implications, for it is these implications which
give rise to the more advanced practices of the Warrior's Path.

With respect to implications, and in relation to what was
stated in the introduction to this book, realise that if humanity is
to seize its fleeting moment of chance, then it is vital for man to
break out of his intensely rational approach to life, and to
embrace the mystery of his beingness in a fully conscious and
meaningful way. Seeing the opportunities inherent within a
challenge is the true meaning of *chance*, and making the best
possible use of those opportunities is the very essence of *seizing
the fleeting moment of chance*.

Seizing the fleeting moment of chance implies both action and materialisation, and since strength is needed for both, it seems appropriate to begin this volume in the North, the place of strength, of action and, in the final analysis, also of materialisation. However, because the North, by virtue of its nature, is also the warrior's battleground, any approach to the North entails entering into battle – an act requiring the use of the warrior's shield.

The nature and the use of the warrior's shield has already been discussed in *Return of the Warriors*, but since this was merely by way of introduction, it is now necessary for us to return to this important concept and consider its deeper implications. In this respect realise that using the warrior's shield is not what it appears at face value, for everything warriors do is in the nature of a strategy. Realise also that all strategies are in reality techniques, or composite techniques, and that each of these techniques is a versatile tool with multiple applications. This point is of particular relevance in considering the warrior's shield, for although the overt use of this technique is indeed what was described in *Return of the Warriors*, one of the more profound applications of the warrior's shield results in the act of *not-doing*, which of course concerns the *art of stalking*.

The art of stalking is *the riddle of the heart*, and in considering what this really means it becomes apparent why this technique is considered to be one of the three areas of expertise required upon the Warrior's Path. As we take a closer look at stalking, it is important to know that it has its basis in the *act of perception*, one of the greatest mysteries known to man.

Although most people look upon the act of perception as a very mundane act, Toltecs have always been fascinated by this stupendous phenomenon, knowing that it is the ultimate key to all acts of true *power*. Why different people should perceive the same event differently, and why some people are capable of perceiving something others are oblivious to, are only two of the great many questions that have kept highly skilled Toltec seers occupied for generations upon generations. And yet, in spite of all their dedicated research, Toltecs today are still not much closer to deciphering the mystery of perception than at the outset of their work. Their only success to date is to have become ever more skilled in the act of perception, and as a result to have gained enormously in experience, and consequently also in knowledge; but the real secret inherent within this most funda-mental act still evades us all.

> BECAUSE THE ACT OF PERCEPTION ENCOMPASSES THE MYSTERY
> OF INTENT, IT TOO IS A MYSTERY, AND THESE TWO MYSTERIES
> INTERACT TO PRODUCE THE MISTS OF DRAGON LORE.

As the aphorism above points out, the reason why Toltec seers have not yet been able to crack the mystery of perception is because it entails the use of that mysterious force termed *intent*. Thus it is therefore quite literally a case of a mystery within a mystery; the one interacting with the other to produce yet a third mystery, namely that phenomenon Toltecs have termed the Mists of Dragon Lore.

It has already been mentioned in the introduction to this book that Dragon Lore is not at all easy to express in terms of the logic demanded by the rational mind of man. In fact, in many ways it is easier to rationalise about the act of perception, and even about the force of *intent*, than to rationalise about the Mists of Dragon Lore. The reason for this is that the concept of Dragon Lore is one of those strange paradoxes which arises from the rational mind itself for, logically speaking, this concept seems to make a great deal of sense, and yet the moment logic is applied to it, it suddenly appears to become completely irrational. Therefore from what has been stated so far concerning the art of stalking, it should not be too difficult to understand why it should be termed a riddle. The act of perception, which seems to be such a very logical and mundane act, is in reality three mysteries in one, and since stalking has its basis in this threefold mystery, it cannot be taken at face value, but must instead be approached as a mystery in its own right.

> WE CANNOT WORK WITH A MYSTERY FROM THE OUTSIDE. IF WE
> WISH TO SOLVE A MYSTERY WE MUST IMMERSE OURSELVES
> WITHIN THAT MYSTERY, FOR ONLY IN THIS WAY CAN WE MAP
> OUT THE UNKNOWN.

The face value of the aphorism above speaks for itself, in that it alludes to the fact that a mystery implies the unknown, and that the unknown can never become the known unless we explore it. This is the same principle that is involved in charting a map for an unknown territory. In order for a cartographer to draw such a map, he must physically go into that territory. However, to enter and to explore an unknown physical location is easy enough, but to enter the unknown regions of the human psyche is altogether a different ball game, and this is what gives rise to the deeper implications of the aphorism.

The clue to this deeper meaning lies in the phrase "we must immerse ourselves within that mystery". This is one of the most difficult concepts to get across to an apprentice, for the simple reason that we cannot truly verbalise its real import. As a result, every apprentice at first makes the mistake of assuming that to immerse oneself in mystery is merely a figure of speech. However, the talented apprentice quickly enough comes to the realisation that stalkers do not as a rule speak in terms of metaphor, and that even when a stalker is forced to use metaphor, such a metaphor is always the expression of an abstract reality which transcends the limitations of the finite mind. Therefore "to become immersed in mystery" is a statement which by far transcends the normal meaning of becoming "engrossed in", or "fascinated by", or "obsessed with". In fact this statement holds the key to the true art of stalking, especially the art of stalking oneself or, in other words, not-doing.

It is particularly noticeable when it comes to not-doing, how often apprentices do take the teachings at face value, and thus fall into the trap of assuming understanding. The only possible way in which to teach not-doing, as with all the other concepts and techniques, is in rational terms. All of us can only start from where we are at, and since every apprentice starts off by being completely caught up in the logic of the rational mind, it stands to reason that apprentices will at first always approach the teachings in terms of the rational. This is especially true for those techniques which are assigned to right side awareness, for apprentices quite unconsciously assume that this means they are given a licence to apply only their rational minds to these practices. The fact that they do not as yet grasp the true nature of right side awareness does not even occur to such apprentices, for they automatically assume that their own particular perception of right side awareness must be correct. As a result, the technique of not-doing is inevitably taken at face value, and then left at that.

It is indeed true that both stalking and not-doing are techniques which apply to right side awareness, but this does not mean that we can afford to take this at face value. The real reason why these two techniques apply to right side awareness will only really become clear as we continue to consider their deeper implications, but let it suffice for now to say that the real value of both techniques lies in applying them to the act of perception, which the majority of people can only register in normal awareness.

However, unlike the average man or woman, warriors do not make the mistake of assuming that their perception of anything is the ultimate reality. Having learned through experience that the act of perception is always relative to our view of the world, warriors do not take their perceptions at face value, for they know that whenever our view of the world changes, so too does our perception of both life and ourselves. Therefore warriors accept what they have perceived without accepting it, and believe what they have perceived without believing it. This is the not-doing of the warrior, and by practising this, he or she avoids becoming obsessed with the face value of anything, no matter whether it is a problem, a joyful experience, a statement made by another person, the behaviour of that person, or a concept or technique of the Toltec tradition.

Consequently, when it comes to the statement that we have to immerse ourselves within mystery, the warrior knows for a fact that he is dealing with a metaphor for a reality which cannot be verbalised. Knowing this, the warrior also knows that it would be plain stupidity to ask how this is supposed to be accomplished, for if this was possible to explain, then there would have been no need to use metaphor in the first place. Instead the warrior practices not-doing, by starting to stalk his perception of this statement. It is exactly at this point where the apprentice's rational mind will inevitably do a backward somersault to land on its head, and without even thinking about it, the apprentice will voice the invalid question, "How?"

Stalking one's perception is not nearly so difficult to do as it is to explain. In fact this is true of everything warriors do, for until you know how to do it, it always seems to be very difficult, but this is only because the rational mind of man insists on complicating everything. Once you know how to do something, then you discover that it is not the doing that is difficult, but the explaining of it to someone who is bent on complicating everything. In order to overcome this difficulty Toltecs devised certain guidelines for apprentices to follow in learning for themselves that which cannot be verbalised. Such guidelines are called postulates, or premises, and are usually given in the form of a set. The set given to apprentices to help them learn what it is to stalk their perception, is known as *the four postulates of stalking*, traditionally given in the form of the following aphorism.

YOU SHOULD KNOW, FIRSTLY, THAT THE WHOLE WORLD AND EVERYTHING IN IT IS AN ENDLESS MYSTERY; SECONDLY, THAT IT IS OUR DUTY AS WARRIORS TO SOLVE THIS MYSTERY, BUT WE SHOULD NEVER ENGAGE THE HOPE OF BEING ABLE TO DO SO; THIRDLY, THAT BECAUSE WARRIORS ARE AWARE OF THE ENDLESS MYSTERY SURROUNDING THEM, THEY ACKNOWLEDGE THAT THEY TOO ARE A PART OF THIS MYSTERY, AND BECAUSE THEY KNOW THAT IT IS THEIR DUTY TO SOLVE THIS MYSTERY, THEY BECOME AT-ONE WITH THE MYSTERY; FOURTHLY, BEING AT-ONE WITH THE MYSTERY, THE WARRIOR COMES TO UNDERSTAND THAT THE CRUX OF THIS MYSTERY IS THE INFINITE MYSTERY OF BEINGNESS, IRRESPECTIVE OF WHETHER BEINGNESS MEANS AN ATOM, A MINERAL, A PLANT, AN ANIMAL, A HUMAN, OR EVEN A SUPERHUMAN ENTITY. HAVING COME TO THIS REALISATION THE WARRIOR ENTERS INTO A STATE OF TRUE HUMILITY, FOR WITHIN THE MYSTERY OF BEINGNESS, ALL ARE EQUAL.

Needless to say, every apprentice at first finds it very difficult to put these guidelines into practice in his or her daily life. It is simply not easy to regard the world as being a mystery when one has been taught that there is a rational explanation for everything, nor is it easy to think of oneself as being a mystery when one has spent most of one's life believing that one knows oneself. Likewise it is not easy to look upon an insect as being equal to one, when we have all been raised to believe that the human being is the superior life-form. And yet, it is precisely because of this that Toltecs devised these postulates. Knowing full well that apprentices are incapable of living up to these guidelines, nagals have since time immemorial stalked their apprentices into true learning by giving them these postulates.

In order to understand how this works, realise that it is in struggling to put these postulates into practice that the apprentice has no option other than to start questioning himself as to why he invariably fails again and again. Therefore when such an apprentice comes to the nagal to ask why he cannot put these guidelines into practice, the nagal will usually reply by suggesting that perhaps it is because the apprentice does not really want to change, or that perhaps the Warrior's Path is not really for him a path with a heart. Being challenged in this way, the apprentice is immediately thrown back upon himself, and in utter frustration he will try his best to convince the nagal that it is indeed for him a path with a heart, and that he really does want to change. Of course, it is not the nagal who needs to be convinced, but the apprentice himself, and thus he is brought to the real crux of the matter.

Had the nagal not been convinced of the apprentice's sincerity he would have ended the apprenticeship forthwith, which the apprentice himself also knows. By throwing the apprentice back upon himself, it is clear that the nagal is stalking the apprentice. However, the beauty of this manoeuvre is that even if the apprentice is aware of being stalked, he also knows very well that a stalker never lies, and as a result he finds himself in the uncomfortable position of having become the victim of his own invalid question.

Caught between the devil and the deep blue sea, the apprentice now has only two options open to him; either he accepts the nagal's statement at face value, in which case he must acknowledge that what is holding him back is the fact that he is not trying hard enough; or else he must acknowledge the fact that he is being stalked, in which case he knows that there is a truth in the nagal's guidance which he has not yet figured out. But irrespective of which option the apprentice chooses, it still boils down to the fact that he now has to reassess his motives as well as his endeavours. In doing this, whether by himself, or with the assistance of the nagal, the apprentice automatically begins to stalk his own perception of both himself and his circumstances. Finally, realising that he cannot afford to take his perception at face value, the apprentice begins to look at his beliefs and his behaviour in a completely different light. No longer so sure in his knowledge of himself, such an apprentice will start to question everything about himself quite ruthlessly.

However, the real value in this manoeuvre goes far beyond what has been explained. By giving the apprentice a set of guide-lines which he knows that the apprentice will never be able to implement, the nagal has effectively tricked the apprentice, firstly, into stalking his own perception; secondly, into quite unconsciously beginning to see himself as something of a mystery; and thirdly, into starting to coalesce the Mists of Dragon Lore. This threefold effect comes about even if the apprentice knows nothing about any of this beforehand, and even if he knows all along that he is being stalked. Herein lies the wonder of the rational mind of man. Being far too clever for its own good, it is exceedingly easy to trip up the rational mind with its own cleverness. In fact, the rational mind is so 'clever' that it will even co-operate in this operation if it is explained before-hand, for the rational mind can always be tricked by its sense of logic, its sense of fear, or its sense of ambition, even when it knows this!

In the final analysis it is his expertise at being able to trip up the rational mind with its own cleverness, or fear, or ambition, that reveals the art of the true stalker. But once again we cannot afford to take this at face value, for the art of the stalker can only be acquired by practising on oneself. It is impossible to learn to stalk others if one cannot even stalk oneself, and therefore it is only once an apprentice has begun to see how his own mind works, and how easy it is to trip it up with its boring insistence on wanting to be in control, that it becomes possible for him to start stalking others. Even more importantly, through having started to see just how limiting his perception can be, and how very seriously he has always believed in his own rightness, the apprentice is now in a position truly to stalk his own perception, and therefore also his own rationality.

Ceasing to regard his perception as being inviolate, the apprentice soon finds that the rewards this freedom brings far exceed the effort that was involved in getting to this point. Firstly, the desire to justify his actions has begun to fall away and, as a result, the apprentice does not expend valuable time and *personal power* in trying to defend or justify either his opinions or his actions. Instead the apprentice now begins to see his own folly, and with this realisation comes the freedom of being able to laugh at himself. Secondly, through being able to see from his own experience that we are indeed mysterious creatures, the apprentice learns to stop worrying that he has not yet acquired understanding. Slowly but surely realising that this lifetime is never going to be enough to solve the mystery of our beingness, the apprentice gradually acquires that state of mind which can only be termed true patience. Thirdly, through seeing the benefit in stalking himself, the apprentice no longer tries to *practise* not-doing, but instead starts to *live* not-doing, and so learns that he can apply this same principle to everything else on the Warrior's Path.

Living the teachings, as opposed to practising the teachings, is a concept the apprentice can least afford to take at face value, for the accumulated effects of living the teachings is that mysterious phenomenon termed Dragon Lore, which the perceptive reader will have noticed is a concept I keep skirting

around. The best way to grasp all this, is to consider the following aphorism.

> AT FIRST THE WHOLE CONCEPT OF BEING A WARRIOR IS FOR THE
> APPRENTICE NOTHING MORE THAN A ROMANTIC IDEAL. THEN,
> AS HE STARTS TO LEARN, HE BEGINS TO WONDER IF THE TASKS
> ASSIGNED TO HIM ARE REALLY POSSIBLE TO ACCOMPLISH. AS A
> RESULT THE APPRENTICE IS NO LONGER AS CONVINCED ABOUT
> ANYTHING AS HE WAS WHEN HE FIRST STARTED OUT. BUT IN THIS
> LOSS OF CONVICTION, THE APPRENTICE WALKS NEATLY INTO THE
> TRAP SET FOR HIM BY THE NAGAL. WITHOUT EVEN REALISING IT,
> THE APPRENTICE HAS STARTED TO LOOK UPON THE WARRIOR'S
> PATH AS BEING SOMETHING OF A MYTH. THE MOMENT THE
> NAGAL BECOMES AWARE OF THIS, HE BEGINS TO CHALLENGE THE
> APPRENTICE'S SENSE OF CONVICTION IN EVERY WAY POSSIBLE,
> AND IN HAVING NO OTHER RECOURSE BUT TO FIGHT BACK, THE
> APPRENTICE WILL TRY HIS UTMOST TO CONVINCE THE NAGAL
> THAT HE IS TRYING HIS BEST. HOWEVER, IN DOING SO, THE
> APPRENTICE GETS CAUGHT UP IN THE MYTH WHICH HE HIMSELF
> HAS CREATED. BEING CAUGHT IN THAT MYTH, THE APPRENTICE
> WILL UNCONSCIOUSLY START LIVING THE MYTH IN HIS EFFORTS
> TO BE IMPECCABLE, UNTIL EVENTUALLY HE HAS LIVED THE MYTH
> FOR SO LONG, THAT HE BECOMES THE MYTH.

In view of what has been imparted so far, it should now not be
too difficult to grasp the import of this aphorism. All of us come
to the Warrior's Path with our baggage, and that baggage is
never much different to the next person's, for the contents of
this baggage are the prejudices and preconceived ideas that all of
us have acquired by virtue of our social conditioning. From out
of all this junk, by far the worst idea is the expectation that we
are going to be *taught* to be warriors. Whilst apprentices continue to hold onto this idea, they learn precious little, for the
simple reason that, firstly, the true teachings cannot be verbalised; and secondly, *power* is knowledge which can only be
acquired through personal experience. Furthermore, whilst
apprentices are expecting to be taught, they will not call forth
the teachings, but will instead sit back and wait for the nagal to

give them the teachings. However, realise that we cannot be given knowledge; we cannot be given *power*. If we are to have *power*, then we must *claim* that *power* through personal experience. Therefore the only teaching a nagal can offer is guidance in how best to face our challenges and how to extract from out of them our own *gifts of power*.

This is quite the most difficult point to get across to any apprentice, because apprentices are very rarely willing to believe that all the knowledge and *power* they could ever possibly hope for is to be found in their own daily life. Somehow or other apprentices always come to a nagal expecting that he has a magic wand somewhere, and that when he feels the apprentice is ready, he will suddenly take out that wand and wave it around dramatically so as to transform the apprentice into a formidable warrior. But alas, although there are some unscrupulous characters who do perpetuate this superstition in order to get apprentices to hand over their wallets, Toltecs themselves, in spite of all of their knowledge and *power*, have not yet managed either to find or make such a clever little stick.

Nagals are indeed powerful beings and, depending upon their own particular training, they can even be extraordinarily powerful. But irrespective of how powerful a nagal may be, he cannot use his *power* to transform an apprentice who does not believe in himself. A nagal can, if he wants to, and as was often done in the past, perform like a circus animal non-stop, in the hope that this will make his apprentices learn. He can push his apprentices in and out of heightened awareness like yo-yos. He can amaze them, or frighten them, with one impressive ritual after another. He can move his apprentices' assemblage points with just the sound of his voice, until they feel quite dizzy, or laugh, or cry. He can alter their perception by capturing their attention with only his eyes. And if all else fails, the nagal can resort to using his abilities as a seer to put the fear of hell into his apprentices. But after all of this, even though the apprentices will be suitably impressed, and even though they will gather in corners to whisper in bated breath about all the wonders they have witnessed, they will still be none the wiser, and they will still be just as impotent as they have always been.

All that a nagal can really do for his apprentices is to guide them into discovering their own inner strength, and explain how to use that strength to claim their *power*. However, this is only possible once the apprentice is willing to start working with the challenges in his or her own life, and in this way to call forth those aspects of the teachings which are of relevance in the moment. Every bit of teaching received must be put into practice if it is to be of any benefit, but it is equally impossible to practise teachings for which one has no use in facing one's challenges. Herein lies the greatest difficulty of all, for invariably apprentices never see their true challenges, and even if they do, they would prefer the nagal to perform some magic trick, rather than face those challenges and extract from out of them their *gifts of power*.

The very first thing a nagal has to do with a newly-recruited apprentice is to shake that apprentice out of his belief that the nagal is going to do it for him. If the nagal does not do this, he will end up with a dependant who will never learn to claim his *power*, but if the nagal is too vigorous in shaking the apprentice out of his expectations, he runs the risk that the apprentice will lose all sense of self-confidence, and therefore will still end up being a dependant. In other words, the apprentice must be brought to the point at which he can see for himself that his beliefs are nothing more than wild expectations based upon a view of the world which is mostly not true, but at the same time care must be taken that the apprentice does not fall apart once he starts to realise that his whole life has been based upon lies and misconceptions.

The only way in which the nagal can really guide an apprentice through this tricky manoeuvre is to set the apprentice up in such a way that he will quite unconsciously begin to look upon the teachings as being some sort of a myth. Realise that a myth is something which the majority of people are never too sure whether they should take seriously or ignore. This is a most important point, for once an apprentice starts to look upon the teachings in this way, he has, even though he does not realise it, been shaken out of his expectations, but because he is also not too sure whether or not to believe what is happening to him, he is in no danger of losing confidence in himself or in his own judgement. Nevertheless, no longer convinced either that he is ever going to learn anything of real value, or that he can go back to his old way of life should he quit, the apprentice finds himself caught up in the myth which he himself has created, albeit with some subtle help from the nagal. In this respect the nagal will start to stalk an apprentice into the correct frame of mind from day one, by imparting to him the four postulates of stalking, usually in a covert fashion at first, for traditionally these postulates are only given to an apprentice in a formal manner much later on in his training.

Once an apprentice has become caught up in the myth, the nagal will continue to challenge him in one way or another, with the result that the apprentice will be forced into starting to fight for his own self-worth. Furthermore, by continuously trying to convince the nagal that he really does want to become a warrior above anything else in the whole wide world, the apprentice is in reality constantly affirming to himself that he is capable and worthy of becoming a warrior, and that he will do anything it takes in order to succeed.

This is a fine state of mind, and the only one which ensures that the apprentice will really make the required *effort* to live like a warrior. Making the effort to live like a warrior is what is termed practising the teachings, and it is this *practising* of the teachings, rather than living his old way of life, that is the real not-doing of the apprentice, even though he is hardly ever aware of it. Apropos this, realise that all of the apprentice's conscious not-doings will have no real value other than to aid him in the effort it takes to practise living like a warrior.

At this point in his training the apprentice is very aware of the fact that he is desperately *trying* to live like a warrior, but that he is still a long way off from being able to claim that status – a fact he will be reminded of constantly by the nagal. In other words, the apprentice knows he is living a myth, but by being caught in this myth he also knows that he cannot afford to quit, and therefore has no option but to do his utmost to live that myth impeccably. What this really means is that the apprentice is now no longer just trying to practise not-doing in his pursuit of a romantic ideal, but has instead become so absorbed in his attempts to survive the constant onslaughts of the nagal, that he actually starts to live a not-doing.

The moment the apprentice has started to live his life like a not-doing, he initiates a chain reaction within himself which cannot be stopped. From this moment on he will stalk his own perception ceaselessly, and will no longer feel the need to ask invalid questions, but will start to formulate those questions which he instinctively feels will lead him into a deeper understanding of his own potential. Now that he has ceased sitting around disgruntled because the nagal is not fulfilling his expectations, but instead taking full responsibility for his life, his knowledge, and therefore also his *power*, the apprentice makes every effort to live the impeccable life of a warrior, and in doing so, comes to the realisation that he can only do this within the context of his daily life.

This total change of attitude marks the all-important point at which the transformation process is initiated, not because the nagal has waved a magic wand, but simply because he has tricked the apprentice into starting this process within himself, by forcing him to fight for his own survival, his sense of sanity, and ultimately, his own self-worth. This is the greatest *gift of power* a nagal can possibly give to any apprentice. To be shaken lose from the debilitating restraints of our social conditioning, and to be given back confidence in one's own worth and in one's own potential, is a great gift indeed, and yet even this gift pales into insignificance next to the gift of transformation the apprentice gives himself in the process of getting to this point.

By far the most important aspect of the act of transformation is that elusive phenomenon known as the Mists of Dragon Lore. As a result of this necessary preamble it is hoped that the reader will no longer be tempted to take this concept at face value, but will instead strive to see the many intricate implications which every nagal since time immemorial has found so difficult to verbalise.

The most trying issue to verbalise with respect to Dragon Lore is that man has the ability to materialise a dream. For the majority of people this is not difficult to accept in the sense of material things. For example, most will readily agree that if it is your dream to own your own business one day, or to own a sports car, or a beautiful home, then provided you make the effort, you will be able to fulfil those dreams. Most will also agree that if your dream is to invent a new kind of air transport, or even a new kind of space travel, then you can do it if you are prepared to make it your life's ambition. But when it comes to the concept of having to materialise one's own true potential as a magical being of the universe, most people will suddenly fall quiet and begin to look askance at whoever is trying to tell them that they do have the ability to do so. And yet, this *is* man's true potential.

As incredible as it may sound, every man and woman does have the ability to materialise their dreams in the sense of conjuring. Man is a creature of magic, and therefore conjuring is as much his birthright as are the Toltec teachings. In life man has two options. The first is that he can continue to believe that he is the victim of his birth and his circumstances, that he is powerless to change any of it, and that there is no life before birth or after death. If this is true, then life upon the physical plane is a meaningless exercise with no special significance or any real value. The second option is for man to believe that he exists beyond the confines of the physical plane, and that the only reason he does periodically come into physical existence is to learn how to materialise his full potential upon the dense physical plane by overcoming the many challenges this form of existence brings us. If this is true, then we cannot possibly be victims, and if we are not victims then it stands to reason that we do have the ability to change both ourselves and our lives. However, such an ability implies conjuring in the truest possible sense of the word, irrespective of whether we use the magic of a wand, or the magic of *transmutation, transformation* and *transfiguration*.

The only reason why men and women do not believe in their magical abilities, is either because they are looking for a magic wand in their pursuit of superstition and old wives' tales, or else because they believe that everything can be explained in rational terms. At the end of the day, though, it is not the ability to pull a rabbit out of a hat, or the ability to materialise a pair of ear rings out of thin air, that constitutes true conjuring, but the magical ability to create and to destroy – the ability to transmute our shortcomings into *power*, the ability to transform ourselves into impeccable warriors of the spirit of man, and the ability to transfigure ourselves into true man, the microcosm of the macrocosm. Herein lies man's greatest *power* as a magical creature of the universe.

As was explained in *Return of the Warriors*, there are basically two kinds of magic, termed *the first ring of power* and *the second ring of power*. Both these forms of magic are today part and parcel of the Toltec tradition, but the Warriors of Freedom no longer teach *the first ring of power*, for the simple reason that this form of magic does not lead to freedom.

It is still too early in the teachings to be able to explain the real differences between these two forms of magic, but maybe an analogy will suffice for now. Think of *the first ring of power* as being like atomic fission, and *the second ring of power* as being like atomic fusion. The first form of magic is subtractive in quality, in that it separates, divides, removes something and, in short, destroys. The second form, on the other hand, is *additive* in quality, in that it unites, heals, adds something that was not present before and, in short, upholds, uplifts, and creates. The first form of magic is the *power* of the *tonal*, or the matter aspect, whereas the second form of magic is the *power* of the *nagal*, or the spirit aspect. When these two forms of magic are united they bring to birth a third form of magic – Dragon Lore – the true *power* of man.

From the above it should be clear that it is not a case of the Warriors of Freedom having spurned *the first ring of power*, for destruction does have its place in the greater scheme of things, but rather that it is a case of not allowing either themselves or their apprentices to get caught up in this form of magic. Furthermore, if *the first ring of power* is developed before *the second ring*, then because of its separative nature, the power of this first form of magic prevents the apprentice from ever being able to learn *the second ring of power*. And yet, realise that because it is the will of the spirit of man to materialise its full potential upon the dense physical plane, which means the ability both to create and to destroy, acquisition of *the second ring of power* automatically yields also the use of *the first ring.*

A strange quirk of human reason is that people will believe readily the negative, but not the positive. Therefore, if you tell someone who has never been able to conjure that they have the ability to do so, they will simply not believe you or, worse still, they will sit back wide-eyed and expect you to teach them, or at least until such time as they have become caught up in the myth. But strangely, paradoxically, it is also a quirk of human reason that if you challenge someone, you will arouse in that person the spirit of the rebel. Therefore if someone is caught on an idea, and you keep telling him that you doubt he will ever succeed, then out of sheer frustration that person will drive himself to incredible heights, even if only to prove you wrong.

It is in recognition of these odd quirks of the human mind that a nagal who is dedicated to the Path of Freedom will always guide his apprentices into fighting for what they perceive to be their rights, and through this they begin to materialise their true potential. In other words, in their efforts to survive the on-slaughts of the nagal, or in their efforts to prove him wrong, apprentices will begin to coalesce the Mists of Dragon Lore. In either case the apprentices, without realising it, will have begun to materialise some-thing out of what was before no-thing.

This is the only way in which I can verbalise this concept, but it does not imply that there really was nothing to start with, for the apprentice's potential has always been there. However, un-realised potential is as good as nothing until it is made to become something. That some-thing is what is referred to as the mists of what will in time become Dragon Lore, the true *power* of man.

The reader of this book will by now probably be wondering why I have chosen to reveal the way in which a nagal stalks his apprentices in getting them to this point, but if the truth be told, it makes very little difference what either the apprentice or the reader is told beforehand. The reason I have chosen to reveal this tactic is twofold. Firstly, since the readers of these books are most unlikely to be working with a nagal, if anyone at all, the only way in which I can possibly be of use to the reader through the medium of books, is by revealing this tactic. This is because the readers of these books are mainly men and women who have already decided to work for themselves, by themselves. If this was not the case, then the reader would not be reading, but spending his or her time in trying to find a qualified nagal. Thus it does not matter that the reader knows the whole tactic beforehand, for it will work just as well as if he or she had not known it. Secondly, in revealing this tactic, I am not only able to explain the meaning of the mists of Dragon Lore, but I can also begin to demonstrate the deeper implications of both stalking and not-doing, and in relation to these, two final points need to be clarified.

The first point concerns what I have referred to as pulling a rabbit out of a hat, or materialising a pair of ear rings. Apart from sleight of hand, this type of magic does exist, but those who are capable of such feats are very few and far between, and they do not normally accept apprentices. This is because humanity as a whole is a long, long way away from being able to handle such *power* wisely, and consequently the dreamers of mankind themselves block its flow and use.

This kind of *power* is not really a form of magic that can be taught in the traditional sense, but is instead the end result of having lived the impeccable life of a fully trained warrior for a great many lifetimes. Unfortunately, or perhaps fortunately, there is no other way in which to acquire such *power*. If there were, the world today would be filled with a great many naive men and women so busy trying to satisfy their greed for material riches that the evolution of awareness would cease, or else they would be so totally absorbed in trying to rid the world of what they regard as unsavoury characters, that there would be no life-forms left to evolve awareness.

The second point concerns giving an apprentice the four postulates of stalking prematurely – something which could not be explained fully before. At first an apprentice cannot possibly fulfil the requirements demanded of him or her in the four postulates of stalking, but when he or she has started to live the teachings, and has therefore started to coalesce the mists of Dragon Lore, a moment comes when the apprentice does indeed start to fulfil these requirements. This point is made here so that the reader does not come to the erroneous conclusion that the four postulates of stalking are nothing more than a stalker's tactic, for this would be very far from the truth. The four postulates of stalking are not only vital to the *stalker's rule*, which we will be looking at in the next chapter, but are also the very essence of the Mists of Dragon Lore. The best way to grasp this is to look at a short summary of the apprentice's training.

Progressing upon the Warrior's Path, the apprentice goes from pursuing a romantic ideal, to seeing a myth, to living a myth, and finally to becoming that myth. In other words, once the apprentice has seen the myth, sufficient sobriety has been acquired to drop romanticising, and to acknowledge the fact that a great deal of hard work lies ahead. This is the point at which the apprentice starts to put the teachings into practice and initiates the process of transmutation. At this stage, the apprentice starts to live the teachings, rather than just practising them and paying only lip service to the life of a warrior. In starting to live the myth, the apprentice not only initiates the process of transformation, but also begins to coalesce the Mists of Dragon Lore. And then, finally, through living like a warrior for so long, the apprentice crosses an invisible threshold beyond which his entire life becomes transformed into a not-doing, and the last vestiges of his personal history melt into a nebulous fog. This is the point at which it can truly be said that the apprentice has become the myth, and provided that he continues to live the life of an utterly impeccable warrior, transfiguration is the inevitable end result.

By now *power* is at his command, and to all intents and purposes the apprentice has completed his apprenticeship. Having reached the end of his journey as a *human* being, it is now only a matter of time before the apprentice will shed his *human form* by entering into that state of awareness known as the *totality of the self*. This is an act which marks the beginning of a new journey – *the definitive journey* of the warrior. On this new journey, which is the true journey of *man*, the warrior learns that we are all universal creatures who hold two *rings of power*, and that our divine nature is the magic of Dragon Lore.

THE UNSPEAKABLE MANIFESTS AS THAT INCOMPREHENSIBLE DUALITY TERMED THE NAGAL AND THE TONAL – THE TWO RINGS OF POWER. STANDING BETWEEN THESE TWO RINGS IS MAN – THAT UNIVERSAL POINT AT WHICH THE PERCEPTION OF NAGAL AND TONAL ARE ASSEMBLED. AT FIRST THE INTENT OF MAN IS SO VAGUE AND SO INSUBSTANTIAL AS TO BE NO MORE THAN A NEBULOUS MIST INTERACTING WITH THE TWO OUTER RINGS, BUT AS HE CONTINUES TO FOCUS HIS INTENT, IT BECOMES A THIRD RING BINDING THE OTHER TWO TOGETHER. THESE THREE RINGS FORM THE TOTALITY OF THE SELF, A COALITION OF FORCES BASED UPON THE LORE OF THE DRAGON.

CHAPTER TWO

CONTROLLING FOLLY

WE ARE CAUGHT IN A DREAM. IF YOU BELIEVE THAT DREAM TO BE REALITY YOUR ACTIONS WILL BE SHEER FOLLY.

Having touched upon the four postulates of stalking ever so briefly, we will now move on to the intermediate teachings concerning the art of stalking, for it is only by putting these teachings into practice that it becomes possible to begin to grasp the real import of these all-important premises. However, bear in mind that time and time again we will return to the four postulates of stalking, each time to gain a deeper insight into the truths they reveal, that insight in turn revealing a deeper understanding of the stalker's rule, and therefore ultimately of the art of stalking itself. All the while remember that the four postulates of stalking and the stalker's rule are interdependent. In other words, without the four postulates of stalking there can be no rule, and vice versa.

The above point is vital to this section of the teachings, but before it can be clarified further, one other matter must first be explained, namely, that in order to get the stalker's rule into its proper perspective, it is necessary to know that the four postulates of stalking are determined by the four directions. (Fig. 1) In time, as we keep returning to the four postulates, it will become progressively clear why this should be so, and what the implications are, but let it suffice for now to point out that the four postulates of stalking can only really be grasped by putting into practice, not only the technique of stalking, but in fact all four major techniques, which are of course also determined by the four directions of *power*. (Fig. 2)

THE FOUR POSTULATES
OF STALKING

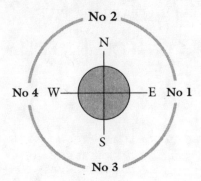

Figure 1

THE FOUR POSTULATES OF STALKING
AND THE FOUR MAJOR TECHNIQUES

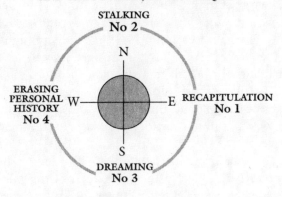

Figure 2

Having clarified this much, let us now return to our consideration of the interdependence of the four postulates of stalking and the stalker's rule. Think of the four postulates of stalking as being like the fabric used for making a piece of embroidery, and think of the seven aspects of the stalker's rule as being like the different types of stitches used in such an embroidery. (Fig. 3) The threads used in this embroidery are the threads of life, whilst the pattern is determined by the many challenges, big and small, encountered throughout life. The end product is of course the embroidery itself which, in this analogy, is the impeccable life of a warrior created upon that base we term the four postulates of stalking. Furthermore, the overall quality of the warrior's life is obviously dependent upon the skill with which he or she uses the stalker's rule, and this in turn is dependent upon the measure of the warrior's understanding of the four postulates of stalking. Therefore the four postulates of stalking, the stalker's rule, the challenges of life, and the possibilities inherent within life, are four inseparable units, each unit reflecting the deeper implications of one of the four postulates of stalking. These four units are traditionally referred to as *the four components of the dream*.

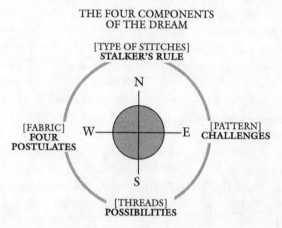

THE FOUR COMPONENTS
OF THE DREAM

[TYPE OF STITCHES]
STALKER'S RULE

N

[FABRIC]   W ——————— E   [PATTERN]
FOUR   CHALLENGES
POSTULATES

S

[THREADS]
POSSIBILITIES

Figure 3

From the above analogy it is clear to see that life is not at all what most people believe it to be. As the aphorism at the beginning of this chapter indicates, life for the average man and woman is nothing more than a dream, and their actions nothing more than folly. And yet this does not imply that life is not real, or that it cannot be real, nor does it imply that our actions are useless. What this aphorism does imply is that life is not what men and women believe it to be, and that if we base our actions on this false sense of reality, then our actions must perforce amount to folly.

> LIFE IS NO-THING. LIFE IS AN ENDLESS CHAOS OF POSSIBILITIES.
> BY SELECTING SOME OF THOSE POSSIBILITIES WE WEAVE A WEB
> DETERMINED BY A PATTERN WE CANNOT KNOW BEFOREHAND.
> IT IS THIS SELECTION OF POSSIBILITIES, OR THE WEAVING, OR THE
> WOVEN WEB, WHICH PEOPLE MISTAKENLY LOOK UPON AS LIFE.
> YET REALISE THAT LIFE REMAINS FOR EVER UNTOUCHED BY THE
> WEAVING OF MAN. WE MAKE OUR UNDERSTANDING OF LIFE
> WHAT WE WILL, BUT LIFE IN ITSELF IS A TRANSCENDENT STATE
> OF FLUX HAVING NO FORM, AND YET GIVING RISE TO ALL FORMS.

The aphorism above describes life beautifully, even though it is perhaps one of the most radical statements with which any apprentice has to contend. People have been so conditioned into believing that they know what life is, that it is not easy to put aside all the many misconceptions, preconceived ideas and prejudices with which all of us have grown up.

The best way of grasping the true nature of life is to refer again to the analogy used earlier. In this analogy "the threads of life" refer to the infinite number of possibilities which exist at any one given moment of time, and from out of which we choose the one which most appeals to us as individuals. It stands to reason that such a choice will always be influenced by the nature of the challenge we happen to be facing in that moment. The chosen possibility is quite literally that thread of life which is figuratively portrayed as the thread we have inserted into our needle, and with which we will 'sew' or work those actions that are termed our life. However, realise that the challenge itself is determined by fate, and ultimately by destiny, and therefore the challenge is part of a pattern which we cannot know beforehand, but which is gradually revealed by each successive challenge. Depending upon how well we follow this pattern, the end result, which we term life, will be impeccable, or it will be a mess.

As can be seen from the aphorism depicting the nature of life, the traditional way of explaining this process is to refer to it as weaving a web, but I personally prefer using the analogy of doing embroidery. Not only is the concept of embroidery easier to grasp in relation to the stalker's rule, but it also clearly conveys the difference between the four postulates of stalking, portrayed by the fabric used for embroidery, and the stalker's rule, portrayed by the intricate stitches used in following the pattern of destiny.

Following on from this preamble, we now need to look at what all of this really means, but before doing so, a word of advice is appropriate. Although the art of stalking is rightfully assigned to right side awareness, it must not be forgotten that it is the riddle of the heart, and that the heart concerns itself with feelings, and not with rationality. The implication here is that the art of stalking enables us to work with the left side in normal aware-ness. In the final analysis, this boils down to mapping out the unknown and making it practical upon the physical plane. How-ever, in considering the left side in normal awareness, we are as always horrendously limited by the inadequate scope of words. In this respect, realise that it is not so much a question of not being able to find words to convey left side knowledge adequate-ly, but that in dealing with the left side the implications are always so astronomically vast that words fail to express the extent of that vastness.

From the above it is clear where lies the trap of taking words at their face value, and where lies the dilemma of every nagal whenever it comes to expressing the left side in terms of words. The end result of this is that we can at best verbalise snippets here and there if we are not to become lost in trying to verbalise the vastness inherent within the left side. But to verbalise only snippets is to take things out of context, and anything taken out of context will of necessity be subject to misinterpretation. In order to minimise misinterpretation, a nagal will always endea-vour to give as many snippets as possible, but in doing so lays himself open to being accused of rambling. No nagal ever does ramble, but in attempting to give as many different snippets from as many different angles as possible, it will often appear as if he is rambling, going off on tangents, and meandering through what at first appear to be unrelated byways.

The nature of the teachings from this point on is such that we will often have to consider concepts which take us far into the left side, and in this respect I must warn the reader right now that it will all too often appear as if I am rambling on and on, and going off on tangents. However, if you bear in mind what has been stated concerning the nature of the left side, you will not be tempted to throw your hands up in dismay, or to use this book as a soccer ball in utter frustration. To grasp the left side is a skill which can be mastered by everyone, but it does take time, patience and, above all, the acquired ability to *feel* with the heart, rather than to *understand* with the rational mind. In this respect the reader will do well to bear in mind that *life is a feeling, and not an intellectual exercise.*

Generally speaking people *spend* their lives, as opposed to *living* their lives, never realising that what they consider to be life is not life at all. People tend to believe that the circumstances surrounding them, or the conditions they find themselves in, are life, but these are merely the challenges forming the pattern upon which we are meant to structure life. People also tend to believe that their actions and behaviour, or the actions and behaviour of others, are life, but our actions are merely the materialisation of the possibility we have chosen to use, and our behaviour is merely the *re-action* to such materialisation or possible materialisation.

However, in all of this, by far the worst belief is that life is an intellectual process which can be approached rationally. This disastrous belief makes no allowance for the mystery of perception or for the mystery of beingness, and as a result people's lives have no real meaning. Not acknowledging the fact that life is a feeling, rather than an intellectual process, people do not base their lives upon the mystery of their true beingness, nor do they base their lives upon the four postulates of stalking. Instead people base their lives upon an intellectualism that is devoid of true feeling, devoid of irrational knowledge. Consequently, life for such people has no "fabric" to it and, having no fabric, there is nothing to hold the "stitching" together – no basis for action – no base to support action. It is therefore not surprising that people content themselves with empty intellectual abstractions, with endless talking, and with erudite philosophising that has no basis in action.

To entertain any of the beliefs mentioned above is to be caught in a dream – a dream which for a great many people today is a nightmare, or at least very close to it. Believing that dream to be reality, people are powerless to take action in the true sense of the word, for it is simply not possible to take action in a state of non-reality. When one is caught in an illusion, any action taken will be determined by that illusion, and therefore the action itself must be considered sheer folly. Being incapable of true action, people have no other recourse than to perpetuate their folly by constantly reacting to everyone and everything in their lives. This, in the final analysis, boils down to *re-enacting* the behaviour they have acquired as a result of their social conditioning. This social conditioning is of course the result of humanity's common dream and, therefore, common illusion.

So we see that it is not life that is an illusion, but rather humanity's perception of life that is the illusion. Life is no-thing, and therefore cannot possibly be an illusion, for by definition an illusion is some-thing which is mistaken for something else. However, once again we see how erroneous man's perception can be, and how often people will *assume understanding* rather than check what they *think* they have perceived. In this respect most people generally look upon illusion as being nothing, and through this prove their ignorance of, and their disrespect for, the value of words.

An illusion is based on some-thing. For example, if I am walking down a path in the dark and notice something moving in the bushes ahead of me, I could well assume that I have encountered another person, or an animal, or even a ghost. If I now make a closer inspection of what I have seen, but discover that it is only an old plastic bag caught on a bush and moving in the wind, I could conclude that what I had thought to be a person, or an animal, or a ghost, was merely an illusion. Yet such reasoning would not be sound, for the plastic bag is very real, and is certainly no illusion. It is instead my initial perception of the plastic bag that is the illusion. But realise that this illusion is based upon my perception of some-thing, which in this case was the plastic bag.

Although the example above pertains to a material illusion, this same principle applies also to emotional and mental illusions. Never pausing to consider the fact that the world is not what it appears to be, people jump to all sorts of conclusions which are based upon an assumed understanding. Caught in this trap of rational assumption, men and women are incapable of taking *action* based upon the reality of life, but instead are forced to *re-enact* old behaviour patterns. Such people are not *living* their lives in the true sense of the word, but are merely *spending* their opportunity to live in re-enacting their folly.

To begin with, all of us are caught in the common dream, the common illusion, and as a result all our actions amount to nothing more than folly. This is the way *power* has set it up. It is a set-up which is really quite weird, in the true sense of the word, for on the one hand we are powerless to change it, but on the other hand we do have the *power* and the freedom to change it all. This is perhaps the ultimate paradox – a paradox which is so complex that it is completely bewildering, but concealing a truth that is stunning in its simplicity.

The truth concealed by this paradox forms the innermost core of the Toltec tradition – a core that is the ultimate source of *power* – a core that can be the key to freedom, or the key to sorcery, the key to creation, or the key to destruction. This core is *Azoth*, the great secret of Hermes Trismegistus. It is also the mythical *elixir of life*, and the much sought-after *Lapis Philosophorum*, the Philosopher's Stone. It is the miracle *staff* of Moses, and *Excalibur*, the unearthly sword of Arthur. It is *Miölnir*, the hammer of Thor, and then again the *Plumed Serpent*, the magic *wand* of the great Toltec votan, Quetzo-Cohuatl.

Such are the legends and myths which have grown up around the truth concealed by this strangest of strange paradoxes, but considering its nature, it is hardly surprising that so many legends and myths should have evolved around this one truth. The reason why Toltecs look upon this truth as being the core of their tradition is that once it has been grasped in its entirety and put into practice, this truth yields a dual force, metaphorically termed the ancient *Spear of Destiny* when touched by the left hand, and the invincible *Sword of Power* when touched by the right hand.

Since it is the key to both creation and destruction, a great many people throughout the ages have made it their sole purpose in life to find this core. However, not all of these seekers can be said to have had motives that were pure. In fact, the vast majority of these seekers had motives that were very far from pure. Of these, the lucky ones died without ever finding the hidden core. The unlucky ones were those few who did find it, but because of their greed and ambition could touch it only ever so briefly. Yet, even for that brief touch, for those few moments of bliss, these unfortunate wretches paid grotesque prices with their sanity.

Such is the nature of this core. It is truly the source of all *power* – a raw *power* which is ancient beyond belief, and yet which is also constantly being renewed by having to turn in upon itself under the unimaginable force of inherent awareness and the truly staggering momentum of evolving awareness.

To touch that core is to journey to the "centre of the world"; a state of awareness which is termed *the pivot of the three rings*, that is, *the three rings of power*. Existing as that unity which is termed the *spirit of man*, the *nagal*, this is a level of awareness which demands the *totality of the self*, and to survive the journey to this centre requires a level of impeccability of which very few have ever been capable. It is primarily for this reason that the Warriors of Freedom were forced to break away from their inherited tradition, and to seek out that knowledge which enhances impeccability above anything else. From our perspective there is absolutely no point in acquiring *power*, if that *power* is going to destroy you.

It was in their pursuit of the required level of impeccability that the Warriors of Freedom discovered the deeper implications inherent within the *Third Attention*. These implications revealed aspects of the teachings which had never before even been considered, aspects which seemed so simplistic that the Old Seers had dismissed them as being trivial. And yet it was these "simplistic" aspects of the teachings that catapulted the Warriors of Freedom into a completely new dimension of knowledge.

As a result of this new knowledge, the Warriors of Freedom once again restructured all of the teachings, this time putting the accent, not so much on the acquisition of *power*, but on acquiring the necessary level of impeccability, which automatically yields an extremely fine and high level of *personal power*. This change of accent brought into being a new method of teaching, and the manner in which the teachings are being presented in these books is in accordance with the new method. In this regard the perceptive reader will by now have noticed how the accent is continually being placed upon impeccability in every respect, for it is only once the required level of impeccability has been reached that the inner core of the Toltec tradition stands revealed and it becomes possible to approach it safely. Only then can the *totality of the self* begin to emerge, and only then can the warrior grasp the *Spear of Destiny* without loss of sanity, and wield the *Sword of Power* without being destroyed.

This then brings us back to our consideration of the core, but to grasp the import of this concept is not at all easy within the context of our social conditioning. To say that all of us are caught in the common dream, and that as a result all our actions amount to nothing more than folly, is one thing, but to say that the answer is as simple as waking up in that dream, is a different thing altogether. Such statements make very little sense to the rational mind, and yet these two statements together reveal the truth of all truths. However, if we are to achieve any real understanding of this concept, then it is vital to bear in mind the following two aphorisms.

YOU ARE BUT THE DREAM OF YOUR DREAMER. YOU ARE NOT YOUR BODY, OR YOUR MIND, NOT EVEN YOUR LUMINOUS COCOON. THESE ARE ONLY THE ELEMENTAL UNITS THAT HAVE BEEN DREAMED IN BY THE EAGLE, AND WHICH ARE COALESCED BY THE DREAMER THROUGH A FOCUSING OF ITS INTENT. THIS COALITION IS KEPT INTACT THROUGHOUT LIFE BY THE INTENSITY WITH WHICH THE DREAMER FIXES ITS ATTENTION UPON THE SUBJECT OF ITS DREAM – YOU.

ALL THE QUALITIES OF YOUR TONAL, INCLUDING ACADEMIC ABILITY AND TALENT, ARE A MATTER OF FOCUS AND INTENSITY. THE MOMENT THAT FOCUS IS SHIFTED, OR THE INTENSITY IS ALTERED, YOUR TONAL CHANGES.

The implications of these two aphorisms are vast – so vast that this one volume is not enough to do justice to them all. Although some of these implications have been covered in the first two volumes, and even though more of them are covered in this volume, there are still many that we will only be able to consider in later volumes. One of the implications that has already been introduced but not dealt with in any depth, and the one that is of uppermost concern here, is the concept of *intelligent co-operation*, given in *Cry of the Eagle*. Therefore in our consideration of these two aphorisms, it is assumed that the reader is fully familiar with the fundamentals of this particular concept, for we now need to look at intelligent co-operation in greater depth.

Before we can continue beyond this point, it is important first of all to clarify what is meant by the dreamer of man. Realise that part of the illusion in which man is trapped is based upon the fact that average men and women do not know their true nature, and consequently believe themselves to be their physical bodies, or their minds, or both. However, as is pointed out in the first aphorism under consideration, man is neither his body nor his mind. Instead man is essentially a spirit being of the universe, termed the *spirit of man*, or the *nagal*. Great care must be taken that this statement is grasped properly, for apprentices all too often make the mistake of assuming that the phrase the *spirit of man* means that every man and woman has his or her own *nagal*.

In a sense the assumption made by the average apprentice is true enough, but strictly speaking it is not entirely correct, for there is only one life, evolving one awareness, through the medium of one material universe. In other words, there is only one *nagal*, *one spirit*, which has many different facets to its awareness, one of which is that creature we term man.

Technically speaking, the awareness of the *nagal* manifests as an untold number of energy fields arranged in various sequences of clustering, and one of those clusters forms that macrocosmic *band* which is termed man. It is this macrocosmic *band of man* that is loosely termed the *spirit of man*, and since the clustering of its energy fields is identical to that of the macrocosm, the *spirit of man* is an exact replica of the manifestation of the macrocosmic *nagal*.

In the final analysis there is only one *spirit of man*, contained within which are millions upon millions of energy fields, each one having the potential to register awareness in terms of itself as an individual. Therefore, what apprentices often consider as one's own personal *nagal*, would in fact be only one energy field within that greater whole termed the *spirit of man*, and what is termed the dreamer, is that energy field registering an awareness of itself as an individual. In other words, the dreamer is the manifestation of the *nagal's* awareness.

However, the point which must be stressed here is that in reality these individual energy fields, at their own level, always remain one coherent whole, for they are completely inter-dependent and interactive, and in this respect form the very basis of the interrelationship of life. It is only really at the level of life upon the physical plane that there is a true sense of separativeness. The reasons for this are diverse and complex, but let it suffice for now to say that the sense of being a separate individual comes about partly because of the separative quality of the mind, and partly because the luminous cocoon of man is also an exact replica of the *spirit of man*, which is of course *one*.

In our consideration of the dreamer, realise that the energy fields that constitute the *spirit of man* all have their own specific rate of vibration, which is determined by their inherent awareness. These energy fields are clustered in the same sequences as the energy fields of the manifested universe, but because they have their own rate of vibration prior to clustering, the original rate of vibration *colours* the vibration brought about by the clustering.

Within the *spirit of man* there are seven colours produced in this way, each colour consisting of a vast range of shades. These colours, which exist as a result of the clustering, each denote a specific overall vibration in the nature of a chord of resonance, and each chord is composed of a huge spectrum of allied frequencies which are in the nature of sympathetic tones, or "shades" of colour. It is these seven colours that determine the seven types of dreamers, and it is the sympathetic resonance of each shade that determines the destiny, and ultimately also the actions of the individual.

From the explanation above it should now be clear why it is not at all accurate to think in terms of my *nagal* as opposed to your *nagal* or, for that matter, my dreamer as opposed to your dreamer. Nonetheless, when it comes to the use of words, we are forced to do just this for the sake of clarity. Therefore the reader is asked to please bear in mind that what follows here is only a verbal approximation of a reality which completely transcends the scope of words.

What then is the dreamer? Put quite simply, the dreamer is the *awareness* of one unit of the *nagal* – the awareness of the individual. The overall vibration of the dreamer is determined by the *potential* of its inherent awareness, and this overall vibration causes it to fall into one of seven spectra seen as a colour. The actual shade of this colour is determined by evolving awareness, and is therefore progressively altered through the process of evolution.

In order to evolve its awareness, the individual units of the *nagal* explore their potential through the *act of dreaming*, and are therefore termed the dreamers. In this respect, the imme-diate challenge for all organic life-forms upon this planet, includ-ing some forms of inorganic life, is to materialise their full poten-tial upon the dense physical plane. In order to do so, the dreamers of man periodically fixate their attention by focusing their *intent* upon the physical plane, and the result of such fixation is physical incarnation. However, it is important to know that incarnation is only feasible if the dreamer concerned can find within life upon the physical plane those conditions which will aid it in its evolution of awareness. Therefore, any incarnation is dependent upon the constantly changing possibilities determined by the destiny of all life. As a result, incarnation is much in the nature of seizing a fleeting moment of chance.

Thus if it were not for the fact that there is only one *nagal*, that life is thoroughly interrelated, and that the dreamers of man are fully group conscious, physical incarnation would be well-nigh impossible. In fact, notwithstanding any of this, physical incarnation is still exceedingly difficult for average men and women, for in spite of the group consciousness of the dreamers, the evolution of awareness at this moment in time entails developing aspects of awareness that are separative in quality, and do not uphold the interrelationship of life. From all of the above it can be seen that co-operation is not only intelligent in that it is vital, but since it forms the very basis of the interrelationship of life, it is also the bedrock of evolution.

Intelligent co-operation exists in many different forms, but the one that concerns us here is co-operation with one's own dreamer. In order to grasp how this is accomplished, it is important to start working from the basis that we are not our physical bodies or our minds. This can very easily be corroborated by using the following simple technique.

Sit down somewhere quietly, make yourself comfortable, and then close your eyes. Now allow yourself to experience each of your senses, with the exception of physical sight. Hear the sounds in the world around you. Smell the air you breathe. Be aware of the taste in your mouth. Feel the touch of clothes against your skin, and the pressure of your body on the furniture and of your feet on the floor. Realise that all these sensations come to you via your physical body, and that you are not your body.

Now concentrate upon your mind. Watch your thoughts as if they are playing off on a television screen in front of you. Allow your thoughts to meander by themselves, but realise that because you can observe them you are not your thoughts, but that they are the product of your mind. Now actively and consciously change your thoughts as many times as you want to, and realise that through your ability to do this, you control your mind, and therefore you are not your mind.

If you are not your body, or your mind, then ask yourself what you are. You will not find an answer, only thoughts and more thoughts. But behind those thoughts you will sense an intelligence observing silently – an intelligence which is you.

Now realise that if you are not your body or your mind, then you are not a physical entity, and because of this, life cannot possibly be what you have always believed it to be. Your name, your circumstances within life, your career, your social standing, your marital status, in fact your everything, is dependent upon you having a physical body which is controlled by your mind. Yet it is your physical body which has a name and an age, which gives you social standing, and which makes it possible to be married and to have children, to have a career, to have money, to have a home, a car, life insurance, and so forth. By having a physical body, and a mind with which to direct and control it, all of this becomes possible – life upon the physical plane becomes possible. But behind this, behind your body and your mind is you, the indwelling intelligence.

This is as far as the technique will take you, but for our present purposes it is far enough. Knowing that you are the intelligence within your body, and that you can control and direct your mind, ask yourself the question, "Do I control my mind, or am I the victim of my own mind?" This little technique is simplicity itself, and yet apprentices using it for the first time are invariably struck dumb by the overpowering realisation not only that they identify one hundred percent with both the body and the mind, but worse still, that they are always the victims of their own thoughts, their own minds!

From the above it must follow that to indulge in the belief that you are a victim is tantamount to admitting that you are your own worst enemy, and that if your life is not what you would like it to be, then it is only because you are not doing anything constructive towards changing it. Furthermore, realise that the only reason why people believe that they are trapped by their circumstances in life, is because they *think* they are trapped or, more accurately, because they *indulge* in the belief that they can only live their lives according to the dictates of circumstance. In the final analysis it is only your physical body which can be trapped in the true sense of the word, and your mind to a certain extent, by indulging in the belief that you are bound by circumstance. You, the indwelling intelligence, can never be trapped, but the belief of being trapped is so all-absorbing, that not only are people generally completely debilitated by this belief, but they might just as well really be trapped.

It is this belief that we are the victims of circumstance, and that we are bound by those circumstances, that constitutes the common illusion of humanity. This is the dream in which all men and women are caught until they have woken up to the fact that they are neither their body nor their mind, and that life does not mean having a name and a position within society. It is in every possible respect as simple as this – waking up – but even just a little bit of reflecting will quickly enough reveal that the implications of such an awakening are truly astronomical.

In order to understand what all of this really means, we must return to our consideration of the dreamer. However, it must first be pointed out that, from the angle of the reader, the concept of the dreamer must for now be regarded as nothing more than a theory, to serve as a working hypothesis until such time as the theory can be corroborated through first-hand experience. All apprentices have to put the teachings into practice if they hope ever to be able to corroborate the truth of the teachings, and the reader should realise that this same rule applies equally to him or her.

As was mentioned earlier, the dreamer evolves its awareness, or rather *dis-covers* or *un-covers* its potential, through the act of dreaming, and in this act periodically fixates its attention upon the physical plane. This fixation, which results in physical incarnation, is brought about whenever the dreamer focuses its *intent* upon certain aspects of its continuous dream. These aspects pertain to manifesting its full potential upon the physical plane – an act which by its very nature demands not only life upon the dense physical plane, but also challenges that can only come about because of physical incarnation. However, realise that as a result of clustering, the dense physical world has a much lower vibration than the world of the dreamer. Therefore, physical incarnation causes the dream of the dreamer to become "deeper", and therefore also more *intense*.

This deepening of the dream, and its intensification within the slower vibrations of the physical world, coupled with the fixation of the dreamer's attention, is what creates the illusion of being trapped. Yet, it must also be remembered that incarnation is only a partial materialisation of the dreamer's awareness. That "portion" of awareness which comes into incarnation is composed of those aspects of itself upon which the dreamer has focused its *intent*, and which it dreams into physical existence by fixating its attention upon incarnation. This partial materialisation of awareness is what results in the human being not knowing his true nature, and this lack of knowledge is further compounded by the fact that there is always an eclipse of consciousness which happens at birth. Consequently the human being identifies completely with both his body and his socially conditioned mind, and it is therefore hardly surprising that the illusion of being trapped is so powerful.

As long as this identification with body and mind persists, the dreamer is not able to control its dream fully and, as a result, its human counterpart, which is the dreamed, temporarily exhibits a will of its own. However, the will of the dreamed is not really *will* in the true sense of the word, but rather the random effects of the dreamer not being able to control the dreamed fully. This lack of control is in the nature of what can only be termed psychic cerebral palsy, and the results of it are almost identical to the physical ailment, in that the dreamed behaves in a 'spastic' manner until such time as the dreamer can gain full control. It is therefore not the dreamer on its own plane which is out of control, but its physical counterpart which, because of the identification taking place, is resisting control. Seeking this control of its physical counterpart is the first step towards being able to unfold its full potential upon the physical plane, and is therefore part of the reason for engaging in physical incarnation.

YOU ARE YOUR DREAMER. THEREFORE TO RESIST YOUR DREAMER IS TO RESIST YOUR OWN SELF – AN ACT WHICH MAKES NO SENSE.

From what we have seen so far it should now be clear why co-operation between oneself and one's dreamer should be so import-ant. However, this co-operation must be *intelligent,* for it must not be forgotten that although the dreamer focuses its *intent* upon the evolution of its awareness, it is nevertheless the dreamed that has to take action upon the physical plane, physically, emotionally and mentally. In other words, the dreamer holds its *intent* focused upon the desired goals, but it is the dreamed who has to figure out how best to accomplish these goals. What this boils down to, is that instead of the dreamed resisting its fate, it must embrace it fully, which amounts to the same thing as taking control of the dream – taking control of one's own life.

To take control of the dream does not mean controlling your dreamer, but rather that you take control of what is happening in the dream. This means that instead of being a victim within the dream, and simply allowing life to *happen* to you, you deter-mine how the course of events presented in the dream is to unfold. In this respect, realise that once we are in incarnation, the attention of the dreamer is fixated, and therefore we cannot alter the desired *goal* of the dream, for this constitutes our fate for this lifetime, but we can determine how to achieve that goal, and therefore can control the *contents* of the dream.

The contents of the dream are what we experience as our challenges in life, and these are designed by the dreamer around the actions of the dreamed. In other words, the *nature* as well as the *form* of any challenge is dependent upon the co-operation, or lack thereof, between dreamer and dreamed. It therefore stands to reason that because it is the dreamed that takes action, it is also the dreamed that dictates both the nature and the form of a challenge. This once again shows the futility of believing that we are the victims of circumstance. Furthermore, from this it is also clear that the more we co-operate with our dreamer, the more we control the contents of the dream, and the more intelligent this co-operation is, the more powerful our control will be.

Controlling the contents of the dream is what is known as *controlling folly*. Our folly comes about, firstly, because we believe in the illusion that we are the victims of circumstance, and secondly, because of the fact that within incarnation we cannot alter the goal of the dream. No matter whether we take control of our lives or not, we cannot avoid the end product of the dream and, therefore, at the end of the day, we have to acknowledge the fact that all our actions amount to nothing more than folly – and yet there is a difference. This difference lies in the fact that if we try to avoid our fate by constantly running away from our challenges, we set up only more challenges and, through this, compound our folly by *submitting* to it. If, on the other hand, we face our challenges by taking *control* of our lives, then not only do we control our folly, but we actually also decrease it.

> INTELLIGENT CO-OPERATION MEANS CONTROLLING YOUR FOLLY. THIS ACT IS THE ULTIMATE KEY TO ALL FORMS OF MAGIC, AND LEADS TO AN UNDERSTANDING OF DRAGON LORE – AN UNDERSTANDING WHICH YIELDS THE ABILITY TO CAST THE SPEAR OF DESTINY AND TO WIELD THE SWORD OF POWER.

As the aphorism above implies, controlling our folly is that ultimate key to what was referred to earlier as the core of the Toltec tradition. However, it must be pointed out that although controlled folly is a concept that is widely practised amongst all warriors, it is only upon the Path of Freedom that its real nature and import can be grasped in its entirety. The reasons for this are far too complex for this volume, but let it suffice for now to say that inherent within the act of controlling folly lies the ability to manipulate the force of *intent*.

In *Return of the Warriors* it was explained that what the un-initiated look upon as magic, are in fact miracles brought about by the manipulation of *intent*. There is no magic as such, although it cannot be denied that the manipulation of *intent* is truly formidable and does indeed appear to be magical. Nevertheless, it must be remembered that *intent* is a quality of the dreamer's awareness, and therefore where there is no intelligent co-operation, where there is no controlled folly, there can also be no manipulation of *intent*. True manipulation of *intent* can only come about where there is a full and conscious control of folly; an act that implies acknowledgement of the interrelationship of life, for it must not be forgotten that there is only one *nagal*, and that because of this, all the dreamers of mankind are fully group-conscious.

In order to grasp this fully we must once again digress slightly in order to explain the difference between the *mind* and that which we term the *rational mind*. Apprentices often make the mistake of assuming that these two are the same, but it will be remembered from *Cry of the Eagle* that mind is one polarity of the dreamer's awareness, and *intent* the other. The rational mind, on the other hand, is an expression of the dreamer's ability to compute, in the sense of working out practical details upon the physical plane. In other words, the rational mind is only the physical expression of a fraction of true mind.

It must also be remembered that the function of mind is to separate and divide for the purposes of evolution, whereas the function of *intent* is, firstly, to pressurise mind into separation, and secondly, to unite, also for the purposes of evolution. In the final analysis mind and *intent* are one and the same thing, namely, the awareness of the dreamer. Therefore, what is termed *the first ring of power* is that aspect of the dreamer's awareness termed mind, whereas *the second ring of power* is that aspect termed *intent*, and inherent within *the first ring of power* is the reflection of *intent* in the form of the urge to separate or to discriminate. It is because of this fact that *the first ring of power* is subtractive in quality, and why it is stated that true *intent* only becomes operative when using the *second ring of power*. However, because *intent* unites, it is additive in quality, and this means that in order to manipulate true *intent* it is necessary to practise the interrelationship of life.

What in effect all of this means is that the only form of *intent* that can be used where there is no practising of the interrelationship of life, is the *reflection* of *intent*, which is separative in quality, and therefore subtractive. This is what can rightfully be termed the *power of the mind*, as opposed to the rational mind, which has no real *power* in itself. The *power of the mind* is, of course, *the first ring of power*, and it is this reflection of *intent* which is utilised by those warriors who are dedicated to the Path of High Adventure. It is primarily for this reason that this path does not lead to freedom, for being concerned only with the acquisition of *power* for personal gain, any use of *intent* results in calling forth the separative quality of mind. Needless to say, this only compounds division, with the result that these warriors become ever more separative in their ways, and therefore do not uphold the interdependence of life.

The trap of the Path of High Adventure is subtle indeed, for it lies in the fact that it is perfectly possible to wield this *power* by achieving only a measure of intelligent co-operation. So as to gain a proper understanding of this, it should be noted that although the dreamers are undeniably group-conscious, yet separativeness, which is an aspect of the dreamer's awareness, plays a vitally important role in the evolution of awareness. Consequently, warriors upon the Path of High Adventure do not *directly* oppose the will of their dreamers by being separative. On the contrary, by being separative they are actually aiding the evolution of awareness by developing the faculty of *discrimination* in both themselves and those around them. Furthermore, because the dreamers are group-conscious, and as the Law of Economy will always cause the actions of the individual, irrespective of whether these are good or bad, to be utilised for the good of the greater whole, such warriors can actually manipulate both the mind aspect of their dreamers and the universal Law of Economy to their own advantage in their selfish pursuit of *power* for the fulfilment of ambitions which have nothing to do with the interrelationship of life.

Yet, realise also that because the dreamers are essentially group-conscious, this is not a state of affairs that can last for ever. Sooner or later the inherent urge to unity must emerge. However if, as sometimes does happen, the sense of separativeness within any one particular incarnation has become too great, the dreamer can lose control to such an extent that the whole of its awareness becomes seriously impaired. Such a dreamer has to all intents and purposes become trapped in its own fixation by the actions of the dreamed, and the illusion of the dream causes it to become destabilised to the extent that it is caught in the one polarity of its awareness, namely, mind. Trapped in this way, such a dreamer is termed a *lost star*, for it will usually take it aeons upon aeons to extricate itself from this trap. Of course, relative to the human time scale, this period of time does seem to be an eternity, and hence the term, a lost star.

Having explained this much, it should now be clear why it is stated that the Path of High Adventure does not lead to freedom, and why it is that upon the Path of Freedom so much accent is placed upon the interrelationship of all life. As was mentioned earlier in this chapter, the key to all this lies in intelligent co-operation, a key which can be used for separation, or unification, the key to both *the first and the second ring of power*, and ultimately the key to creation and destruction. That which makes this key safe to use, and that which balances creation and destruction, and which therefore binds together *the first and the second ring of power*, is that force termed *the third ring of power*. This third ring is gradually brought into being whenever we practise the ultimate form of intelligent co-operation which, in the final analysis, means that we control our folly to the extent that we take control of the dream.

To take control of the dream is not quite as simple as it appears to be at first glance, for to take control implies that we must first of all wake up *in* the dream. Realise that we cannot wake up *from* the dream, for the simple reason that during physical incarnation the attention of the dreamer is fixated, and the moment that fixation is released, it means that the dreamer has withdrawn its *intent*, the result of which is physical death. Therefore what is referred to as waking up in the dream, is that the dreamed becomes aware, firstly, that he is dreaming; secondly, that what is happening to him is therefore only a dream; and thirdly, that he can control the contents of the dream. This is a point which every apprentice at first finds to be very abstract, but only because such an apprentice always tends to forget that a dream is not what his social conditioning has led him or her to believe, but that any dream is in reality an altered state of perception.

It is in failing to understand what is really meant by an altered state of perception that apprentices will often resort to asking questions such as: "Do you mean this rock is only a dream?" "Do you mean this rock is only an illusion, that it does not really exist?" The rock is real enough, as is the dream, and neither of them are an illusion as such, but our perception of both changes radically as we bring about different alignments of perception. Therefore it is not that the rock or the dream is an illusion, but rather that the illusion lies in the fact that we think and believe our present perception of the rock to be the one and only reality.

From the above it stands to reason that in order to take control of the dream we must be able to shift the focus, which in turn implies that we must have a fluid assemblage point, so that we can bring about altered states of perception. If we cannot shift the focus, then obviously we remain a "victim" in the dream. In this respect, the first shift in focus comes about when the apprentice begins to realise that even without being able to move his or her assemblage point to any great extent, it is nevertheless possible to perceive life differently. From the moment this much has been accomplished, the apprentice is well on his or her way to waking up in the dream, and when sufficiently awake, he or she will start to take control of the dream.

It is once the apprentice has started to wake up that the technique of intelligent co-operation becomes so very important. If freedom is to be achieved and the temptation posed by the Path of High Adventure is to be avoided, then it is imperative for the apprentice to come to the realisation that his or her life is just perfect the way it is, and that rather than fighting fate, there must be a fully intelligent co-operation with his or her dreamer. The act of waking up is really very much a question of acknowledging the fact that life, with all its challenges, is not something to run away from, but that it presents an opportunity to materialise our full potential upon the physical plane. Materialising our potential is, of course, the true purpose of the dream, and once we embark upon this, we not only become at-one with the *will* of the dreamer, but we also automatically begin to control our folly so as to bring about only those challenges and effects which aid us in the process of materialisation. It is for this reason that waking up in the dream is termed *having learned to dream true*; that is, dreaming true to our fate.

In order to dream true, we obviously need to refine our skill in the art of dreaming – we need to refine our skill in the ability to bring about altered states of perception. However, as we saw in the example of illusion, there is no point in achieving altered states of perception if our *interpretation* of what we are perceiving is inaccurate. Dreaming will always bring about an altered state of perception, but the only way in which we can be sure that our interpretation of that perception is correct, is to stalk our perception both of ourselves and the world around us.

Here it must be pointed out that in order to do full justice to the fundamental teachings concerning the art of dreaming imparted in *Cry of the Eagle*, it is also necessary to put into practice the teachings on stalking imparted in this book. Likewise, in order to grasp the teachings in this book, the reader will need to be familiar with the fundamentals of stalking imparted in *Return of the Warriors*. In this respect it is important for the reader to know that in many ways the art of dreaming and the art of stalking are two inseparable techniques, both of which are inextricably tied up with the Mastery of Awareness. Essentially the Mastery of Awareness is exactly what the term implies, and within this area of expertise it is the art of dreaming that is used for mapping out unknown aspects of our awareness. However, since the evolution of awareness must take place in a practical manner upon the physical plane, it is the art of stalking that is used for making practical that which the art of dreaming yields, for it must never be forgotten that it is in the practicability of new knowledge that lies its efficacy, and therefore also its authenticity. Never has there been a truer axiom than the old proverb, "the proof of the pudding lies in the eating".

It will be recalled from *Return of the Warriors* that the art of stalking is regarded as one of the three areas of expertise in which every apprentice has to become proficient if he or she hopes to become a true warrior. The reason why the art of stalking is singled out here, rather than the art of dreaming, is not at all easy to explain in a few words, but hopefully this will become progressively clear to the reader in the course of this volume. Let it suffice for now to say that dreaming is dreaming, and that there is not much more we can do with dreaming other than to dream, and to become ever more proficient in the art of dreaming. The reason for this is that the dream of the dreamer is fixed, and nothing we can do in dreaming is going to break the fixation of the dreamer. Therefore we cannot change the dream in any way. This, after all, is our folly. However, we can control our folly, and by doing so, we can manipulate the contents of the dream. Controlling our folly, and manipulating the contents of the dream, is the true purpose and meaning of the art of stalking. Therefore stalking is defined as *the mastery of controlled folly*, and a stalker is defined as *a master of controlled folly*.

We have already noted that controlling our folly is the ultimate form of intelligent co-operation, but in order to control folly it is necessary to wake up to the fact that we are caught in a dream. The act of waking up implies sobriety, a quality of awareness which is rightfully assigned to the east, and the acquisition of which requires recapitulation. There is no better way of waking up than to recapitulate our life so as to be able to see it for what it truly is. But sobriety is also much more than this, for once even just a small measure of sobriety is achieved, we rapidly begin to realise that neither we, nor the world around us, is what we have always believed. In other words, recapitulation yields not only sobriety but, through that sobriety, also reveals the first postulate of stalking – the fact that the whole world and everything in it is an endless mystery. From this moment on it becomes impossible, even for a relatively inexperienced apprentice, to look upon his or her life in the same way as before, and without even realising it, such an apprentice will have begun to stalk him or herself. However, stalking is a skill which can only be acquired by following the dictates of *power*, for it is important to remember that it is not we who create the rules, but *power*. The evolution of awareness is *power's* game, and it is therefore also *power* that has set the rules of the game.

As is always the case with *power*, the rules are deceptively simple, but the implications are vast. On the one hand we have the *rule of the hunt*, and on the other we have set out for us a board – the board of life, given in Figure 3, which, as we already know, are the four components of the dream. This game is the ultimate form of solitaire, except that all four quadrants are completely interdependent and interactive, and that for every move we make, the *power* inherent in the board of life reacts. If the move we have made supports the evolution of awareness, we score one point in gaining a measure of *personal power*, and this point grants us a greater freedom in our choice of subsequent moves. But if the move we have made is contrary to the evolution of awareness, we lose one point, which not only diminishes our *personal power*, but also limits our freedom. The object of solitaire is to eradicate all the pegs until we are left with only one, and likewise in the game of life we are also required to overcome all the challenges in our life in order to achieve all-one-ness or, in other words, the *totality of the self.*

To play the game of life requires action and strength, both of which are placed in the North. But in order to acquire strength and to act with wisdom we must be able to stalk efficiently, and in order to learn this skill, we need to use the stalker's rule by applying any one or any combination of its seven aspects to everything we do in life. It is in using the stalker's rule that we slowly but surely begin to grasp the deeper implications of the second postulate of stalking. These implications lead us directly into Dragon Lore which, being the essence of *the third ring of power*, must of necessity arise in the South, the place of *power* and of dreaming.

It is not feasible to cover everything pertaining to the four postulates of stalking, the stalker's rule and Dragon Lore in this one volume, and yet these three concepts are so inextricably interwoven that it is imperative at least to introduce them as one whole. In the first part of this book I have endeavoured to give as much guidance as is possible for now on how best to view and work with the four postulates of stalking. In this respect the reader should understand that, although it has not been mentioned before, so as to avoid unnecessary confusion, all the teachings imparted in Volumes One and Two pertain primarily to the fundamentals of the first postulate of stalking. Likewise, I have so far in this book also placed more accent on the first postulate than on the others. The reason for this is because even though the four postulates are interdependent, they nevertheless do follow each other sequentially, in that each gives rise to the following one. Therefore, if we are to gain an understanding of them, we must tackle them in their natural order.

In this book we will be concentrating on the stalker's rule, which pertains to the second postulate, and which is placed in the North, the place of strength and of action. Because the second postulate arises from the first, it now becomes necessary to look also at the more advanced aspects of recapitulation, which only really become understandable in studying the second postulate. Although we will throughout this book continue to touch upon the third and fourth postulates, as well as Dragon Lore, it will only be in subsequent volumes that we will be able to explore these advanced teachings fully. For our present purposes we must confine ourselves to the stalker's rule, and thereby learn what it is to coalesce the mists of what in time will become Dragon Lore, for without this understanding we have no hope of ever being able to grasp Dragon Lore, much less utilise it.

We cannot at this point define Dragon Lore with any degree of clarity, but having got this far, we are now at least in a position to consider the following aphorism, which we will use as our point of departure for what follows.

HAVING LEARNED TO STALK HIS OWN DREAM, AND THE DREAM OF OTHERS, THE WARRIOR LEARNS THE LORE OF THE DRAGON. DRAGON LORE ENABLES THE WARRIOR TO ENTER THE DREAM OF THE EAGLE, AND IN SO DOING TO LEARN TO CREATE POSSIBILITIES THAT NEVER BEFORE WERE PRESENT. THE ADVANTAGE IN THIS IS THAT IN HAVING TO DEAL WITH THE UNPREDICTABLE WHIMS OF POWER, THE WARRIOR CAN ALWAYS CREATE A WILD CARD WHENEVER THE NEED FOR ONE ARISES. THEREFORE DRAGON LORE IS THE ULTIMATE KNOWLEDGE IN THE ART OF STALKING – THE ABILITY TO SLIP OUT OF ANY TRAP.

It is not possible to grasp the concept of Dragon Lore without having to consider the reality of alternative worlds, and in this respect Dragon Lore reveals much about that world known as *The World of Sorcerers.* The Warriors of Freedom no longer adhere to the ancient practices of sorcery, for these practices do not lead to freedom, and yet the name of this world has remained intact, for the simple reason that it is a most apt name for this particular world. I wish to make this point here, for although in this book I will be preparing the reader to take his or her first steps in being able to align and access this world, I want nonetheless to make it clear that there are several gateways into The World of Sorcerers. All of these gateways open up into a maze – a maze in which it is very easy to become lost, and which yields one illusion after another. There is only one gateway, which looks exactly the same as all the others, that leads to the heart of this world. It is here, at the very centre of this world, that the truth concerning Dragon Lore stands revealed, and where it is possible to look upon the reflection of the *pivot of the three rings,* as well as the reflections of both the *Spear of Destiny* and the *Sword of Power.* It is to this gateway that I will be guiding the reader, and not to any of the others which are so well known to our modern-day sorcerers.

PART TWO

THE STALKER'S RULE

THE STALKER'S RULE
Mixed Media: Tony Butler

THE STALKER'S RULE

1. *A WARRIOR CHOOSES HIS BATTLE, AND THEREFORE WILL ALWAYS ASSESS BOTH THE CIRCUMSTANCES AND THE CONDITIONS OF EVERY BATTLE WITH THE UTMOST CARE.*

2. *BY STRIVING FOR SIMPLICITY, A WARRIOR DISCARDS ALL UNNECESSARY ACTS.*

3. *A WARRIOR IS ALWAYS READY TO MAKE HIS LAST STAND RIGHT HERE AND RIGHT NOW.*

4. *ONCE HE HAS ENTERED INTO BATTLE, A WARRIOR ABANDONS HIMSELF TO HIS ACTIONS BY ALLOWING HIS SPIRIT TO FLOW FREE AND CLEAR. ONLY THEN DO THE POWERS OF DESTINY GUIDE US BY PAVING THE WAY.*

5. *WHENEVER FACED WITH IMPOSSIBLE ODDS, A WARRIOR OPENS HIMSELF UP TO THE WORLD AROUND HIM BY ALLOWING HIS MIND TO BECOME OCCUPIED WITH THE LITTLE DETAILS OF LIFE.*

6. *A WARRIOR ALWAYS COMPRESSES TIME. ANY BATTLE, NO MATTER HOW BIG OR SMALL IT MAY BE, IS A BATTLE FOR ONE'S LIFE, AND IN A BATTLE FOR ONE'S LIFE AN INSTANT BECOMES AN ETERNITY – AN ETERNITY WHICH DETERMINES THE OUTCOME OF THE BATTLE.*

7. *A STALKER NEVER REVEALS HIS IDENTITY, NOT EVEN TO HIMSELF.*

CHAPTER THREE

WAKING UP IN THE DREAM

YOU CANNOT TAKE CONTROL OF THE DREAM IF YOU ARE NOT AWAKE. TO BE AWAKE MEANS THAT YOU KNOW EVERY FACET OF YOUR LIFE FOR WHAT IT REALLY IS. IN ORDER TO HAVE SUCH SOBRIETY, YOU MUST RECAPITULATE YOUR ENTIRE LIFE, FROM THE PRESENT MOMENT RIGHT BACK TO THE MOMENT OF BIRTH. WITHOUT THAT SOBRIETY YOU WILL ALWAYS BEHAVE LIKE A CLOWN RE-ENACTING FOLLY.

If we are to co-operate intelligently with our dreamers, then clearly it is necessary to wake up to the fact that the dream we have been dreaming for so long is not reality, but an illusion which is perpetuated through our social conditioning. However, it is at this point that the majority of people who expressed the wish to become warriors suddenly turn around and walk away from the challenge. To accept, even if at first just as a working hypothesis, the possibility that everything they have always believed in, worked for, and hoped for, could be an illusion, is normally too much for most people. But even of those few who do decide to stay with the challenge, only a mere handful will prove to have what it takes to master the Warrior's Path. The reason why this should be so, is really quite simple – people do not really want to change. And, indeed, why should any of us want to change just because some man who calls himself a nagal has said that we must.

THE WARRIOR'S PATH CAN ONLY BE MASTERED IF MASTERING IT MEANS SURVIVAL.

Realise that for as long as people are reasonably happy with life the way it is, then there is no real motivation to change anything.

In fact, rather than change anything, most people prefer simply to add some form of enrichment to their lives. Consequently there are a great many people who would like to have the *power* and the ability of a warrior, but only as an extra something that will enrich their lives. However, it is not possible to have the *power* of a warrior without becoming a warrior, and to become a warrior requires a total transformation of the *island of the tonal*.

Generally speaking it is only those people who have reached a point in their lives where they feel honestly that they have nothing to lose, who will gladly subject themselves to a total transformation. Whilst there is still something to lose, the apprentice will resist change, and in resisting change, will automatically cling to his or her old life.

It is because of this state of affairs that a nagal is never keen to take on just anyone as an apprentice, and especially because the normal apprenticeship has an average duration of anything between fifteen and twenty years. Therefore before a nagal will invest this amount of time and energy in an apprentice, he has to be convinced, or at least as far as is possible, that such an apprentice has what it takes to make the grade.

The reason I am explaining this here, is because it has much relevance to this particular section of the teachings, and especially at this moment in time. In the past, when it was the principal duty of every nagal to preserve the teachings, it was vital for the nagal to ensure the continuation of his lineage. Failure to find suitable successors for his own unit meant that the knowledge which was in his custody became lost. In the context of this, the question most often asked is why Toltecs have never resorted to writing down the teachings. Yet, hopefully by this stage the reader will have at least some idea why this has never really been a feasible option.

Realise first of all, that we cannot adequately verbalise much of the teaching, and secondly, because the Warrior's Path is a practical path, the teachings would have become frozen in time, and outdated, had they simply been recorded in writing. The only way the teachings could be kept alive and practical, as well as abreast with evolution, was to pass the knowledge from one generation to the next, making sure that each generation would evolve their knowledge by living like warriors, and in their turn train a new generation. Had the teachings merely been written down, they would no doubt have become lost and forgotten many thousands of years ago, and there would now be no warriors or Toltecs left, and neither would humanity ever have known that it did once upon a time have a heritage.

Today, because man has come of age, and is therefore ready to receive its heritage, all of this has changed quite dramatically. The fact that the teachings are now being recorded in writing has only become possible because there are enough men and women in the world who can and will take charge of the teachings. Accordingly, it is no longer necessary for nagals to keep their lineages alive, for the underlying purpose of lineages has now been fulfilled. Toltecs have kept intact the sacred trust bestowed upon them, and at this moment in time are fulfilling their final duty towards humanity by handing over to man his birthright. The role Toltecs have played for so long, as the custodians of man's heritage, is now finished, and therefore the lineages will be no more.

The implications of this momentous change are vast, but will only really become apparent as more and more of the teachings are imparted. The only implication which is of immediate concern to this section of the teachings, is that in many ways Toltecs are once again resuming their original role in the life of humanity, except that this time it is not in the sense of having to think for people, but in the sense of being mentors and advisors only. Having come of age, this is humanity's *hour of power*, and if man is to claim his *power*, then he has to take responsibility for the fact that he has now come of age, and that he therefore can and must act on his own. Toltecs will continue to play their part in showing man the way, but the onus will be upon man to seek out for himself that guidance. Gone are the days when Toltecs were forced into having to keep man's birthright intact. If man squanders his heritage now that it is being handed over to him, by not putting it into practice and therefore losing the knowledge, or by not seeking out guidance on how best to utilise this heritage and therefore corrupting it, then it will be his responsibility, and his alone.

This point must be carefully considered, for it affects the teachings in a major way, especially what follows here. Although a nagal has always had to ensure that his apprentices have what it takes to become warriors, mainly so that the teachings would be preserved through the continuation of the lineage, this is no longer the case. Nagals today are no longer under any obligation to maintain their lineages, and therefore there is also no longer any pressure upon a nagal to find suitable successors. In other words, although all nagals still have an obligation to lead others to freedom, they are no longer forced into having to teach personal apprentices, nor do they have to worry about whether or not those who do come to them for guidance are going to succeed. What in effect this means is that a nagal can now afford to be even more selective in his choice of apprentices, for it no longer matters if he ends up with none.

As far as these books are concerned, this is a most important point for it is in no way my responsibility what the reader does with the teachings imparted. In this respect, an opportunity has now come about which was never before present. What this opportunity amounts to, is that because the teachings are now being recorded in book form, anyone who wishes to do so can avail themselves of the teachings. However, the conditions for becoming a warrior are still the same as before, except that now it is possible to work from these manuals rather than having to receive oral instruction from a nagal.

That is all very well, and it is truly wonderful that the teachings are now available to everyone, without any form of discrimination, but I would be doing the reader an injustice if I do not point out the pitfall in this new set-up. The danger in this new set-up is to believe that you can bend the rules to suit your purposes. To indulge in such a belief is just a stupid waste of time and energy, for let me once again reiterate that there is absolutely no way of acquiring the skills, the abilities and the *power* of a warrior without becoming a warrior. To think that it is possible to add warriorship to your existing life is exactly the same as thinking that you can become a world champion in tennis, but without making tennis your career, your life, your everything.

Today it is possible for anyone to become a warrior, but only if the age-old requirements are fulfilled. However, this does not preclude people from taking out of the teachings only that which they find to be useful and enriching. There is nothing wrong with this, in fact, it is to be encouraged, provided it is understood that if you are not prepared to change, and you only want to take out of the teachings that which suits you, then you will also never become a warrior. This principle is the same as for those people who learn to play tennis, not to become world champions, but just for their own enjoyment and enrichment. But just as you would be a fool to think that you can compete in world championships if you are only an average tennis player, so too would you be a fool to think that you should be able to do what a warrior does when you are not a warrior. Should you even be dishonest enough to claim such status by calling yourself a warrior a hundred times over, there is no way in which you can fake the impeccability of the warrior's spirit, nor is there any way in which you can imitate his *power*. Sooner or later your actions will reveal your charade.

This then, brings us hard up against the stalker's rule, for if you as the reader intend claiming your *power* as a warrior, and are not simply wishing to enrich your present life with the teachings, then you are going to have to learn how to stalk yourself impeccably. In this respect the very first thing you should do, is to ask yourself: "Do I really want to become a warrior? Am I honestly prepared to undergo a total transformation?"

If every fibre of your being screams out at you that there is no other way, then you will make every effort to put these teachings into practice, no matter how many times you try but fail. Remember that it does not matter if you fail again and again, for we learn far more from failure than we do from beginners' luck. In learning to play tennis, we quite simply do miss the ball countless times, but every time we miss it, we learn from our mistakes. This is a fact of life, and something which is undeniably true about all learning, and yet in learning to become a warrior, and most especially in learning to stalk yourself, anything that seems to be so very logical should never be taken at face value.

To learn to play tennis is one thing, but to learn what it is to be a warrior is altogether very different, for the simple reason that the only way we can become warriors is by putting the teachings into practice in our lives, as opposed to on the tennis court. If you keep missing the ball on the tennis court the worst thing that can happen is that you will lose the game, but every time you miss the ball in life, there are serious repercussions, not only for you, but also for all those around you. Consequently, none of us has a license to make mistakes, for in learning to play the game of life we are not just practising to play one day in a real tennis tournament. Instead, every practice is a real event with real effects, and this is true no matter whether we are learning to become warriors or not. But in the case of someone who is learning to become a warrior, not because it seems like a good idea, but because for that person the acquisition of warriorship means survival, every practice, every event, is a very real battle – a battle for life. Clearly, in a battle for one's life, it stands to reason that we can ill afford to make mistakes. Yet mistakes you will make, and you will learn from your mistakes, but that learning will be done the hard way. At the end of the day, all of us pay for every lesson with something from our life.

Therefore, one of the very first things that every apprentice learns quickly enough when he or she comes to the Warrior's Path is the first aspect of the stalker's rule, namely, that *a warrior chooses his battle, and therefore will always assess both the circumstances and the conditions of every battle with the utmost care*. The phrase 'chooses his battle' should not be taken at face value, and this is something we will be considering presently, but let us first of all understand that those apprentices who consistently ignore this first aspect of the stalker's rule, and who therefore stubbornly cling to their old way of thinking and behaving, are doomed to failure, in that they refuse to wake up. Such an apprentice will never become a warrior, for the simple reason that he or she persists in the folly of the dream.

The point to be grasped here, and one which I cannot possibly over-emphasise, is that the initial act of waking up in the dream is not so much a technique, or an acquired ability, but is instead an *act of survival*. Why should you want to wake up when you like your dream? It is only once the dream of the person concerned has started to become a nightmare in some way, that the person will want to wake up in order to escape the contents of that dream.

Realise though, that what can be a nightmare for one person will not necessarily be the same for someone else. Every one of us is different, and therefore what constitutes a nightmare for each individual is also always very different. For example, for one person poverty could be a nightmare, whilst for someone else, running a huge financial empire could be their nightmare. Likewise, for one set of parents, having a delinquent child could be for them a nightmare, whilst for another set of parents, a nightmare could be to have a child that is mentally retarded. However, in all cases, what makes a dream a nightmare is the fact that the person concerned begins to feel that their sanity, and perhaps even their life, is being threatened in a very real sense, and that there is no place in the dream to run to, no place in the dream to hide. It is then, and only then, that such a person will struggle to wake up.

Notice that earlier I used the phrase the *initial act* of waking up. These words were carefully chosen for a reason, namely, that to wake up is not quite as simple as gaining instant sobriety overnight. Waking up in the dream starts when we make the momentous decision to change, but to acquire true sobriety is a long process of struggling to see the contents of the dream for what they really are. The initial decision is truly a cataclysmic change, but that decision must be followed by the required action, and all action takes time to unfold and to bear fruit. It is simply not possible to plant the seed of a tree today, and to have a fully grown tree by tomorrow.

Traditionally a nagal will only accept an apprentice for training if he can see that the apprentice is already struggling to wake up. Once an apprentice has reached this point, he or she does not need to be convinced that every occurrence is a battle for life. Of this the apprentice is already convinced, but what he or she needs now, is to know what to do about it. The only way forward, is for the apprentice to learn how to stalk perception or, in other words, how to stalk the dream. However, because such an apprentice is invariably a new recruit, he or she does not yet have the sobriety to be able to grasp the real import of the stalker's rule or, for that matter, the four postulates of stalking. Therefore let us look at an example of how an apprentice is expected to approach stalking the dream, and in this we will look at the example of one of my own apprentices, although obviously for the sake of privacy I have changed his name.

Sean and his brother, Willis, are in business together. As the company was originally started by Sean, he has always, but by unspoken mutual agreement, been managing director. However, all of a sudden the undercurrents which have been developing in their relationship for some time have come to a climax, with the result that Willis informs Sean that he is taking over the company, and is going to run it his way from that moment on. Willis furthermore makes it clear to Sean that if he has a problem with this, then he is free to leave, on condition that he walks away with nothing.

In this turn of events, Sean is faced with a very real dilemma, for not only is everything he had worked for and hoped for now on the line, but he also has the problem that he is the one who has signed surety for all of the company's liabilities. Therefore, if Sean stays on in the company, he will be in the uncomfortable position of having to answer to his brother for everything, and in a company which he himself started, primarily for himself! If, on the other hand, Sean lets his brother have his way, and just walks away, Sean will legally be held responsible if Willis ends up making a mess of the company.

What is Sean to do? In order to answer this question the first thing to be taken into consideration is the fact that Sean is an apprentice to the Warrior's Path, for this determines what his options are. Had Sean not been an apprentice, then his options would have been very different, and it is primarily for this reason that at the beginning of this chapter I explained the difference between someone who is serious about wanting to become a warrior, as opposed to someone who just wants to use the teachings to enrich his or her life. Since the teachings in these books are being imparted in their purity, that is, on the assumption that the reader is a serious student, the onus lies squarely upon the shoulders of the reader to implement the teachings with due consideration and discrimination. In other words, if you as the reader land yourself in some very hot water because you have never seriously wanted to become a warrior, then know that you will have absolutely no right to blame either the teachings, or me. If you want to dabble in the Toltec teachings, then by all means feel free to do so, but take care that you do not burn your fingers or, worse still, lose a whole arm!

Returning now to Sean, who is an apprentice to the Warrior's Path, we see that he cannot possibly choose any of the options which would be applicable to the average person who is not an apprentice, for these options will merely lead Sean into perpetuating the illusion of the dream, and will force him into re-enacting his folly. Because Sean is learning to become a warrior, he has no other choice than to try his best to act like a truly impeccable warrior. This is an important point, for apprentices all too often tend to forget that the only way you can learn to claim your *power* as a warrior, is to be challenged by *power*, and this is exactly what has happened to Sean.

Yet, when this happens, the apprentice concerned will normally try his utmost to back out of the challenge somehow, protesting wildly that he is not yet ready to handle the challenge like a warrior. However, we are not talking about practising on the tennis court – we are dealing here with a real challenge from *power* – a challenge which constitutes for Sean a very real battle, and the outcome of which will affect him for the rest of his life, and not only him, but also his brother, his parents, and everyone else who is involved. Such is the nature of the Warrior's Path. If you want to become a warrior, then you must be prepared to stand up and fight to the very best of your ability – ready or not.

If Sean is going to handle his challenge like a true warrior, then the first thing he must do is to apply the first aspect of the stalker's rule, namely, *a warrior chooses his battle*. Choosing the battle does not mean that a warrior chooses to fight some battles and ignores others. Every challenge is important in that it brings us a *gift of power*, and therefore we cannot ever afford to ignore any battle. What this statement means is that we must be clear on *what* constitutes the real battle. Depending upon our level of perception, any challenge can be viewed in several different ways, and each of these different perspectives amounts to a battle. People generally speaking have so little clarity on the issues in their lives that they mostly tend to concentrate on the "wrong" perspective of a challenge, and consequently end up fighting the "wrong" battle.

Now, if Sean is going to ascertain what the real battle in his challenge with his brother is, then he cannot just choose any perspective at random, and regard this as being the battle, but must instead *assess both the circumstances and the conditions of the battle with the utmost care*. In this respect, it is important for Sean to remember that the world is not what it appears to be. In trying to do this, Sean is encouraged to remember that he must accept the face value of his challenge, for it is this that sets the stage for battle, but he must not fall into the trap of accepting the face value of the challenge as constituting the real battle. Sean is also reminded that he must strive to use the warrior's shield at all times, for unless he is wide awake, and approaches this battle with fear, with respect, and with absolute assurance, he is just asking for a beating.

Having got at least this much clarity on what he is facing, Sean now still needs to ascertain what for him personally constitutes the real battle within this situation. If Sean is not going to stare himself blind at the face value of his challenge it is vital for him to shift the focus away from the manner in which he is accustomed to view a challenge of this nature. This implies that he must stalk his perception, otherwise the habits of a lifetime will simply keep him stuck in his normal perception. In order to accomplish this, Sean must strive to use the stalker's rule, but he must also remember that this can only be done by taking into consideration all four components of the dream. Realise that because these four components are completely interactive, it is the interaction between them that is going to determine, firstly, Sean's perception of the challenge; secondly, his strategy; and thirdly, the outcome of the battle. Any use of the stalker's rule will always set up a chain reaction, the outcome of which, because of the unpredictable whims of *power*, cannot be determined beforehand. In other words, to use the stalker's rule means jumping into the unknown, but simply to jump into the unknown willy-nilly, is the ultimate foolishness. Anyone who is foolish enough to implement the stalker's rule in such a fashion is asking for more trouble than he or she can possibly bargain for.

The true art of the master stalker lies in the ability to improvise, but such improvisation cannot be any old rubbish played off the cuff in the moment. Remember that we are dealing here with real life, and therefore if we are to avoid the arrows of the sharpshooters of the universe, then every improvisation must be highly skilled, must be extremely accurate and, above all, must be grounded in truth. The whole point in stalking is to gain the advantage in order to survive, but anyone who indulges in a sloppy undisciplined performance based upon lies, will not survive for too long, especially if that person is trying to use the stalker's rule.

The art of improvisation is a skill which can only be acquired by following a carefully demarcated set of guidelines. Note that I say guidelines, and not rules. Rules are no good for improvising, simply because every situation that arises is different, and will therefore be an exception to the rule. The only thing we can safely prescribe for stalking is a strategy, and it is this basic strategy that is looked upon as being a set of guidelines.

The set of guidelines referred to above are not really guidelines in the normal sense of the word, but are more in the nature of *feeling your way in the dark*. Traditionally these guidelines are verbalised in the following aphorism which, although very accurate, is somewhat difficult to grasp with the rational mind.

> ANY STALKING MANOEUVRE IS ESSENTIALLY IMPROVISATION. SUCH IMPROVISATION MUST BE BASED UPON DUE CONSIDERATION OF THE POSSIBLE INTERACTIONS BETWEEN THE FOUR COMPONENTS OF THE DREAM WHICH AUTOMATICALLY COME INTO BEING WITH EVERY ACTION, MENTAL, EMOTIONAL AND PHYSICAL. THE ONLY WAY IN WHICH THIS CAN BE DONE IS TO ASSESS THE TENSIONS INHERENT WITHIN THE WEB OF LIFE. THESE TENSIONS ARE ALWAYS PERCEIVABLE WHENEVER THE FOUR POSTULATES OF STALKING ARE BROUGHT INTO PLAY.

Let us carefully consider the implications of this aphorism, so that we can grasp what is meant by the set of guidelines we are referring to. "To assess the tensions inherent within the web of life", is not at all easy to explain without becoming very technical, but for the purposes of this book I shall try to keep the technical theory down to a bare minimum.

Realise that because all of life is interrelated, every challenge that arises in anybody's life is but the result of interactive energies brought into being by the cumulative effects of *power*. In simpler, but less accurate terms, this means that in the example we are considering, Sean is not the victim being unfairly attacked by his brother. Instead Sean is being challenged, and that challenge is the accumulated outcome of an untold number of perceptions, both present and past. In order to gain a proper understanding of this, realise that these perceptions are not only Sean's perceptions, but also those of his brother, his parents, the relatives of both Sean and his brother, the perceptions of their teachers at school and at university, the perceptions of all their friends and acquaintances, their clients in business, and so on. Now, remember that all of these perceptions are interactive, in that the *personal power* generated by each ultimately gives rise to *universal power*. Furthermore, remember that the secondary impulse in the act of perception is emotion, and that these emotions are also interactive. Needless to say, all of these interactions give rise to even more perception, so that we get ripple upon ripple of perception, each ripple giving rise to new *power* and, in addition, also becoming charged with emotion.

These ripples always give rise to certain effects in the lives of all concerned – effects which the individual will express in terms of some sort of action, irrespective of whether it is mental, emotional or physical action. Such action is determined by what is known as the *intensity* of the ripple which gave rise to the action. The intensity of a ripple comes into being when the *personal power* and the emotion generated by the perception of one person interacts with that of another person. Obviously if more people are involved, then the intensity of the ripple will be determined by the interaction between the products of everyone's perception.

The quality of this intensity is what people generally recognise as being a mood of sorts, and is directly proportional to the actual *degree of perception*. For example, if two people are talking together, and both have a perception which is very clouded by their social conditioning, they will not be perceiving very well. As a result there will be a lot of misunderstanding between them, and the mis-interpretation of what is actually being said will cause the conver-sation to take on a very definite type of mood. This is true, not only of individuals talking together, but for all forms of perception, and at all possible levels, even at the level of a whole race of people, at the level of a country, and at the level of the world as a whole. Therefore, depending upon the degree of perception that is preva-lent at any given time, the overall *quality*, or *mood*, could be one of aggression, melancholy, peace, agitation, etcetera.

These qualities always generate some form of *tension*, and as all of life is interrelated, these tensions are present in the web of life at all times, and are sensed, or *felt* by everyone. These are the ten-sions that the master stalker uses as his guidelines during improvi-sation, and it stands to reason that his skill in improvisation is dependent upon how well he can *read* and *assess* the nature of those tensions. This implies that the master stalker is not only highly sensitive to the slightest shift in tension, but is also able to read every nuance of that tension with deadly accuracy, and can assess its potential from split second to split second.

These tensions are in the nature of energies which affect indivi-duals as well as the web of life itself. Exactly how this takes place is far too technical for the purposes of this book, but let it suffice for now to say that tensions tend to interact together in such a way that they materialise what people recognise as the challenges in their lives. Herein lies the truth of statements such as, "Take care what you wish for, it may come true"; "You materialise your worst fears"; and "You call forth the challenges in your life".

From the above it should be evident that if we wish to see a battle for what it really is, rather than becoming obsessed with its face value, we need to be able to ascertain what the tensions are that have brought it into being. The only way this skill can be acquired is to have a working knowledge of the four postulates of stalking, for the *power* flow in life, which is revealed by the four postulates of stalking, always follows an ordered structure, even though the actual outcome of that flow is completely whimsical and unpredictable. In order to grasp how this is done, let us now revert to our example of Sean.

If Sean wishes to work out what is actually transpiring in his life, he must endeavour to use the four postulates of stalking, so as to ascertain which tensions have brought about his challenge. The flow of *power* as revealed in the four postulates of stalking, is East, North, South, West, and therefore every challenge should be viewed in this order. As the East is the place of *sobriety*, it is clear that in approaching any challenge the first requirement is to achieve clarity on the issues facing us. However, the first postulate of stalking tells us that *the whole world and everything in it is an endless mystery*, which of course includes our challenges. Therefore Sean cannot approach his challenge rationally, for such an approach does not allow for mystery, and consequently will only give him clarity on the face value of the challenge.

Sean also cannot run away from his challenge, for the second postulate tells us that *it is our duty to solve this mystery*. So just by looking at this second postulate Sean already knows that he cannot let his brother have his way, and leave it at that. This second postulate belongs to the North, the place of *action*, and therefore Sean is required to take some form of action, and clearly this action must be an attempt to solve the mystery, of which Sean's challenge is a materialisation. Yet, the second half of this postulate warns us that *we should never engage the hope of being able to do so*. What this really means is that any challenge is only a fractional materialisation of the overall mystery. In other words, what is transpiring between Sean and his brother is not a whim of the moment, but is rather the outcome of something that has been brewing for a long time; in fact probably for all of his life up to that point, and the outcome of which will affect him for the rest of his life. This very important point is something we will look at much more closely in the following chapter.

Moving now to the third postulate, Sean realises that if he is going to solve this mystery by handling his challenge correctly he must acknowledge that *he too is a part of that mystery*, and must strive to *become at-one with it*. Nothing else in the teachings points out more clearly that we cannot afford to indulge in the belief that we are victims than this third postulate. In other words, Sean must acknowledge that he is partly responsible for his brother's change in attitude and behaviour. Since perception and its products are fully interactive, this is hardly surprising, but what is surprising, is how often people will insist that they are completely innocent victims.

At this point I would like to stress once again that there are no victims in this world, and even if there were, innocent they could never possibly be. I know that those who believe in victims will always want to dispute this point, but with people such as these I have absolutely no argument. If you *choose to believe* that you are a victim, then indeed you are a victim, and I fully agree with you that you are a victim. Therefore there is nothing further to discuss. If, on the other hand, you choose to be a warrior, rather than a victim, then realise that you are responsible for whatever happens in your life. If you walk across the road, and someone runs you down with his car, then you are just as guilty as the one who ran you down. First of all, you decided to cross the road at that particular moment. You could have crossed somewhere else, or you could have crossed later, or you could have crossed faster or slower. In short, you could have been more alert. Secondly, realise that although man-made law will essentially be on your side, these petty laws will not relieve you of the fact that you are guilty of having damaged that person's car, and of the fact that he might even be found guilty of negligent driving.

Likewise, if you are raped, it is because you needed that experience. Perhaps it was to teach you humility. Perhaps it was to teach you what it is to be humiliated. Perhaps it was to teach you something about your behaviour. In other words, what could you have done to attract rape? If you are extremely sexy, or pretty, or like to advertise your sex appeal, then take responsibility for it. If, on the other hand, your attitude towards others is so snooty that someone felt the need to humiliate you with rape, then you must likewise accept responsibility for this. Furthermore, accept the fact that if the rapist is caught and jailed, or perhaps even sentenced to death, you will be guilty of that man's sentence, even though thousands will hail the justice of the courts, and will flock to your defence.

Those who want to believe in victimhood will often argue that children who are born with some handicap are truly victims of their birth, and yet by the same token these people choose to forget wonderful examples like Helen Keller. Deaf, blind and dumb, Helen refused to vegetate in a home for handicapped children, although she could have done so had she wanted to be a victim. However, having said this, I must in all fairness also point out that there are cases which can be seen as exceptions to the rule. An example of this is where children are born with mental retardation, or some other form of severe mental handicap. Such children cannot possibly lead a normal life in the true sense of the word, and as a result their true value in life is the gift of experience which they bring their parents and relatives. I cannot do adequate justice to cases such as these in this book, for the truth behind these most loving and loveable orphans of the world is a long and somewhat tragic story, but let it suffice for now to say that my argument is not with these children. Children such as these will never become warriors in this lifetime. But my argument is with the parents of some of these children, who could use the challenge posed by such a child to their full advantage instead of, as is so often the case, wanting to run away from it, and therefore confining these children to a home for the mentally handicapped.

In the examples I have given, I can already hear the angry wails of the "victims" of this world. However, remember that I have not said that a rapist has any justification for raping another being, neither have I claimed that a driver has any right to drive recklessly. But, by the same token, neither does someone have the right to make another person guilty of rape by calling forth a rape, or to make a driver guilty of negligent driving by calling forth a driver that is either half-asleep or just plain reckless. Remember also that I have already agreed that victims are truly victims, and in this respect are lucky in that they will always have the judicial system to protect them in their victimhood. But remember above all that these books are not being written for victims, but for those who refuse to be victims, and who wish instead to claim their *power* as warriors. For people such as these there can be no pretence and there can be no lies. A spade remains a shovel, and we must face the bare facts with every bit of honesty we can possibly muster, for without that honesty, there can never be true sobriety.

We all have our part to play in whatever happens to us in life, and therefore we are always just as guilty as the one who has committed some wrong against us. This is equally true of parents who spawn a mentally retarded child, for it is not only the child who needs this experience, but also the parents. Therefore, if Sean is to get clarity on what is really happening in his life he must start to look at what his role in all of this has been. In other words, Sean cannot afford to stand back in self-righteousness to complain about his brother's behaviour, but must instead become at-one with the mystery, for only in this way will he be able to see his own contribution to what has transpired.

In considering the fourth postulate, Sean is reminded that the *crux of the mystery is the infinite mystery of beingness.* This is most valuable guidance because, in the final analysis, every challenge that comes our way is there so that in struggling to overcome it, we may learn more about who and what we really are. If Sean is to shift the focus in order to achieve sobriety he cannot look at his brother's actions in terms of what his brother is doing *to* him, but instead must view his brother's behaviour in terms of what it is doing *for* him.

Once again the whole concept of being a victim falls away neatly, and in the place of that self-pity comes the awesome realisation that by having perpetrated an injustice against Sean, Willis is actually helping his brother on his way to becoming a warrior. This does not excuse Willis from his actions, but what it does point out, is that both Sean and Willis need this challenge in order to move forward in life. In this respect, always remember that we cannot possibly condemn another person, for the simple reason that we don't know who or what that person is. But we can, and have every right to, condemn the actions and the behaviour of another person, provided that such condemnation is justifiable. Therefore it is not that Willis is a "baddy" because of what he is doing, or somehow less than Sean, but that

Willis' actions and behaviour towards Sean are bad. Yet, Sean's behaviour towards Willis is also not much better, for by needing this particular challenge, Sean called forth this bad behaviour from his brother, and therefore he is indirectly just as cruel as Willis.

I want to stress the fact that I am not inferring that Willis can in any way justify his actions. What Willis has done is wrong, and through that mistake he will learn whatever it is he has to learn. But just because Willis has made a mistake, it does not automatically mean that Sean is innocent. In fact, the moment that Sean came to this realisation, he could start to see how although he had the best of intentions throughout his whole life, he kept doing a great many things that must have made his brother feel terribly inferior to him.

Sean has finally begun to see how he himself called forth this challenge, and what his own role has been in bringing the relationship between him and Willis to this point. By using the mirror concept, Sean can now see that the bottom line is that both he and his brother have always struggled to feel good about themselves, and to believe in their own value. Sean has expressed this in terms of wanting to be the proverbial "good shepherd" to his brother; Willis has expressed it through being a rebel who is for ever at odds with the world around him, and now finally, in wanting to curb the actions of the good shepherd. Although the two brothers are as different in their behaviour as can be, yet deep down inside they are as identical as twins and, in the final analysis, there is no real difference between them. In his acceptance of this, Sean is forced to admit that *within the mystery of beingness, all are equal.*

Sean has now been brought full circle, for he clearly has a great deal of recapitulation to do on his relationship with his brother which, of course, brings him straight back to the East, the place of recapitulation. Nonetheless, even with just this preliminary use of the four postulates of stalking, Sean has already acquired far more sobriety than he would normally have been capable of. This is a point of enormous relevance, for realise that to recapitulate the relationship with his brother fully would more than likely take Sean many years to accomplish, years which he does not have. Therefore, any bit of sobriety he can lay his hands on right now is extremely valuable to Sean, and from what he has already gleaned so far, Sean can now clearly see that it is not the company he and his brother are fighting for, but that both of them, in their own way, are having to fight for their sense of self-worth. Herein lies the real challenge, and the real battle, and therefore the tensions upon which Sean should be concentrating are not those which have to do with material possessions or with a power struggle, but those which concern the self-image of both him and his brother.

Having got to this point, Sean in fact has all the sobriety he needs at the current moment. He now knows what constitutes for him the real battle, and in this respect he now also knows which tensions are going to be his guide. Having ascertained this much, Sean has fulfilled the first aspect of the stalker's rule, namely, that a warrior chooses his battle, and in this has effect-ively started to implement the stalker's rule. What Sean now needs to do is to devise a strategy that will enable him to use those tensions in fighting this battle with his brother. However, before we look at Sean's strategy, let us not forget the most important reason why we are challenged in life. Apprentices, on the whole, usually become so excited about how a technique works, and can get so carried away when it does work for them, that they tend to forget to absorb what they have learned from the exercise. Therefore, let us first of all look at what Sean has learned from his challenge so far.

Perhaps the most important thing Sean has learned from this challenge is that Willis is not victimising him, but has instead provided him with a wonderful opportunity to work at improving his low self-image. Even with just this little bit of recapitulation he has done on his relationship with his brother, Sean can already clearly see that it is only because of his low self-image that this challenge was called forth. With respect to recapitulation, realise that the only recapitulation Sean has done to date, as far as Willis is concerned, has been the little bit of *spontaneous recapitulation* mentioned earlier. And yet, because that recapitulation was done in the *context* of his present challenge, the sobriety it yielded is invaluable to Sean. This is a point which cannot ever be over-emphasised.

Apprentices so often despair at the fact that they struggle to recapitulate and, as a result, unconsciously try their best to forget that such a technique exists. Such apprentices somehow seem to believe that if they can manage to forget, then so too will the nagal. And yet all of this is so unnecessary if only apprentices will make the effort to remember one of the first basic aphorisms they are ever taught:

> THE ONLY TRUE LEARNING IS PRACTICAL EXPERIENCE, AND
> THEREFORE EVERYTHING YOU DO MUST BE IN THE CONTEXT OF
> THE PRESENT MOMENT.

I hear myself repeating this over and over again in many different ways, and apprentices nod their heads wisely, scribble it down in their journals, and then three months down the line when I ask them how their recapitulation is coming on, the look of guilt that comes over their faces says it all.

When the assemblage point is still firmly fixed we cannot recapitulate the past with any real success. Why? Simply because the assemblage point is stuck. I do not need to repeat what has already been dealt with in *Return of the Warriors*, except to point out once again that intellectual memories of the past are not much good, and are certainly not what is meant by recapitulation. However, if it is remembered that whatever is happening to you right now is but the result of the past, then the *feelings* and the *emotions* generated by the present will guide you back in time. It is for this very reason that apprentices are always told to recapitulate backwards. We always start from the present moment and then work back to the moment of birth; never the other way round, for this would be impossible for most people.

We have already seen how this works in the example of Sean. The reason why Sean had this bit of spontaneous recapitulation on his relationship with his brother, is because of his present challenge. Therefore, this is the most beneficial time for Sean to recapitulate the relationship because, in fighting this battle, he will again *experience* many of the emotions and the feelings which have always come up in his relationship with Willis. If Sean is aware of this, and therefore stays on the lookout for these emotions and feelings, they will, when they come up, enable Sean temporarily to move or even shift his assemblage point to realign energy fields which hold clear memories of forgotten events and issues surrounding Willis. But this can only happen if Sean is going to be aware of the value of these emotions and feelings. If he is not, when they do come up, he will ignore them by becoming obsessed with the face value of his current challenge, and by indulging in endless internal dialogue stimulated by the rational mind.

I cannot stress this point enough. There would be absolutely no point in Sean trying to recapitulate a past love affair at this time, for it has nothing to do with his current challenge. If, on the other hand, Sean is trying to recapitulate his relationship with Willis, and this past love affair keeps coming to mind, then Sean must bring it into the equation, for it is obvious that this affair must somehow be connected to his relationship with Willis. The point is that everything the apprentice tries to put into practice must relate to the present moment. This is especially important with respect to recapitulation, for otherwise the apprentice will become disheartened by the difficulty of this practice.

The same principle holds good for all the practices and techniques. For example, you cannot practise not-doing by having a conversation with another person in your head. And yet, how often is this not the case? People will spend hours thinking of what they should have said, but didn't. Alternatively, they work themselves up into a stew about what they are going to say, except that when the moment arrives, they somehow never say what they had planned to say. Either the occasion to blurt out what they have rehearsed never arises or, if it does, their courage fails them in the moment. Likewise, in trying to analyse a dream, or in interpreting an omen, it is vital to work from the basis that it must have relevance to what is happening in your life right now. This is especially true of prophetic dreams, for what is taking place right now is the foundation for tomorrow. The *power* always lies in the moment, and therefore we should always start working from where we happen to be at the time.

The reason why apprentices find it so difficult to remember this is twofold. Firstly, humanity today is very separative in its thinking, and apprentices are no exception to this. Consequently, at the beginning of their training, apprentices never do see the relationship between what is happening in their lives now to everything else. Secondly, caught up in their social conditioning, apprentices see life in the same way as everybody else, and as a result of this common view of the world, time and time again walk into the trap of taking things at face value. This is especially true of self-importance, for apprentices are so very conscious of not being self-important, that most of the time it is quite hilarious to see how self-important they can become in being holier than thou.

Being separative in their way of thinking, and taking most things purely at face value, apprentices are usually at first so busy trying to be warriors, in the sense of what they believe a warrior to be, that they completely forget they can only become warriors *within* the context of their daily life. As a result, these apprentices fall prey to the temptation of wanting to measure their performance against that of others. This in itself is a most excellent exercise, provided that the apprentice remembers, which he or she hardly ever does, that it is the *performance* they are judging, and not the person. Without even realising it, apprentices time and time again make the fatal mistake of comparing *themselves* with others. The end result is that they inevitably start to see their shortcomings, but in trying to feel better about themselves, they forget that our shortcomings are our road to *power*, and instead try to cover for these shortcomings by pretending that they are already impeccable warriors, or at least better than others, in the sense that they are well on their way to becoming warriors. Without even realising it, self-importance has whipped round to hit such apprentices squarely on the back of the head!

Whilst self-importance is still intact, recapitulation never amounts to much more than bringing forth huge doses of self-pity whenever the apprentice concerned recalls how hard done-by he or she has been in the past. True recapitulation can only really start taking effect when apprentices make the conscious effort to stop indulging in the belief that they are victims, and because of this, come to the realisation that it is only their self-importance which makes them feel victimised. This is a point of huge import, for where there is true humility there never can be any sense of being victimised – there can only be the sure know-ledge that one is being challenged.

To be challenged is a far cry from being victimised. But because people all too often succumb to their fear, yet choose not to admit their cowardice to themselves, they cover for it by becoming most awfully self-righteous and complaining bitterly that it is not right that other people should be allowed to bully them. In the example of Sean, it is clear to see how, if left to his social conditioning, he could very easily believe Willis was bul-lying him unjustly. Sean would then feel very justified in sniffing indignantly, sticking his nose in the air and walking around with a hurt look on his face, so that the whole world may know how much he is suffering. However, to indulge in such behaviour is the height of arrogance and the very epitome of self-importance, for it implies that your holiness is so untouchable, and your perfection so complete, that you are the only person in the world who does not need the *gifts of power* challenges bring us. There-fore how *dare* anyone challenge you? Or, more precisely, how dare anyone be so beastly to you?

Eradicating self-importance is much the same as undoing our social conditioning, in that there is no one specific technique for doing so. Instead, we need to put into practice all of the teach-ings and all of the techniques if we are ever going to eradicate self-importance and undo our social conditioning. However, it is worthwhile to point out here that the quickest and surest way of giving self-importance a death blow is to use the four postulates of stalking and the stalker's rule in learning to stalk perception. As we have seen in Sean's case, whenever this is done, true and valuable recapitulation becomes possible, and once we can begin to see our life for what it truly is, all sense of having been victimised, and therefore all sense of self-importance, begins to fall away naturally and easily.

In this respect, we always have the people who challenge us to thank for the opportunity they invariably give us to acquire the necessary sobriety with which to eradicate self-importance. In Toltec terms such people are called *petty tyrants*, but because the true petty tyrant is a scarce commodity, Toltecs have classified petty tyrants into four categories.

In the first category are to be found the true petty tyrants – men or women who will stop at nothing to get at you for some reason or other. Such people are cruel and capricious and, being clever enough always to stay just beyond the reach of justice, they are utterly devious and underhanded. Such a man will not hesitate to rape you, "just to teach you a lesson", and such a woman will not flinch at quite literally skinning you alive. To get on the wrong side of these people is truly life-threatening, for they will kill at the drop of a hat!

In the second category we have men and women who are essentially the same as those in the first, except that they avoid physical cruelty, but instead use all forms of emotional and mental abuse with which to undermine a person's strength and break his spirit. This type is most often encountered in the workplace, and they always get away with their behaviour as a result of instilling the fear of hell into their employees.

The third category is comprised of people who do not normally behave like petty tyrants but, when their anger is aroused in some way, will do everything in their power to make your life a total misery. Not being nearly as clever at avoiding justice as the first and second groups, these people will usually resort to getting the law on their side in tormenting you. Once angered, such men and women will suddenly turn upon you in the most unexpected manner and when you least expect it. If you retaliate in some way, they will be quick to start a law suit, and if it is going to serve their purposes, they will resort to reporting you to the authorities for even the smallest of offences. Put your garbage out on the street on the day before the garbage is to be collected, and they will report you to the city council. Park your car on the pavement in front of your own house for five minutes only, and they will report you to the traffic department. Such people are most commonly found amongst neighbours, and very often amongst relatives and jilted lovers or spouses.

The fourth category consists of the proverbial nags. Such people will find fault with absolutely everything you do, and will nag you to total distraction. They won't report you to anyone, but they will constantly be coming to you to complain. Wash your car on a Sunday, and you are disturbing their peace. Mow your lawn with a petrol lawnmower, and they will complain about the noise and the unhealthy fumes. Mow your lawn with an electric lawnmower, and they will be telling you that we all have a responsibility and duty to save on electricity consumption!

If and when an apprentice does find him or herself a petty tyrant, the nagal will always encourage the apprentice to look upon that person as a most valuable treasure, for by learning to stalk a petty tyrant, we learn far more, and also far more rapidly, than in the absence of one. This is true of all types of petty tyrants, and most especially those in the first and the second categories. In struggling to survive the onslaughts of these people we not only learn to drop our sense of self-importance in a hurry, but we also claim an enormous amount of *power* in terms of self-confidence and self-esteem. However, needless to say, petty tyrants in the first and the second categories should be handled with great care for, if given half a chance, the first type will kill you and the second type will destroy you for life.

Apropos the above, I must issue a fair warning here by pointing out that, generally speaking, apprentices can only handle the true petty tyrant with relative safety when they are under the guidance of a fully-trained nagal. Therefore, my advice to the reader, who is most unlikely to be working with a nagal, is if you find yourself a true petty tyrant, give it a miss and get the hell out of it if you possibly can. Since you are intending to become a warrior you need to stay alive and in one piece. Therefore, submit to whatever the demand in the moment may be, then turn tail and run, remembering that in all cases of inexperience discretion is the better part of valour.

Should it be necessary for you to run in order to save your life, then realise that this does not necessarily mean that you are running away from a challenge. This is a very important point which warrants some careful consideration, for we are never given challenges which we cannot handle. If a challenge comes our way, then it is because we need that challenge, and can handle it, but also remember that a warrior chooses his battle. Therefore when we do suddenly find ourselves facing a challenge which demands instant action, but find that we are incapable in that moment of ascertaining wherein lies the true battle, then it is always better to adopt a stance of self-preservation until such time as we can figure out why we were faced with that challenge. In this respect an analogy will help to clarify this important point.

If you are not a doctor, but should suddenly find yourself having to tend to a person who is seriously injured, it would be utter foolishness for you to assume that you are being challenged to tend to this person. If you don't know anything about first aid, or about healing, then run to find help for that person as quickly as you can. Once you have done what you can to get help for that person, then try and figure out why it was necessary for you to be challenged in this way. This same principle holds good in dealing with petty tyrants, especially those in the first and the second categories. In all such cases, the first and foremost battle to be fought is to stay alive, or to keep your job, for the simple reason that dead people don't ever become warriors, and if you get fired you will have lost your petty tyrant and your income on top of it. In the next chapter we will return briefly to our discussion of petty tyrants, for this is especially relevant today with respect to the escalating number of parents who are turning to child abuse as an expression of this type of behaviour.

In the example of Sean we see that Willis is temporarily playing the role of petty tyrant for him. Willis in this instance falls into the third category of petty tyrants, that is, people who do not normally behave like petty tyrants unless provoked in some manner. How Sean should handle his brother, and how any apprentice, for that matter, should handle a petty tyrant, is what the stalker's rule teaches us, for it is only by learning to stalk both ourselves and others that we can finally rid ourselves of all sense of being victimised.

By looking at what Sean has learned from his challenge so far we can also see how much this situation with Willis is helping Sean, not only to recapitulate and thereby to acquire sobriety in his life, but also to eradicate his self-importance, to gain skill in using the warrior's shield and, most important of all, to learn to stalk both himself and others in his endeavour to wake up in the dream, in his pursuit of warriorship. Everything Sean has learned up to this point will aid him greatly in understanding how he is to devise a strategy for entering into battle with Willis – a concept we will look at in the following chapter.

CHAPTER FOUR

THE WARRIOR'S HONOUR

TO HAVE THE HONOUR OF THE WARRIOR REQUIRES A PROPER TONAL.

In the previous chapter we saw that if Sean is going to handle his challenge impeccably it is necessary for him to devise some sort of a strategy based upon what he has learned so far. In order to understand how this is to be done, it is important to remember that Sean is striving to become a warrior and that all his challenges are therefore in the nature of opportunities to claim his *power* as a warrior. Nevertheless, to become a warrior requires a total transformation of the *island of the tonal*, and so it stands to reason that we can equally well say that every challenge in our lives is an opportunity to gradually transform the *island of the tonal*. In Volumes One and Two this was explained in terms of acquiring what is known as a *proper tonal*, an act which not only brings about the saving of *personal power*, but also the acquisition of self-respect and self-confidence, all of which adds up to a very real knowledge of what it is to be a fully responsible human being whose honour is reflected in his or her every action; mental, emotional and physical. Consequently, whatever strategy Sean is going to adopt will be a reflection of his honour, or lack thereof, and will equally be a measure of his impeccability as demonstrated by his actions which, of course, will be determined by the present condition of his *tonal*.

From the above it is clear that a stalker's approach to formulating a strategy is vastly different to that of someone who is not a warrior. People, generally speaking, want to win all of their battles, all the time, and always want to be right.

Yet, ironically enough, most men and women spend their lives trying to run away from the battles they should be fighting and, when forced to fight, end up fighting mostly the wrong battles, with the result that, even if they do win their battles, they have in effect achieved very little, if anything at all. From a stalker's perspective such behaviour is sheer idiocy, for not only is it an utter waste of time and *personal power*, but it is also hardly honourable.

The question of honour is a vital consideration in the life of the warrior, for without a very real sense of honour there can be no self-respect, no self-confidence, and most certainly no belief in self. Without these characteristics it is impossible to think and to act in terms of warriorship. Therefore, if we intend becoming warriors, then every challenge in our lives should be seen as an opportunity either to enhance, or to uphold our honour. Yet very few people ever act in an honourable manner, for the simple reason that very few people really know what the true meaning of the word entails. Most people assume that honour implies upholding their social image, or upholding their sense of pride but, sadly, this has nothing to do with honour. Our social image is but the product of the common dream, whereas pride is usually based upon the sense of superiority, and to defend these two illusions is to uphold social conditioning, and not honour.

The honour of the warrior lies in the fact that his every thought, feeling and action is impeccable, as is his skill in handling his emotions. But remember that to be impeccable means that you act to the very best of your ability upon whatever knowledge is available to you in the moment. In other words, to be impeccable means that you take full responsibility for yourself, for your life, and for your knowledge, for it is that responsibility, or lack of it, that influences all our actions; mental, emotional and physical. Here it is important to bear in mind that the word "responsibility" means the *ability to respond*, that is, the ability to respond, not only to all of life, but also to yourself, your own life, and your own knowledge. In this respect, people are generally so busy trying to uphold their social image and their social conditioning, that they very rarely have the time or the energy to respond to themselves.

Consequently, most people lead lives which are completely unimpeccable, in that they are for ever upholding someone else's ideas or, more accurately, someone else's prejudices, rather than acting upon their own knowledge.

The example of Sean demonstrates this point beautifully, for had Sean not been on the Warrior's Path he would have adopted one of three options. Either he would have become a beggar and accepted his brother's unfair proposal; or he would have taken the coward's way out by running away without putting up a fight; or he would have done the big macho thing by strutting and crowing around town like an over-confident cockerel who is going to use the law to put Willis in his place. But where is the honour in any of these options? What would Sean have accomplished by adopting any one of them? The only thing Sean would have accomplished in the case of the first two options is loss of self-respect, and in the case of the third option, provided he won the court case, he would only have succeeded in proving to himself that he was right and his brother was wrong – something which only reinforces the idiotic belief that in order to be someone and something you must prove yourself right and others wrong!

Sean's strategy must instead be so designed as to enhance his sense of honour and aid him in transforming his *island of the tonal*. Sean already knows that the transformation which is currently required concerns his self-image and his belief in his own worth. In fact, having given due consideration to all his other shortcomings, it is clear to Sean that his low self-image and his consequent lack of belief in himself, is central to all of his shortcomings and, therefore, if he can change his self-image it will be so much easier to change everything else on the *island of the tonal*. This is true of everyone for, generally speaking, it is always people's low self-image which is the cause of most of their shortcomings, and which also always gets in the way of everything they do. However, the reason why the majority of people today suffer from a low self-image is because they have no real sense of what it is to be honourable.

The honour of the warrior is summed up in a nutshell in the following aphorism.

A WARRIOR IS AN HONOURABLE BEING IN THAT HIS HUMILITY
DOES NOT ALLOW FOR ANY ACTION WHICH DOES NOT UPHOLD
THE INTERRELATIONSHIP OF LIFE.

The implications of this aphorism are extremely far-reaching, but by far the most important implication that concerns us here is that to have the honour of a warrior demands not only a recognition of the interrelationship of all life, but also a conscious upholding of this law. In other words, the true warrior cannot just pay lip service to the interrelationship of life, but must live it in every possible sense of the word. What this means is that the warrior acknowledges the fact that *if he uplifts himself, then through the interaction of life he also uplifts all those around him.*

From the above it is apparent that any strategy devised by a warrior must of necessity be of such a nature as to benefit, not only him or herself, but also the rest of life, of which he or she is but a unit. Therefore, the true warrior can never react out of anger, or retaliate reflexively as a result of having been slighted or offended in some way. Nor can the warrior react out of a sense of revenge, or spite. All such reactions will only "benefit" the person's sense of self-importance, and will certainly not do anyone any good at all. Because of the interrelationship of life, whatever course of action the warrior is going to adopt must benefit all concerned, including him or herself. This also means that the warrior cannot afford to play the role of martyr or victim, for such a role will most certainly not benefit the warrior, and if it does not benefit the warrior, then it also cannot benefit those around him or her. Such is the Law of *Light and Reflection*, summed up in the concept Toltecs refer to as *mirrors of the soul*.

Although the concept of mirrors has already been covered in *Return of the Warriors*, it is necessary here for us to expand somewhat upon this concept in order to grasp how a warrior goes about devising a suitable strategy. In this respect, realise that all people, all beings, and the world at large, merely reflect for us what we most need to learn about ourselves. This is an immutable universal law that none of us can escape or afford to ignore. It is impossible to hold up a rose in front of a mirror and have a tulip reflected back to us.

Therefore if we see aggression reflected to us by the people around us, then it is because we need to address the aggression within ourselves. If we see dishonesty reflected in the people around us, then we must likewise look at how or where we too manifest dishonesty. If, on the other hand, we see beauty and harmony reflected for us, then we must look for, and give ourselves honest credit for those areas in our lives where we too manifest beauty and harmony. If it is the mirror of the world at large we are looking into, and if in that mirror we see violence, then it is because we as a community, or race of people, need jointly to address the violence within us all. Although people, generally speaking, are so engrossed in playing the *blame game* that they do not want to recognise this most fundamental of universal laws, the fact remains that our mirrors are incapable of lying to us, and the reader would do well here to reread what has already been imparted in *Return of the Warriors* with respect to this concept.

It will also benefit the reader always to bear in mind that mirrors are of three types, namely, past, present and future. In other words, although most mirrors generally reflect for us what we most need to learn about our present behaviour or beliefs, it does happen that some of our mirrors will reflect either past behaviour, or the potential for manifesting behaviour of which we are not yet aware. However, the point to be stressed here, is the need for absolute honesty, for it is the easiest thing in the world to brush aside a mirror as being irrelevant to the present moment. To do so, though, is sheer idiocy for anyone wishing to become a warrior, and normally results either from a sense of superiority or inferiority, or else, because the person concerned believes that to *acknowledge*, and therefore to *own*, one's shortcomings is somehow bad. Such a belief inevitably stems from social conditioning, and anyone adhering to it does not acknowledge the fact that *our shortcomings are our ticket to freedom and our passage to power*.

There are two reasons why we are sometimes shown a mirror of past behaviour. The first, and by far the most common reason, is because there are still subtleties or nuances concerning this past behaviour which require our attention. The second reason concerns the fact that apprentices to the Warrior's Path often tend to swing from being dishonest to the polar opposite where they become so *obsessed* with trying to be honest, that they will usually become destructively self-critical. Caught in this process, such apprentices choose to forget to give themselves *honest credit*, and thereby fall prey to the mistaken assumption that self-criticism is the sign of humility. Nothing could be further from the truth, for self-criticism implies a rather heavy dose, albeit in a subtle form, of self-importance. Such apprentices make the fatal mistake of believing that they are somehow powerless to change their own behaviour, or else just *too good* to have to endure the embarrassment of taking ownership of such behaviour. Consequently, instead of taking ownership of their behaviour, and acknowledging the value inherent within their shortcomings, such apprentices indulge in self-criticism by believing that this will in some way solve the problem.

The purpose for being shown a mirror which pertains to the possible future is much the same as concerning past mirrors, but realise that because we are being shown potential behaviour, the need for exercising vigilance is dire. It is a fatal mistake for anyone to assume that if he or she is not displaying a certain behaviour at present, he or she never will be. We are never given guidance, and never shown something for which we have no need. The very fact that we are being shown a mirror of the future is indication enough that this behaviour is already starting to manifest, although often at first in ways that are so small as to appear completely insignificant. That potential might as yet only be a tiny trickle, on rare occasions, but it will become a raging torrent if it is not stemmed right now. The acorn is small and beautiful, but it nevertheless has the potential of growing into a massive oak if placed in fertile ground.

Our potential shortcomings are exactly the same, and just because our shortcomings are our passage to *power* we should not assume that this means we have been given a licence to develop all manner of vices. For example, if a person has the potential for becoming an alcoholic, then it only takes two or three drinks occasionally to develop that potential into a terrible addiction. However, if such a person is sufficiently aware and honest enough to acknowledge the fact that he or she is becoming obsessed with the very idea of drinking, then that person will use that shortcoming as a challenge to be wide awake and thoroughly impeccable every time he or she is around alcohol. If such a person is an apprentice to the Warrior's Path, he or she would not be expected to avoid the use of alcohol, but would instead be encouraged to use that challenge in order to develop a finely-honed sense of self-discipline and self-respect. This the apprentice would do by allowing him or herself to enjoy the occasional social drink or two, but without ever indulging in alcohol.

The most important point with respect to mirrors, and the one that concerns us here, is the fact that any strategy devised by a warrior, irrespective of the form it may take, is geared entirely towards the upliftment of self *and* the world around him or her. This is a paradoxical statement when taken at face value, for, on the one hand, the *theory* of the concept appeals to most people's sense of morality in the sense of doing something which is to the mutual benefit of all. On the other hand, the actual *practising* of this concept is something most people normally frown upon heavily as being selfish. Because of social conditioning, people do not like to be seen as selfish in any way, and yet few people ever come to realise that life is a selfish process, and that there is also a huge difference between being *selfish* as opposed to being *self-centred*. As a result, most people who do not want to be seen as being selfish invariably end up manifesting the very behaviour they do not want to be accused of.

There is nothing wrong with being selfish, for if we accept the fact that people only mirror for us our own behaviour, then time and time again we are thrown back upon ourselves. If we practise the mirror concept, then the only work there is, is work on *ourselves*. The warrior is not a being who will even consider wasting his time or his *personal power* in indulging in the stupidity of the blame game, for he knows full well that if he does not like the reflection he is seeing, then it is not the fault of the mirror, but something in himself that he does not approve of. Therefore, as far as the warrior is concerned, if you do not like what you are seeing in the mirror, then *do* something about changing *yourself*, and don't just sit around whining and complaining about the behaviour of others.

We cannot change others, nor do we have a right to want to change them, but we can change ourselves, and if we change ourselves, then our mirrors too must change. If, on the other hand, and as sometimes does happen, the person who is reflecting for us is incapable of changing, or simply does not want to change, then that person will leave our lives in one way or another once we have changed ourselves. The simple truth which comes out here is that a mirror cannot reflect anything which is not true, for all mirrors, including ourselves, are subject to the law of *Light and Reflection*. For example, if you are a totally honest person, then you will just never attract dishonest people, and if you are not a violent person, you will never find yourself confronted with violence. But, if you find yourself having to deal with a person who tells lies all the time, then ask yourself in what ways you too are lying. Remember not to take a mirror at face value, but to look for what is termed the *bottom line*, in this case, lying, irrespective of the form that lying takes. Realise that forms can be exceedingly subtle, and even obscure, but if you accept the fact that a mirror can never reflect what is not there, then you will look for how you too are lying, and if you look for it you will find it. For example, it could be as subtle as trying so hard to keep up your social image that you are compromising yourself, and are therefore no longer true to yourself. If this is the case, then you are quite literally *living* a lie, which is even worse than telling lies.

When it comes to looking into the mirror of the world at large, apprentices usually find it a lot more difficult to find the bottom line, even though the principle is exactly the same as for a personal mirror. For example, if the crime rate in a country is a problem, apprentices will often shrug this fact off with the attitude that they in themselves are not guilty of crime. I use this particular example because it is so very prevalent today in almost every country in the world. Why is it so prevalent? Simply because man has reached adulthood, and must now take full responsibility for being an adult. It is no longer the sole responsibility of the social authorities to curb crime, but it is instead the responsibility of every adult man or woman. This does not mean that people must now rush around stopping crime, but it does mean that people should be looking into the mirror and taking full responsibility for what they are seeing.

Therefore the question that is posed to an apprentice apropos crime is: "How do you perpetuate crime in your own life?" In this respect no two people are identical, and as a result each person will manifest crime in a different way. For example, by blaming the government or the social authorities for not being able to curb crime, you are not taking responsibility for being an adult, but are instead inferring that you as an individual are powerless to do anything about the crime rate. However, such an inference is tantamount to saying that you are a victim and at the mercy of every criminal. If this is what you believe, then you will without a doubt attract those people into your life who will reflect for you the belief that you are a victim. Having attracted these people, then as we saw earlier in this book, you are as guilty of their crimes as they are for perpetrating them. If, on the other hand, you choose to claim your *power* as a warrior, and stop believing that you are the victim of all and sundry, then you will not be attracting crime, but will instead start to attract people who are also strong and willing to claim their *power*. If enough people in a neighbourhood would do this that neighbourhood would be free from crime in hardly any time at all, and what is true of a neighbourhood is equally true for a whole country. Crime can only occur where people are calling it forth, and will always flourish in an environment of fear and tolerance sparked off by the victim mentality.

In the final analysis, we therefore see that life is a selfish pro-cess, for by placing the focus upon ourselves, and by taking full responsibility for our own knowledge and our own state of being, we can and do change the world around us. However, the same cannot be said about being self-centred. To be self-centred means that we do not believe in or uphold the interrelationship of life, for this is the very meaning of the term. To be self-centred quite literally implies that you see yourself as being the centre around which the rest of the world pivots, an idea which expresses a gross sense of self-importance.

Seeing themselves as being so very important, self-centred people can never understand why others around them are failing to live up to their standards and expectations. Wanting everyone to bow down to their will, and to accept their point of view, such people are always at loggerheads with others, and in refusing to accept the concept that others are merely our mirrors, they inadvertently uphold the victim mentality. Such people are forever defending some "good" cause in the name of justice, and instead of taking responsibility for their own state of being, they blame someone else, and invariably get caught up in trying to "save" others from the cruel clutches of the victimisers. Consequently, self-centred people are the original do-gooders of this world, if I may be allowed to coin such a term. These are the people who form the vast majority of those misguided souls who are forever fighting for some good cause, whether it is to hold protest marches to curb the violence, or whether it is to save the penguins from the threat of pollution. Yet such people never pause to consider their own role in perpetuating violence and the appalling rate of pollution.

To adopt the stance of selfishness within the process of life is, therefore, a far cry from what social conditioning has ingrained in men and women in general because, as we have seen, it is in fact the very basis of true humility, in that instead of blaming others, we accept full responsibility for who and what we are, as well as accepting responsibility for our own knowledge and our own state of being. By adopting a selfish approach to life we acknowledge that the only work to be done is on the self, and that through the interaction of life this will also benefit all of the world around us. Self-centredness, however, is the complete opposite, for there is nothing humble about being self-centred. On the contrary, to be self-centred is not only to be self-important, but is also the height of arrogance and conceit, and although the do-gooders of this world will scream and shout in defence of their actions, the truth of the matter is that *charity begins at home*. If you cannot sort out the mess in your own life, then how in hell's name are you ever going to be able to sort out the mess in someone else's life? Likewise, if you cannot stop calling forth people to victimise you, then who gives you the right to demand that the social authorities do a better job at protecting you? Such reasoning makes absolutely no sense to the warrior at all, because since it is you yourself who are calling forth victimisers, you are in effect demanding that the social authorities should protect you from your own behaviour!

Three final points need to be mentioned in connection with what we have been discussing. The first of these is that if one takes into account that petty tyrants do exist, then obviously one could look upon what has been stated about them so far as contradicting the concept of mirrors. But, if one goes beyond the face value of petty tyrants one quickly enough comes to the realisation that there is in fact no contradiction as such. The only reason why it appears to be a contradiction is because not all of us are overtly petty tyrants. Yet, realise that if you do have a petty tyrant in your life, then it is only because you have called forth the experiences you are gaining through your association with that person.

Furthermore, bearing in mind that you should never become hooked to the face value of a mirror, you should first take a very close look at yourself, before assuming that you are not a petty tyrant. This is the same injunction that is given to any apprentice who has found him or herself a petty tyrant, and when such apprentices do look within themselves, they are invariably struck dumb to realise that they are indeed petty tyrants in the sense of having victimised themselves with their own behaviour for as long as they can recall! The irony of attracting a petty tyrant into one's life lies in the fact that if we do, then it is only because our self-image is so low that in our *feelings* we have no value at all. If we do have such a low self-image, it is hardly surprising that we end up having to call forth a petty tyrant who will reflect for us our own sense of unworthiness and lack of value.

The second point concerns the fact that when we change then so too must our mirrors. Although this is true, it nevertheless does happen from time to time that we have mirrors in our lives that are either incapable of changing, in that it is not yet time for them to change, because they still need to learn from their be- haviour; or else mirrors that are unwilling to change for whatever reasons. When this is the case, then generally speaking such people are forced to leave our lives, either because they choose to do so, or because of the circumstances within their lives. For example, let us assume that it is your boss who has been your mirror, but that you have dealt with whatever it is within you that needed to be addressed. However, in spite of the fact that you have dealt with every single nuance you may have over-looked initially, your boss is still not showing any sign of changing his attitude towards you. When something like this happens, either you will find yourself being transferred to another office, or your boss will be transferred, or you will be promoted to some other position, or something to this effect. But one way or another, the mirror of your boss must and will leave your life.

Notwithstanding what has been stated so far, realise that there are mirrors that will not change, and which just simply cannot leave your life for some time. Typical examples of such mirrors are often to be found in parents or children, but even in such cases there is no contradiction in the concept of mirrors. If a mirror is incapable of changing, or does not wish to change, and we find that we are incapable of ridding ourselves of that mirror, then it stands to reason that we still do need that mirror, irrespective of what we may feel or believe about it. For example, if your parents, or your child for that matter, keep on reflecting for you behaviour which you know beyond all shadow of a doubt you are no longer guilty of, then take it as fact that in some obscure way you still need that mirror.

Most of the time when this happens it is because the person concerned needs such a mirror to remind him or her of the fact that a warrior must learn to stand free and detached from the world around him or her, but without ever becoming judgmental. In other words, the warrior must learn that all of life is interactive, and that because of this, all behaviour stems from our interaction with others. Therefore, if you have eradicated the behaviour which is being reflected for you by your parents, or your child, then what still needs to be done is to work on your interaction and your relationship not only with your parents, or your child, but also with the world at large. If this is done, although your parents or your child might still persist with their behaviour towards others, they will nonetheless change their behaviour towards you personally, for the simple reason that no-one can escape the law of Light and Reflection.

The final point to be covered here is that if we have done everything within our power to handle our mirrors impeccably, but the mirror still persists, then we can safely assume that what had been a mirror to begin with has now been transmuted into a challenge. When this is the case the challenge normally lies in being forced to take a firm stand on what it is we are fighting for. Usually this will revolve around compromise in some way. For example, apprentices to the Warrior's Path will often make the mistake of not wanting to end a relationship, even if it means that they are having to compromise themselves by staying in that relationship. Such a relationship could be a romantic one, or a business relationship, or their relationship with a friend, or parent, or even their children. Yet, realise that if you are going to claim your *power* as a warrior, sooner or later you will be confronted by having to take a firm stand on who you are, and in what you believe.

Just standing up for our own rights is often enough to resolve such a challenge, but it does happen that the challenge quite often lies in having to choose between the Warrior's Path and a particular relationship. When this is the case one has no other choice but to terminate that relationship, no matter how difficult this may be for oneself or for the other person concerned. Needless to say, this is especially difficult to do when the other person happens to be one's own child who is still a minor. Nevertheless, even with one's own child there is every need to be utterly ruthless, for if you do not stand up for your own rights you will never be able to claim your *power*, and you will be no good to anyone, least of all your child, or yourself for that matter.

I am not here implying that parents of delinquent children should spurn their responsibility by simply abandoning a delinquent child, but I am stating that if you do have a delinquent child you must take every action that may be necessary in order to imprint upon the mind of that child that its behaviour is totally and completely unacceptable. How this is to be done depends solely upon the circumstances in your life, but you could, for example, send such a child to a boarding school for wayward children or, if need be, even to a reformatory. By taking such action you are to all intents and purposes ending the relationship with that child by not having him or her at home, but you will not have shirked your responsibility towards the child. Such challenges are never easy to handle by any standards, and far more clarification is needed on this subject than what has been given here, but without at least touching upon this kind of challenge this section of the teachings would not be complete.

From all of the above it should now be clear that by having no one to blame, and by being thrown back upon himself time and time again, the warrior has no option but to adopt a humble approach to life. By working with the mirror concept day in and day out, every apprentice, through the experiences in his or her life, sooner or later has to acknowledge the fact that he or she is indeed no better and no worse than anyone or anything else. In the final analysis we are all equal to each other and to every other life-form upon this planet. The only real differences between one being and another are the great many different ways in which we tend to materialise our challenges in life.

Although there are lots of people in this world who deem themselves to be better than others, the warrior is a being who has learned through working with mirrors that he is no angel and, in having learned to accept himself for who and what he honestly is, has no fear of owning all and everything which is on his *island of the tonal*. By having got to know every aspect of his being, from the very worst through to the very best, the warrior is incapable of judging another person, or being for that matter, and here lies his greatest honour. Not being ashamed of the fact that he is no better than a petty criminal, and not bashful about the fact that he also has within him the qualities of the saint, the warrior is capable of facing all of life squarely, standing tall and with head held high. This the warrior can do, not because of arrogance, not because of self-importance, not because of false pride, but because he has acquired that utter humility which comes from the sure knowledge, firstly, that no one is better or worse than himself; and secondly, that he is an honourable being in that he is *honest* enough to own every aspect of his *island of the tonal* and *courageous* enough to fight for impeccability.

Honesty and courage are the two qualities that mark the honour of the true warrior, for in the final analysis honesty and courage are but the two sides of the one coin we term honour. It takes courage to be honest with yourself, and without honesty there can be no real courage, only a false bravado to cover the deep fear that someone is going to find out something about you that you would prefer others, including yourself, not to know. But where is the honour in living a life that is based upon lies, pretences, and the cowardice born of fear? How can we ever hope to claim our *power* as warriors if we have no honesty and no courage? To have *power* we must have knowledge, but since knowledge can only be acquired through life's experiences, how are we to do this if we refuse to acknowledge who and what we really are? Yet, realise that to acknowledge the worst in ourselves, and not to hate ourselves for that, and to acknowledge the very best in us, and to *believe* that we are worthy of such fine qualities, requires unequivocal honesty and unwavering courage.

The only way in which to acquire honesty is to accept the fact that the world around us is our mirror, and the only way in which to acquire courage, is to hold onto the knowledge that if you do not like the reflections you see, then you do have the *power* and the ability to change those reflections by changing yourself. Therefore, although a warrior is incapable of judging another being, he nevertheless also knows that he does not have to condone behaviour which is dishonourable. By not accepting such behaviour in himself, the warrior is not under any obligation to accept it from others. Consequently, it is never the person concerned whom the warrior judges, but it is that person's behaviour which the warrior looks at with *discrimination*. Is this behaviour an act which leads to freedom, or to slavery? Is this behaviour an act which uplifts, or breaks down? In short, is such behaviour honourable, or dishonourable? However, even in this respect the warrior is never so arrogant as to blame another person for their behaviour, for in acknowledging his responsibility in having called forth this mirror the warrior addresses that particular behaviour within himself, or alternatively, the challenge which that person's behaviour brings him. In other words, is this behaviour reflecting aspects within the warrior that uphold his honour?

What we have looked at here in connection with mirrors is vital to take into consideration when formulating any kind of a strategy, for the strategy of the warrior is not geared towards trying to change others by enforcing his will upon them, but is instead so designed as to enable the warrior to uplift himself, and in so doing to uplift all of life around him. This is what the warrior strives for, not because it is the moral thing to do, or because the warrior is such an unselfish person, but merely because his sense of honour is such that he cannot concern himself with anyone other than himself. Therefore even if it does come to having to choose between his relationship with a particular person and the Warrior's Path, the warrior will still put himself and his own evolution first, and in doing what is best for him, he also automatically does what is best for the other person concerned.

This practice is the very basis of stalking, and it is this that has given rise to the statement that *the warrior controls everything without controlling anything*, for realise that in changing ourselves we do change the world around us, and therefore we have no need to resort to the pettiness of dictatorship. Simply by using the law of Light and Reflection, and by practising the interrelationship of life, the warrior in time becomes a truly invincible being with considerable *power* at his or her command. However, this is a statement which every apprentice at first mistakenly looks upon as being perhaps naive or, at best, overly simplistic. Yet it is typical of everything warriors do, in that although all of their actions are deceptively simple and appear to be so common-place and harmless, they nevertheless hold within them unimaginable *power*. This is particularly true of the strategies devised by warriors, for although they will always appear to be harmless, because of their utter simplicity, they are in reality lethal. But in order to see how this works, we will now return to our example of Sean and his brother Willis.

In having to devise a strategy for handling this battle with his brother, Sean has to take into account the second aspect of the stalker's rule, namely, *by striving for simplicity, a warrior discards all unnecessary acts.* From what we have learned concerning mirrors, this aspect of the stalker's rule should now not be so difficult to grasp. Simply by bringing everything back to himself and his own progress upon the Path of Knowledge, the warrior eliminates a vast amount of actions, emotions, feelings and thoughts that can only arise and have any meaning within the context of self-importance and self-centredness.

This is not something that needs any further explanation because even just a little thought upon the concept of mirrors will be enough to speak volumes. The vast majority of people's actions, their emotional state, their endless circling thoughts and higgledy-piggledy mess of feelings, all stem from their self-centred approach to life and the victim mentality. Therefore, from the warrior's point of view, every battle is as simple as fighting for his honour as a warrior. Not at all concerned with trying to perpetuate his social conditioning through not wanting to own his shortcomings, or by trying to defend his behaviour in attempting to justify actions he himself does not approve of, the warrior has very little to consider other than how best to uplift himself into becoming an even more honourable being.

Nothing could be simpler than this, although accomplishing such a feat is not simple at all, for all of us are mysterious creatures and, because of that mystery, tend to operate with a truly astounding complexity. In this respect, it is important to note that people generally always make the mistake of *assuming* that they know themselves, when in effect they only know their behaviour. But even here, people normally do not even have the vaguest understanding of what causes that behaviour, or why they should have the shortcomings they do have. If people do claim to have an understanding, then even just a little probing soon shows that what they term to be understanding is invariably nothing more than some personal version of the blame game.

This brings us straight back to the four postulates of stalking.

As far as Sean is concerned, he must now consider the second postulate of stalking first, for it this postulate that has to do with *action*, and devising a strategy is the very first action he will take in his battle with Willis. The second postulate tells us that *it is our duty as warriors to solve the mystery, but that we should never engage the hope of being able to do so.*

We have already ascertained that the real battle for Sean lies in having to conquer his poor self-image by striving to acknowledge to himself that he does in fact have value as an individual. In this respect, Sean will be able to establish what brought about his low self-image in the first place, by using the technique of recapitulation. However, recapitulation will only reveal the *cause* of his low self-image, but will not reveal the *reason* why having to fight for his self-worth should constitute for Sean one of his major challenges in this lifetime.

Obviously the answer to this last question lies firmly within the realm of destiny, but what is of immediate import here is that the reason as to why Sean has to struggle with a low self-image remains part of the *mystery* of his being. This is the real meaning of the second part of the postulate under consideration, for remember that everything on our *island of the tonal* is there for a reason, and that although we do in time transmute all of our shortcomings into assets of value, those shortcomings nevertheless stay with us for life. In other words, although Sean will in time conquer his low self-image by learning how to use it constructively, rather than allowing it to coax him into behaviour which drains him of his self-confidence and self-respect, Sean will nevertheless for the duration of this lifetime always have a low self-image, for that low self-image is a feature of his *island of the tonal*.

This is true of all our shortcomings, for to transmute our shortcomings simply means that we have learned how to make them work *for* us, rather than *against* us. However, in the process of transmutation we never *lose* or *eradicate* our shortcomings as such, and neither is it desirable to do so, because our shortcomings are our ticket to freedom and our passage to *power*. Without our shortcomings we would never be able to transform ourselves into warriors, for it is only by fighting to transmute our shortcomings that we ultimately manage to eliminate the behaviour that originally stemmed from them. It is through *transmuting* our shortcomings that we manage to *transform* ourselves into warriors, and consequently it is the behaviour which stems from our shortcomings that is eliminated, and not the shortcomings themselves – a fact which is all too often forgotten by the careless apprentice.

It stands to reason that if we have our shortcomings so that we can unravel the mystery of our being, but we can never eliminate our shortcomings, then solving that mystery is very clearly the work of much more than just this lifetime. In other words, the best any of us can do is to start from where we are at in trying to solve as much of the mystery of our being as is possible to do in the space of this lifetime. It is only the arrogant fool who will ever entertain the hope that he or she is going to unravel the mystery of beingness in the few short years of just one lifetime.

As far as Sean is concerned, his strategy should be such as to enable him not only to transmute his low self-image, but also to solve as much of that part of the mystery of his being as he is capable of in this lifetime. This is what is meant by the first part of the second postulate, namely, that *it is our duty as warriors to solve the mystery*. The word "duty" furthermore implies that solving the mystery of our being is not only something which we owe to ourselves, but is in a very real sense also our *duty* because of the interdependence of life. However, this is not something which should be taken at face value, because a warrior's sense of duty is not at all the same as that of the average man or woman. Duty to a warrior means that he acknowledges the fact that it is not the prerogative of some to sit back and wait, whilst others carry out their duties in the sense of having to serve. Each and every one of us has a duty to uplift ourselves, not only so that we may benefit in a personal capacity, but also so that we may benefit universally, in that we are all units of the one life. Therefore, every time a warrior manages to solve some aspect of the mystery of his being, he also solves a tiny fragment of that huge mystery which encompasses the greater life, of which he is a unit. In the final analysis, this is what is truly meant by the phrase *mapping out the unknown,* and it is this that the warrior looks upon as his duty and, ultimately, also as his only justification for the priceless gift of life.

Having got this far, it should be quite clear that Sean must now refer to the third postulate in order to proceed with devising his strategy. Remember that this postulate tells us that we too *are a part of this mystery*, a fact we have already ascertained in our consideration of mirrors. But this postulate also tells us that we should *become at-one with the mystery*. This is an important point for, as we saw earlier in this book, it is only by immersing ourselves within the mystery that we can have any hope of being able to solve it. The reason for this is that in dealing with the mystery of our being, rational thought is of little use, and therefore *feeling* is needed, but it is practically impossible to *get the feel of something* unless we immerse ourselves in it. The importance of accessing feeling at this point is also indicated by the fact that in working with the third postulate we find ourselves facing the South which, as we know from *Cry of the Eagle*, is irrational, and thus we need to approach it with feeling, rather than with rationality.

Sean does not find it at all easy to put his normal rationalising aside in order to access his feelings, for he has always been an academic person relying heavily upon the rational. Accessing our feelings is what is termed *listening to the heart* – a complex skill which is neither quickly nor easily perfected, but in this respect we fortunately have the third aspect of the stalker's rule to aid us. This is a concept which we will explore in greater depth in the following chapter, but we must consider it briefly here in order to grasp how a warrior devises his or her strategy.

The third aspect of the stalker's rule states that *a warrior is always ready to make his last stand right here and right now*. In his consideration of this, Sean found that it was not quite so difficult to put aside all his rational thoughts on how best to handle the situation with his brother. The only thing he needed to do was to focus his attention on the fact that none of us have any guarantee on life, and that accordingly it is only the present moment that is of any real consequence. Therefore, as soon as Sean asked himself what he would like most if this was to be his final moment on earth, he was immediately overwhelmed by an odd feeling which sparked off in him an almost consuming desire to be free of the close association with his brother.

At first Sean cannot figure out exactly what the feeling he experienced really means, but the one thing he is certain of is that he most definitely does want to be free of his association with Willis. However, if Sean is going to free himself from the relationship with his brother he will have to claim his *power* in some way. This is hardly surprising, because in working with the third postulate he is facing South, which is not only the place of *warmth*, but also the place of *power*. This feature is central to all strategies devised by warriors, for at the end of the day, the sole purpose of all challenges is to provide us with the opportunity to claim our *power* and, in so doing, to uplift ourselves.

In considering how best to claim his *power* in this particular battle, Sean recalls that the real battle for him lies in how best to use this opportunity to start transmuting his low self-image. However, once again rational thought is not much good here, for rationality can only guide Sean within the context of what he already knows, which in this case would be to adopt one of the known options, and we have already seen that these would not benefit Sean in his battle. This then is as far as the third postulate can take Sean for the moment, but in order to finalise his strategy Sean is now up against the challenge of having to find an option which is currently unknown to him. In facing the unknown, it is therefore once again feeling that is needed here, which indicates to Sean that he must now turn to face the West, the place of *feeling*, and refer to the fourth postulate of stalking.

Having turned to the West, Sean is quick to realise that because this is the quarter assigned to *erasing personal history*, the implications are that his strategy should somehow be an exercise in erasing his personal history. This insight makes a great deal of sense to Sean, since he knows that it is always our personal history, which as we saw in *Cry of the Eagle*, is our self-image, that tends to be the biggest bug-bear in our lives. This is particularly true of Sean at this moment in his life, for he is indeed suffering from the effects of a poor self-image. However, realise that it is still personal history which keeps even those people who have a very good self-image, firmly stuck in their view of the world and which can therefore be found at the root of all of their challenges in life. The only way in which we can overcome our challenges and solve the mystery of our being, is to erase our personal history, in order to stop the world. Until we have stopped the world, the mystery of our being remains elusive, our challenges always appear to be a burden, and life in general is a dull and dreary occurrence within a very mundane world.

Thinking about erasing his personal history and knowing that this means he must transmute his low self-image Sean recalls that a warrior uses the tensions which are relevant to a battle as his guide. In this particular case these tensions are of course those surrounding his low self-image, as well as that of his brother. Now remember that these tensions are generated by the quality of intensity and that intensity is the product of the interaction between the perception of two people.

In considering this fact it suddenly dawns on Sean that if he has such an intense desire to be free from the association with his brother, then even though he has never consciously realised it up until now, this unspoken desire must nevertheless have been generating tension between him and Willis for a long, long time. Furthermore, since it is Willis who initiated this battle, the chances are that Willis has much the same desire as Sean, and this after all is perhaps exactly what Willis has implied by indicating that he is taking over the company.

Sean already glimpsed this when he worked out what constitutes for him the real battle, but the only thing he could be certain of at that point was the fact that both he and Willis are having to fight for their sense of self-worth. Now, in considering the tensions surrounding this battle, Sean again recalls the odd feeling he sensed earlier, but was not able to fathom, and realising that it was obviously this feeling which sparked off his desire to be free of Willis, the penny finally drops.

Sean can now clearly see that the overriding tension in his

working relationship with Willis has always been of having to keep up with his brother in every respect, simply as a result of being swept along by their mutual desires and visions for the future. Now that he can see this Sean can also grasp the meaning of the odd feeling he experienced, and can finally put a name to it – the feeling of co-dependency! Because Sean and Willis have both had a low self-image for as long as Sean can remember, they have always relied heavily upon each other's support in everything they have ever done, with the result that they developed a co-dependency. So strong had this co-dependency become, that in thinking about it, Sean found it extremely difficult to differentiate his own identity from those aspects of his brother which he has inadvertently come to accept as being his own.

Having realised this, it is now abundantly clear to Sean that the most important thing is for him to break away from his brother and find his own identity. Consequently there is no longer any question of Sean staying in partnership with Willis. Nor, for that matter, would it benefit Sean to try and keep the company, for although it was his company to start with, it had become a reflection of their co-dependency from the day Willis first joined him. The whole operation of the company, the type of clients they have attracted, and the nature of the work contracted to the company, is all based upon the two brothers' co-dependency. Therefore, if Sean is going to find his own identity he must free himself of everything that will in any way maintain that co-dependency. In short, Sean now knows that he must indeed let Willis take over the company, lock, stock and barrel, not because he is too cowardly to fight, but simply because this is what his fate demands.

By taking the pertinent tensions into consideration, it is clear to Sean that the bottom line of this struggle, for both him and Willis, is that they have to rid themselves of their co-dependency. Wanting to take over the company was merely Willis' way of expressing that he too wishes to rid himself of Sean's influence in his life. In other words, from Willis' point of view, being managing director of the company would enable him to feel better about himself and a lot more self-confident, in which case he would be much less dependent upon Sean.

In that moment of clarity Sean felt totally in awe of the fact that people are indeed only our mirrors and, through this personal experience, also came to grasp for himself that, as is stated in the fourth postulate, *the crux of this mystery is the infinite mystery of beingness*, and *within the mystery of beingness all are equal*. Consequently, Sean could feel no anger towards his brother, but now through being able truly to see his own role in all of this, experienced a very deep sense of what is really meant by the phrase, *the warrior enters into a state of true humility*.

Sean also understands that if he is to claim his *power* as a warrior then it is imperative for him to do this in a way that will enable him to improve his own self-image. In this respect, Sean knows that for the first time in his life he is actually willing to take into account his own wishes, by acknowledging his overriding desire to be free of his brother. Therefore, all he has to do is discuss with Willis the practicalities involved in transferring the whole company into Willis' name. Thinking about this, it is immediately clear to Sean that the only thing he really wants out of the whole deal is three months salary to tie him over until he can start up a new business of his own – a very reasonable and simple request and one to which not even Willis could possibly object.

Having formulated his strategy, which is simplicity itself, Sean now only has to implement it, and in doing so he will again use the tensions concerning the low self-image of both himself and his brother to guide him. In other words, knowing that his brother is more than likely going to be highly defensive and feeling sheepish about his unfair demands, Sean will have to make his brother understand that Willis' decision does indeed suit him equally well. What this boils down to is that Sean must convince Willis that he has made the correct choice for both of them and that he therefore holds no grudge against Willis.

Needless to say, Sean's strategy is a far cry from the course which most people would have opted for, but it is also deadly. The last thing Willis will expect is for Sean to be agreeable and helpful, and therefore when Sean approaches his brother, Willis will be totally thrown off balance. At face value it will appear to Willis that he has won the battle, but in reality Sean has only just begun to stalk both himself and his brother in a most surreptitious battle that will take some time before being concluded. In effect, the tables have now been reversed and instead of Sean being the hunted, he has now become the hunter, and in this respect neither he nor Willis as yet know what the cost to Willis will be for having "won" this battle at face value. Realise also that Sean's strategy is not only for his own benefit, but also for the benefit of Willis. Therefore although Sean is acting selfishly, he is not being self-centred.

One further point that should be stressed here is that although a warrior may appear to be very ordinary and harmless, he is still a deadly opponent. As is apparent in this example of Sean and Willis, the warrior may appear to walk away defeated, but what lies behind his strategy? What unseen blows has he already delivered, and what are his blows to come? At this moment even Sean is incapable of knowing this, but one thing is for sure, Willis has through his actions given Sean his gap to freedom and Sean is not about to let his fleeting moment of chance slip through his fingers. Seeing his opportunity finally to be free from his association with his brother, Sean has every intention of using this opportunity to his full advantage. Already he has claimed an enormous amount of *power* by realising that he does not have to play the good shepherd to Willis in order to feel good about himself, and neither is he dependent upon Willis in order to have a successful business of his own. In this respect, Sean has truly shifted the focus from being the victim to being the victor and in so doing has not only taken charge of the *intensity* generated by the low self-image of both his brother and himself, but has already begun to manipulate it.

To manipulate intensity is quite naturally the first step in transforming the *tonal* into a *proper tonal*, but this is not all, for it also happens to be the first step in learning to master Dragon Lore – the ultimate magic. In the following chapters we will take a closer look at what this really implies.

Apropos Dragon Lore, one final point is worth mentioning here. In the example of Sean I am purposely keeping the use of tensions down to a very basic level. The reason I am doing so is because the true use of tensions entails practices which are far in advance of this present book; practices which can rightfully be classified as pertaining to the advanced teachings on the art of stalking. Nonetheless, it is not possible to practise the intermediate teachings without at least a rudimentary knowledge of the use of tensions. In this respect the reader is once again urged to remember never to regard any of the teachings imparted as being complete.

CHAPTER FIVE

STEPPING INTO THE UNKNOWN

TO ENTER THE UNKNOWN REQUIRES THE MANIPULATION OF INTENSITY. WHILST INTENSITY REMAINS INTACT THE ASSEMBLAGE POINT REMAINS FIRMLY FIXED, AND THEREFORE ENTERING LEFT SIDE AWARENESS AND THE UNKNOWN IS IMPOSSIBLE.

Once the warrior has devised a strategy it stands to reason that the strategy must be implemented if it is to bring forth any form of a result. However, as we have already seen, a stalker's strategy is in essence nothing more than the definition of parameters for a chosen line of improvisation. This is an important point which must never be forgotten, for in dealing with *power* we can never determine the actual unfoldment of the battle beforehand, nor what the outcome of that unfoldment will be. The only thing we can be sure of is that the battle will sooner or later come at us like a wave within the ocean of life, and when it comes, the strategy we have worked out should enable us to mount that wave so as to surf it. What will happen once we have mounted the wave, and where the wave will take us, lies securely within the realm of the unknown. Toltecs therefore refer to the implementation of a strategy as the act of *stepping into the unknown*.

Realise how different the approach of the warrior is to that of the average man or woman. People, generally speaking, go about their lives *planning* a course of action as if they can determine the actual course of events, and the moment those events start to unfold in a way that is different to what they have anticipated or hoped for they immediately set about trying to find a way in which to *force* the outcome to conform with their wishes. Such people see this as the security that comes from being in control of their lives, but from a warrior's point of view, trying to force the hand of *power* is a fool's game based upon the illusion that we control the currents in the ocean of life.

To entertain any such belief is to be utterly demented. We cannot control *power*, which, it must be remembered is *universal power*, but because *power* is the product of perception we *can* control our own level of perception, or the alignment of that perception, which of course determines our own *personal power*. Consequently, although we cannot control *power* as such, we nevertheless can choose to perceive the events in our lives in whichever way we want to. This is exactly what people do, and it is this act which is the very basis of all social conditioning, for in spite of man's gross sense of separativeness, all human beings are instinctively group-conscious and, as a result, people love to conform to the group consensus, especially so as to receive their fellow man's approval. The end result of this is that people adhere to the common dream as if it is the ultimate reality, and thus are for ever adjusting their perception to conform to the limitations of that dream. People therefore not only limit their own perception, and thereby fall prey to living a life of illusion, but worse still, also limit their own *personal power*, and consequently disempower themselves.

Maintaining the common dream, and keeping social conditioning intact, requires that the assemblage point of everyone must be kept relatively fixed at one level of perception. Furthermore, since man is constantly striving to feel secure within his experience of life, the point at which the assemblage point is fixed must of necessity be firmly within the confines of the known. From what we have learned so far, this implies that the common dream, and therefore also social conditioning, is dependent upon an intensity which is fixed and maintained by the majority of human beings. This is exactly why average men and women tend to be completely oblivious of the unknown, for whenever they do encounter it, they behave towards it as if it is something from the known that has somehow gone awry, and therefore should be brought under control, or discarded, as quickly as possible. Obviously with such an attitude, men and women are constantly restraining themselves from consciously entering into the unknown, and their lives become a one-sided rational affair in which the random effects of the unknown are perceived to be a higgledy-piggledy chaos of "luck" and "misfortune".

However, the warrior is not a being who is trying to adhere either to the common dream or to social conditioning, and therefore for him every strategy is designed to enable him to co-operate with the forces in his life so as to surf the waves into the unknown of both his potential and his destiny. Consequently, for the warrior who is striving to enter into the unknown, the prime purpose for both devising and implementing a strategy is to alter his intensity in some way. In this respect it must be remembered that the aim of the warrior is to co-operate fully and intelligently with the purpose of his own dreamer, and as the dreamer is already holding the purpose of this incarnation secure by focusing its *intent*, it stands to reason that what is required of the warrior is to make his perception fluid enough so as to be able to handle impeccably any challenge he encounters. Even more important than this is the fact that we call forth our challenges in life by the tensions set up within the web of life as a result of the intensity we generate in our interaction with others during the act of perception. Therefore, although we cannot avoid our fate, in that we cannot alter the *intent* of our dreamer, we nonetheless can dictate the *quality* of our challenges by learning to control the intensity we generate.

Dictating the quality of our challenges is not at all the same as trying to dictate the course of our lives. The analogy which I often use to explain this point is to liken fate to a journey. If it is your fate in this lifetime to travel to Rome, you will go to Rome in one way or another, but how you get there is entirely up to you. In order to get to Rome, you will, whether you are aware of it or not, call forth all sorts of challenges to guide you in the right direction. Some of these challenges you will perceive as being "good", in that they make for a joyful and pleasant journey, whilst others you will perceive as being "bad", in that they make for an unpleasant and miserable journey. In short, you can make your way to Rome into an exciting journey of adventure, or you can turn it into a living nightmare in which you feel as if you are being dragged there by the hair, kicking and screaming all the way. This is what is meant by dictating the quality of our challenges.

Yet, realise that intensity is but the result of a particular level of perception. Therefore if we wish to alter our intensity, and thereby learn to control it, then we must strive to alter our level of perception and learn to control this also. This brings us straight back to the concept of the necessity to have a fluid assemblage point, for without fluidity we cannot control our level of perception or, for that matter, our intensity. However, the easiest way in which to achieve a fluid assemblage point is to learn to stalk our perception, and the best way in which to do this is to learn to read the tensions inherent within daily life, for these tensions are but the product of intensity. Once we can read these tensions, we can begin to change our level of perception and our intensity simply by using the warrior's shield and by practising not-doing. In other words, if we strive to read the tensions in our daily life, instead of getting caught up in the face value of events, then we automatically begin to accept without accepting, and we start to believe without believing and, as a result, our perception is no longer fixed by obsession, and the assemblage point is free to move.

However, to become aware of the tensions in one's daily life, let alone to read them, requires that one is wide awake, fearful, respectful and absolutely assured. This certainly implies using the warrior's shield, but also brings us back to the concept that a warrior lives on the edge, and to this effect bases his whole life on the third aspect of the stalker's rule, namely, that *a warrior is always ready to make his last stand right here and right now*. This third aspect of the stalker's rule has implications that far exceed the scope of this book, but the implications that are of immediate import to us here are primarily concerned with the concepts of *stepping into the unknown*, and *living in the moment*, both of which are thoroughly interrelated.

In the example of Sean, it should now be clear that once he implements the strategy he has devised he will be stepping into the unknown in a very real sense, simply because the outcome is not something that can be predicted. The only thing Sean can be certain of is that his life will change for ever as a result of his action, and so too will his perception of both himself and his life. Only a little thought is needed to realise that for the average man or women such an unpredictable state of affairs is tantamount to a nightmare, but not so for a warrior. For the warrior, who lives by challenge, this is a very fine state of affairs, and it is for him confirmation of the fact that he has become fluid enough to be able to live on the edge, and that he is strong enough to withstand the rigours of mapping out the unknown. In Sean's case this moment marks for him his gap to freedom, but in order to take that gap Sean must consider the implications inherent within the third postulate of stalking.

The third postulate of stalking points out to us that the world and the events in our lives are not what they appear to be, but are instead an endless mystery and, furthermore, because our experience of this mystery changes as our perception changes, we are therefore also a part of that mystery by virtue of the fact that the act of perception itself is a mystery. Consequently, for someone like Sean, the only viable way in which to approach his life from this moment on, is to accept without accepting, and to believe without believing. No longer can Sean afford to take things at face value and leave it at that. From now on it is vitally important for him to live with the sure knowledge that every day of his life, every moment of his life, is going to be spent on unfamiliar ground, and that every sunrise is going to reveal a new horizon that is as yet unknown to him.

Stepping into the unknown is therefore not something in the same vein as deciding to go for the occasional walk, as it is so often mistaken to be, for stepping into the unknown is an irrevocable act which changes one's life for ever. It is only those misguided souls who want to have the *power* of the warrior, but who do not have the self-discipline, the self-respect, or the honour necessary to become warriors, who strive to enter and exit the unknown at will. In other words, such people try to enter the unknown within the context of their existing lives, learn what they can in the unknown, and then attempt to return to their normal lives with the knowledge gained whilst in the unknown. Although such practices do exist they are dangerous in the extreme because they lack both sobriety and impeccability. Entering the unknown is not unlike stepping into an atomic reactor, for immediately one enters the unknown, one's whole being becomes charged with an energy that initiates within one a chain reaction that cannot be stopped. The only way to handle that chain reaction is to flow with it and to set one's *intent* upon total transformation. Through that transformation one becomes immune to the destructive effects of the "radiation", but where there is no desire to change, no desire to become a truly impeccable warrior, the practitioner is quite literally exposing him or herself to the highly destructive energy of atomic radiation. The reader would do well at this point to review the teachings given in *Cry of the Eagle* on the temptations posed by *power* as one of the four natural enemies.

From the above it should be clear that stepping into the unknown is an act which initiates the process of *death*, and the only way to do this safely is to *embrace death*. In other words, at this point in his or her training the warrior must be prepared to die to his or her old life in order to accommodate the transformational process. It is primarily for this reason that it is always stressed that the warrior must come to knowledge fully prepared to die, and that only if becoming a warrior is an act of survival will the apprentice be prepared to do what it takes to become a warrior.

The concept of *embracing death* should not be taken at face value, for it is not at all what the average man or woman believes it to be. Embracing death is not only vital to the process of transformation, but it is also essential for achieving freedom. In the final analysis, embracing death is but the natural result of having learned to live on the edge, and is often referred to as *dancing the edge*. However, living on the edge and dancing the edge are not one and the same thing. Living on the edge means that the warrior has reached a point in his life at which he has, either through his own endeavours, or through the circumstances within his life, been catapulted into the unknown. Once in the unknown the warrior finds that unknown challenges demanding the acquisition of new knowledge are coming his way thick and fast and from all directions, and that any behaviour that is less than impeccable spells physical, mental or emotional annihilation. Dancing the edge, on the other hand, is the acquired ability of the warrior to balance his fear of annihilation with sobriety, and it is this ability that enables him to mount and surf every wave that comes his way, for not to surf those waves would also spell annihilation in one way or another. In other words, dancing the edge is the ability a warrior acquires as a result of having accepted death as his best advisor, for the warrior knows full well that not to do so would be to refuse to acknowledge the actions of the sharpshooters of the universe, in which case he could be annihilated at any moment. Therefore to accept death as one's best advisor boils down to accepting the fact that one has no option but to learn the *dance of death* in order to dance the edge.

One of the most profound implications inherent within the concept of living on the edge is the fact that this is where life is for ever *new*, for ever *nascent*. Consequently, for the warrior living on the edge, life is never stagnant or repetitious, or boring. Instead every moment of his life is filled with awesome wonder and breathless excitement. This is not a point which apprentices find easy to grasp, for generally speaking, most apprentices tend to think of the edge as being akin to the "outer edges of life", if I may be permitted to use such an odd phrase. The only way in which I can really make this point clear is to use an analogy which has been used since time immemorial. Therefore think of life as being like a huge wheel – *the wheel of life*.

In addition to its broad rim, the wheel of life also has many spokes to it radiating outwards from its central hub. The majority of humanity are to be found upon the rim of the wheel, whilst those who are somewhat more free than average humanity are to be found on the spokes of the wheel, the less avant-garde of these being closer to the rim, the more avant-garde being closer to the hub. Those readers who have been on similar devices at amusement parks will know that the centrifugal force generated at the outer rim of a spinning wheel is enough to make anyone dizzy, and is normally so great that it quite literally pins you to your spot. In other words, to be on the rim is not only confusing, but also keeps one stuck to one spot.

However, realise that what normally causes most wheels to spin is the circular force emanating from the hub of the wheel, and therefore what Toltecs refer to as the edge is quite literally the innermost edge of the wheel's hub, that is, the edge closest to the driving shaft, which in this analogy corresponds to the source of manifested life. Here at the centre of the wheel, with the focus kept steadily upon the driving shaft, life does not seem to spin at such an alarming rate. In fact, by comparison to the outer rim, and even the spokes for that matter, the innermost edge of the hub seems relatively still and at peace. The centrifugal force around the hub of the wheel, on the other hand, feels as if it is a raging wind that is threatening to take away even one's breath, and the only way to survive that force is to counteract it with a suitable centripetal force as expressed in the following aphorism.

AT THE CENTRE OF THE WHEEL OF LIFE RAGES AN ALMIGHTY WIND AGAINST WHICH THE WARRIOR'S ONLY DEFENCE IS HIS UNBENDING INTENT TO ACHIEVE AND HOLD THE TOTALITY OF THE SELF, FOR THE DRIVING FORCE OF THE WHEEL IS THE SPIRIT OF MAN.

As the aphorism above points out, that which enables the warrior to move away from the rim of the wheel towards the hub, and that which enables him to retain his position at the centre of the wheel, is in both cases setting his *intent* upon achieving the *totality of the self*. It must be remembered that the *totality of the self* implies that state of awareness at which the *nagal*, the dreamer and the *tonal* are experienced as one whole, or in other words, that level of awareness which can best be described as *at-one-ment*. But as we have already seen so far, at-one-ment, or the *totality of the self*, brings us straight back to the concept of group-consciousness, for not only are all the dreamers of mankind group-conscious, but there is also only just one *nagal*, one spirit of man. It will also be remembered from Chapter Two that the *totality of the self* enables the warrior to journey to the *pivot of the three rings* and to access the *third ring of power*. All in all it should by now be much clearer why it is so important for the true warrior to strive not only for impeccability, but also for freedom, both of which can only really be acquired by achieving the *totality of the self*.

Achieving the *totality of the self* is not something that can be accomplished quickly or easily, but all of the teachings imparted up to this point, if put into practice in one's daily life, will bring about a greater and greater measure of impeccability and *personal power*, both of which take the warrior ever closer to being able to shed the human form in entering into the *totality of the self*. Therefore let us continue with our present consideration of what exactly is entailed in living on the edge.

By far the most important implication as far as our present consideration of the teachings is concerned, is that because life on the edge is for ever new, the warrior is living in a constant state of flux and change and is therefore continuously adjusting his or her perception of life and also of the world in general. This is the very meaning of being a fluid warrior and of having a fluid assemblage point, but fluidity in itself is not a goal as such, but merely the means to a far greater end, namely achieving the *totality of the self*. However, as we have already learned from the third postulate of stalking, we are a mystery and although we also know from the second postulate that it is our duty to solve that mystery, we should nevertheless not engage the hope of ever being able to do so. The implications here are quite clear, but also staggering, for realise that the *totality of the self* is therefore not a goal, but merely a necessary stepping stone into an even greater journey, an even greater adventure of self-discovery.

It is primarily for this reason that, from the true Toltec's perspective, the real journey, that is, the *definitive journey of the warrior*, only starts once the third attention is entered and the warrior achieves the *totality of the self*. The journey up to this point is that of the *hu-man* being learning to become *man*. Once such a being has become man, then, and only then is he or she capable of commencing the *definitive journey of the warrior* in his or her quest of learning what it is to be man, as opposed to hu-man, and only then is it possible for him or her to become Toltec, that is, a man or woman of knowledge. This is a fact which is easily over-looked by the careless apprentice who more than often tends to forget that true man is a hu-man that has shed the human form, and therefore erroneously assumes that it is possible to become Toltec whilst still retaining the human form.

The reason I am belabouring this point here is that there is no other way in which to impress upon the apprentice's mind that to become a warrior is not a goal, and that anyone who comes to the Warrior's Path wanting to know how long it will take him or her to achieve "the goal", is doomed to failure. True warriorship can only be achieved by learning to dance the edge impeccably whilst living on that edge. True warriorship is a level of awareness and involves a skill and expertise in handling that awareness that can only be acquired through prolonged practical experience. There is simply no other way in which to acquire the knowledge and therefore the *personal power* of the warrior. How long it takes to acquire that level of awareness and skill depends entirely upon the individual, but in all cases, it is only once the apprentice has stopped fretting about the imagined goal that any real progress becomes possible.

TRUE KNOWLEDGE IS TO EXPERIENCE THE INNER SELF.

THE COST OF TRUE KNOWLEDGE IS YOUR LIFE. THE KNOWLEDGE
YOU SEEK CAN ONLY BE ACQUIRED BY DEDICATING YOUR LIFE
TO IT.

The two aphorisms above are two of the very first to be taught to every apprentice, and yet it takes all apprentices an awfully long time before they begin to grasp, let alone live according to the guidance contained in these aphorisms. Although a nagal repeatedly admonishes his apprentices to remember that it is the journey, and not the goal, that is important, apprentices time and time again make the fatal mistake of striving to reach "the goal", and consequently become thoroughly disheartened because that goal never seems to come into sight. And yet, paradoxically, it is never long after the apprentice has given up on the idea that he will ever see, let alone reach the goal, that he finds himself beginning to slip into the awareness of the true warrior, simply because he is no longer goal-orientated, but is instead concentrating on living an impeccable life.

SELF-IMPORTANCE LEADS TO IMPATIENCE, AND IMPATIENCE WILL CAUSE YOU TO FRET ABOUT HAVING TO ACHIEVE WARRIORSHIP SOONER RATHER THAN LATER. FRETTING IMPATIENTLY, YOU WILL CONTINUE TO BLUNDER ALONG IN IGNORANCE OF YOUR DAILY LIFE, AND IN THAT IGNORANCE YOU WILL MISS YOUR FLEETING MOMENTS OF CHANCE. ONLY ONCE YOU HAVE ACQUIRED TRUE HUMILITY AND PATIENCE WILL POWER COME TO YOU UNBIDDEN.

The aphorism above is simple enough to speak for itself, and yet it is also quite the hardest one for any apprentice to put into practice, for the social conditioning of every person is such that it is almost unthinkable to work towards what appears to be nothing. However, the observant apprentice is normally quite quick to realise that nothing implies no-thing in the sense of the *nagal*, the spirit of man. Therefore it is not as if the apprentice is working for no gain, but rather that he or she is working towards entering into the awareness of the true warrior, which, of course, is an awareness of his or her *nagal*, and which by definition is *no-thing*. This is an important point with huge practical implications, so let us therefore consider at least some of these implications in greater detail.

The first of the implications we need to consider here is the fact that in not having a fixed goal towards which to work, the apprentice quickly enough learns to start noticing and therefore also appreciating the little things in his or her life. Consequently, instead of worrying about when he will achieve true warriorship, the apprentice starts to pay careful attention to every step of the way and, by doing so, speeds up his progress beyond imagination for, in the final analysis, most of our lives are spent performing what the majority of apprentices tend to look upon as being the very mundane and trivial tasks demanded by life upon the physical plane. Yet if we are ever going to acquire the status of warriorship, it is imperative that we dedicate our entire life to this pursuit. This implies that every single moment of our life must be spent living like a warrior, and this includes brushing our teeth, peeling the potatoes, our duties at work and doing the shopping! If we try to become warriors by striving for impeccability only whilst practising the various techniques, such as recapitulation or dreaming, then obviously most of our day is going to be spent in going about things with our normal doings. It is therefore hardly surprising that whilst apprentices are still caught up in the idea that their pursuit of warriorship is separate from their daily lives, their progress will be exceedingly slow and limited.

The above point is enormously important and can never be stressed enough. The greatest cause of failure upon the Warrior's Path, and the most restraining force that keeps an apprentice back, is the sense of separativeness, and the erroneous idea that to become a warrior requires "time out in some special place". Unfortunately there are today far too many misguided souls who advocate such myths, and consequently most apprentices are for ever wondering when the nagal is going to get on in imparting to them the real teachings, rather than wanting to know how they peel the potatoes, or why they swore at someone who stole their parking spot in front of the shopping centre. And yet the moment the apprentice can begin to see the interrelationship of life, and begins to grasp the fact that practising the techniques leads to being able to peel potatoes impeccably, life takes on a completely different dimension and thus the apprentice's assemblage point becomes more fluid as he or she strives to alter his or her perception and intensity.

The second implication we need to consider here is one we touched upon earlier, namely, that because life on the edge is for ever nascent, the warrior lives in a state of constant flux and change. Where there is continuous change there can be no sense of security, and the advantage in this is that the apprentice, and the warrior for that matter, is constantly kept alert and on his toes. Since there is no opportunity for becoming complacent the apprentice has no option other than to start fighting for sobriety in the moment, so as not to become swamped by a continuously growing pile of uncertain events.

Although apprentices are also taught from day one that *time is the essence of impeccability*, they once again take a while to figure out for themselves that none of us can afford to allow our perceptions of life and the world to heap up like so much unattended paperwork on a desk. Too often do apprentices make the mistake of assuming that tomorrow is early enough to tend to what they have perceived today. *Power* lies in the moment, and if that fleeting chance is not taken exactly when it comes round, "just now", or tomorrow, or next week, is always too late. In this respect, even the thoroughly dedicated apprentice will often walk into this trap by doubting his perception, and therefore delaying taking action until he has had the time to "think things through". Although it is undeniably true that it is not wise to rush into any kind of action in a helter-skelter manner, it is equally true that the only way in which we can live on the edge, and dance that edge, is to try. However, merely to try is not good enough, for merely to try implies that we have a licence to make mistakes, but in living on the edge any mistake costs us dearly. Therefore when Toltecs use the term "try", it is meant in the sense of attempting to do the unfamiliar as if your life depends upon being able to handle that challenge successfully.

The above point is one we will return to again in considering the fifth and sixth aspects of the stalker's rule, but we must touch upon it here so as to grasp fully what is entailed in stepping into the unknown. It must be stressed that in being forced to fight for sobriety in the moment, the apprentice, whether he is conscious of it or not, is constantly forcing himself into trying to move his assemblage point. Not only does this forcing have great value in building *intent*, but it also helps the apprentice to become more and more aware of the deeper implications inherent within the teachings. Having begun to see for himself that golden opportunities can be lost because of careless perception, or because of delayed action, such an apprentice starts to make every effort to be wide awake in the moment and to stalk his perception every minute of every day.

The third of the implications we are looking at arises out of the previous two. Once an apprentice has learned to stalk his or her perception constantly the technique of recapitulation suddenly starts to take on a totally new meaning. Because the apprentice is striving for sobriety in the moment, and has become aware of all the apparently insignificant little details of life, spontaneous recapitulation is considerably enhanced, and in addition, the apprentice starts to become aware of numerous subtle *feelings* which are sparked off by something as small as one word, the melody of an old song, or even just the way in which someone smiles at him. In all such cases, what the apprentice has become aware of are the tensions within the web of life, and simply by being aware of those tensions the apprentice very quickly starts to recapitulate the events that caused them.

However, by becoming aware of the tensions within the web of life the apprentice not only benefits in terms of recapitulation, but also in terms of not-doing. Being now far more aware than ever before, such an apprentice begins to see his normal doings for what they really are, and therefore becomes more detached and objective towards the world around him. Being more detached, it is a lot easier not only to stalk his perception in the moment, but it now also becomes possible for him to check every action; physical, emotional and mental, prior to taking that action. In other words, such an apprentice has acquired what Toltecs term *speed*, and therefore instead of blundering into the traps of his old doings before he even knows it, the apprentice now has the necessary speed to be able to register the intentions that give rise to every act, irrespective of whether this act is physical, emotional or mental. Having this speed, such an apprentice no longer finds it difficult to practise not-doing, and consequently it is not long before he starts to live his life in terms of a not-doing.

One of the greatest advantages in living his life in terms of a not-doing, is that the apprentice becomes ever more detached from the rational mind. As a result, the internal dialogue begins to die out and, above all, the apprentice starts to listen to his heart more and more. Once this much has been accomplished, life once again takes on a completely new meaning. Instead of being constantly caught up in thinking about everything, the apprentice starts to *feel* the world and everything around him and in no time at all, comes to the realisation that feeling the world is far more accurate, a lot quicker and considerably more enjoyable than thinking about everything.

In listening to the heart it is not as if the warrior stops

thinking altogether, but rather that the rational mind is put into its proper perspective, and thus is used only when it is needed, instead of allowing it to run one's life with its incessant internal dialogue. Here the reader would do well to remember that the rational mind is only a small part of man's total mind and that it is nothing more than man's own in-built computer. The program which the rational mind uses is of course our social conditioning, and it is therefore vitally important to get the rational mind into its proper perspective as quickly as possible, for only then does it become possible to reprogram the computer. Reprogramming the computer can only be done by re-evaluating the world and our lives, and there is no better way to do this than by learning to listen to the heart.

Listening to the heart is an acquired skill which takes time to understand and to perfect because social conditioning is such that none of us are ever taught how to *feel* – all the accent being placed on learning to *think*, that is, to think rationally. Apprentices often do not understand the concept of listening to the heart at all well, for the simple reason that they tend to assume understanding of the concept rather than learning through experience what it truly entails. Let us therefore take a closer look at this concept in order to get clarity and also to eradicate some of the misconceptions that have arisen around this subject. However, doing so entails having to take into consideration the seven electro-magnetic centres to be found within the luminous cocoon and which are attached to the physical body along the length of the spine. These centres take us well into technical aspects of the teachings which do not really concern the scope of this book, but without at least touching upon these centres it is not possible to grasp what is entailed in listening to the heart. We will therefore merely touch upon these centres ever so briefly.

First of all, realise that the term "heart" does not refer to the physical heart, but rather to one of the seven major electro-magnetic centres mentioned above. All of these centres control parts of the nervous system as well as certain organs. The one that concerns us here is a centre which is situated in-between the shoulder blades, and the physical manifestation of which is the thymus gland. This centre controls not only the physical heart but, via the thymus gland, also has various other functions, of which medical science is as yet wholly unaware. It is the rate of vibration of this centre which corresponds to that state of awareness at which the interrelationship of life is clearly visible, and this is therefore looked upon by Toltecs as the centre of *fusion* or of group-consciousness. Consequently, because the dreamers of mankind are group-conscious, it is the heart centre which is the principal centre of communication between the dreamer and the dreamed and, as a result, Toltecs say that the dreamer speaks to the dreamed via the heart. (Figure 4). Therefore the act of listening to the heart really implies listening to the dreamer.

THE SEVEN MAJOR ELECTRO-MAGNETIC CENTRES AND THEIR EXPRESSIONS

CENTRE	ORGAN	EXPRESSION
HEAD	Pineal Gland	Intent
BROW	Pituitary Gland	Mind/ Discrimination
HEART	Thymus Gland	Feeling/Fusion/ Inclusiveness
THROAT	Thyroid Gland	Rational Mind/ Fission/ Separativeness
SOLAR PLEXUS	Pancreas	Emotions
SACRAL	Gonads	Reflection of Intent
BASE	Adrenal Gland	Dragon Lore/ Power of Man

FIGURE 4

On the other hand, the rational mind, which it must be remembered is but a faint reflection of true *mind*, is expressed through the throat centre, of which the physical manifestation is the thyroid gland. It is this centre which is primarily responsible for the sense of separativeness, and therefore also for that state of awareness which in the human being gives rise to the sense of being an individual. Consequently Toltecs look upon the throat centre as being the principal centre through which the dreamed, or the unperfected tonal, perceives life and the world around it and, because of its separative nature, it is termed the centre of *fission*.

True *mind*, which is the one polarity of the dreamer's awareness, is expressed through the second head centre, of which the physical manifestation is the pituitary gland. Because this gland is situated roughly opposite the centre of the forehead, esotericists refer to it as the *third eye*, and it is this centre which is the true expression of the real, or the *proper, tonal* of man. Thus it is also this centre which is the source of *discrimination* which, of course, has its reflection in the separativeness of the rational mind. This centre, however, can only be brought into activity through the instrumentation of the heart centre, and hence the necessity for the warrior to open his heart.

Continuing now with our consideration of the heart, remember that *intent* is a faculty of the dreamer, and because the principal centre of communication between the dreamer and the dreamed is the heart centre, the heart is also the principal centre through which *intent* is activated. However, it must be pointed out that pure *intent* is actually expressed through that centre in the head of which the manifestation is the pineal gland. Nevertheless, since it is only through the instrumentation of the heart centre that the pineal gland can be brought into activity, Toltecs look upon the activating of *intent* as originating from the heart, in the same way that true *mind* can only be accessed through the heart. Here, once again, we see how important it is for the warrior to learn to open his heart.

Apropos the above, it will benefit the reader greatly if I also point out here that the *reflection of intent*, mentioned in Chapter Two, is expressed through the sacral centre, of which the physical manifestation are the gonads. It is primarily because of this fact that sorcerers, and those upon the Path of High Adventure, make the mistake of assuming that *will*, or *personal power*, emanates from the lower abdomen.

However, by far the most important point to be grasped in all of this is the fact that because the heart is the principal centre of communication between the dreamer and the dreamed, and because *intent* is activated through the heart, it is hardly surprising that the assemblage point of man should be located on the surface of the luminous cocoon opposite the heart centre. The significance of this lies in the fact that once an apprentice starts to become aware of the interrelationship of life, he is in effect starting to work with that rate of vibration which corresponds to the heart centre, and it is therefore stated that such an apprentice has begun to *open the heart.* In having become detached from the rational mind, and in opening the heart, the apprentice has shifted the focus in a very real sense, for instead of perceiving the world via the throat centre which controls the rational mind, he now perceives the world via the heart centre. In other words, the apprentice is now beginning to perceive true to the purpose of his dreamer, and it is this which constitutes the real meaning of that term *learning to dream true.*

Once an apprentice is in contact with his heart true thinking becomes possible, for instead of rationalising about everything, which invariably ends up in circling thought, or internal dialogue, the apprentice now perceives the world and life in terms of *feeling.* Such feeling is always registered as an instantaneous *knowing* with every fibre of one's being. The reason for this is that because the apprentice is now no longer perceiving everything in terms of separativeness, events and situations are not seen in isolation to one another, but are instead seen as thoroughly interactive and therefore interdependent threads of the one life, and since the apprentice is a unit of this one life, he can sense, or feel, where each of those threads will lead if followed. The result of this new-found ability to feel is that the apprentice begins to act instinctively upon those feelings in much the same way as someone who feels the heat from a fire will snatch his hand away before he burns his hand. For this reason it is stated that true thinking does not entail internal dialogue, and neither does it take any time to perform for, clearly, the thought involved in snatching one's hand away from a scorching fire is truly instantaneous and certainly does not involve the slow, laborious and logical deliberations born of internal dialogue.

It should now be clear what is truly meant by listening to the heart for, in the final analysis, listening to the heart is the act of true thinking, as opposed to the rationalisations born of internal dialogue. Once this ability has been acquired, it becomes possible not only to reprogram the rational mind, but it also paves the way to learning to stop the world, and thereby being able to erase one's personal history completely. However, although from the angle of this book it may appear to be relatively simple to access the true *mind*, I would be doing the reader an injustice if I do not point out that this is far from being true. It takes time, patience and above all, a great deal of hard work to learn to listen to the heart accurately without constant interference from the rational mind, and it is for this reason that an apprentice's dedication to the Warrior's Path must be utterly impeccable. Yet, where there is a total commitment, and where there is patience, diligence and perseverance, one step leads to another, and every step taken brings its own rewards and takes the apprentice one step closer to being able to master this most important technique.

From everything stated so far, it should now also be clear that listening to the heart is the first step in learning to *see*. Technically speaking, the art of the true seer involves the activating and then integrated use of all three of the head centres, of which we have here only considered two. However, since this book is being written for average men and women who are only just beginning to learn how to claim their *power* as warriors, we need not consider the training of a seer at this point in time. I simply mention this fact so as give the reader some perspective on where the teachings ultimately lead to.

Thus we see that to step into the unknown is primarily concerned with the fourth postulate of stalking, placed in the West, the place of *feeling*, and from what we have learned so far, it is not so difficult to understand why it should be the third aspect of the stalker's rule that brings the warrior hard up against having to accept death as his best advisor. The West, the place of the setting sun, is not only the Temple of Death, but it is also here that the warrior comes to grips fully with the interrelationship of life and the fact that the *crux of the mystery of life is the infinite mystery of beingness*. We have already seen that every strategy of a warrior is so designed as to put him into touch with that mystery, and that implementing any one of these strategies is to step into the unknown.

Obviously, once within the unknown, the warrior cannot again step into the unknown unless, of course, he keeps returning to the known of his normal doings afterwards, and this, as we have noted, is not only highly dangerous, but also highly undesirable in that it arrests true transformation. For those warriors who are dedicated to the Path of Freedom, stepping into the unknown is a path of no return. Once they have stepped into the unknown, such warriors never again return to their former lives, and to all intents and purposes such warriors have died to their old doings and to their old selves. Every time a warrior implements a new strategy he does not repeat stepping into the unknown, but that new strategy instead takes him down yet another unexplored path within a different region of the unknown. Therefore, for the Warriors of Freedom, stepping into the unknown happens only once in every lifetime and it marks for them their gap to freedom, their *bid for power*.

Neither do the Warriors of Freedom ever desire a return to their old lives. Having had a taste of what it means to live on the edge, and having witnessed even just a few of the wonders contained within the Temple of Death, such warriors find it totally unthinkable to return to the narrow and debilitating confines demarcated by the rational mind. Possessing first hand experience of what it is to be free within the vast open expanses of the unknown, the only wish of the Warriors of Freedom is to remain free, to remain upon the frontiers where life is forever nascent. This they do by learning the *dance of death*, so as to be able to dance the edge, and in that continuous dance of innovation they rejoice in the creativity of the dreamer flowing through them via hearts that are wide open to the interrelationship, the interdependence and the interaction of all of life.

With regard to the above, it is necessary to point out here that to remain within the unknown must not be taken literally, in the sense that these warriors remain within left side awareness. To do so would be highly impractical and therefore completely undesirable. The reason why this assumption is often made is because the unknown as such can only be accessed directly by shifting the assemblage point into left side awareness. However, this is not what we are referring to here. Realise that even whilst we are in normal awareness we are constantly having to deal with the unknown every time we practise not-doing, and every time we tackle a challenge that is unfamiliar to us, for in all such cases we cannot know beforehand what the outcome will be. We can hazard a guess at what will happen, and we can cast a prediction based on similar cases or events, but if the challenge is vastly different to anything we have known before, then the outcome is equally unknown until it begins to transpire, and the same is true of a not-doing. Therefore, the unknown we are referring to here is the innovation of pioneering, of mapping out the unknown, rather than the unknown encountered within left side awareness. In the final analysis, there is of course only one unknown, but the difference lies in whether we approach it in normal awareness, or whether we approach it from within the left side.

Living with death as their best advisor and in having learned to dance the edge of life, the Warriors of Freedom are incapable of looking upon life in the same way as average men and women have been taught to do through their social conditioning. For the Warrior of Freedom death is not something vague out there that will only catch up with him in his old age, but is instead a very real and vital force that guides his every step, his every decision, emotion and feeling. Knowing that his death can tap him at any moment, the Warrior of Freedom does not waste even an instant of his time or his *personal power,* but strives to make every moment and every act as meaningful and as pleasurable as possible. Such warriors are for ever ready to make their last stand right here and right now, for each and every one of their acts is utterly impeccable and an expression of their innermost predilection. For such warriors there are no regrets, only a breathtaking sense of enthusiasm and exhilaration.

From the above it stands to reason that the true warrior very much *lives in the moment,* a concept which forms the bridge into the fourth aspect of the stalker's rule. By living in the moment the warrior's life becomes completely transformed, for instead of fretting about the future and about future aspirations, the warrior now contents him or herself with enjoying every act, no matter how big or how small. *Enjoyment* is again one of those concepts about which average men and women tend to have a completely wrong understanding, due to their ignorance of words.

The term "enjoy" quite literally means to *enmesh oneself in rejoicing.* However, only a little thought is needed to grasp that it is not really possible to enjoy oneself in the true sense of the word whilst one remains a captive of the rational mind, and enslaved by social conditioning. Only those who are free can enjoy themselves in the true sense of the word, and it is primarily because of this fact that average men and women are generally speaking always looking for some form of escapism which they tend to regard as constituting for them a form of enjoyment. Escapism, however, is a far cry from freedom and to indulge in escapisms is an equally far cry from real enjoyment.

The true warrior does not seek escapisms of any description, for to do so would imply that he or she is not only trying to escape the challenges of life, but also taking time out – two actions that each in their own way, and conjointly, annihilate the possibility of true freedom. Instead the warrior seeks to draw the *gift of power* out of every situation in his or her life and, in order to do so, must live in the moment. Therefore rather than trying to escape life, the warrior participates fully in the process of life which, it will be remembered from *Cry of the Eagle,* is the technical definition of unconditional love. The implication of all this is that the true warrior can, and does, enjoy himself fully every moment of his life, simply because his heart is so wide open that he embraces all of life with a love that is completely unconditional. I do not really know how else to express this, for it is one of those concepts which is so far into the left side that verbalisation is almost impossible. I therefore ask the reader to consider carefully what has been stated here with respect to living in the moment, and enjoyment, and also to consider the implications of the following aphorism.

> IN THE BEGINNING EVERY WARRIOR NEEDS THE WARRIOR'S SHIELD IN ORDER TO SURVIVE THE ARROWS OF THE SHARPSHOOTERS OF THE UNIVERSE, AND THEREFORE THAT SHIELD IS VERY MUCH A SHIELD. HOWEVER, ONCE THE WARRIOR HAS ENTERED THE TEMPLE OF DEATH AND HAS LEARNED TO DANCE THE EDGE, THE STEPS OF HIS DANCE AND THE SWIFTNESS OF HIS MOVEMENTS ARE ALL THAT IS REQUIRED. FROM THIS MOMENT ON THE WARRIOR USES HIS SHIELD, NOT AS A PROTECTION FROM THE SHARPSHOOTERS OF THE UNIVERSE, BUT AS A MEANS WHEREBY HE STRIVES TO EMBRACE MORE AND MORE OF LIFE WITH HIS HEART. IN TIME THAT STRIVING BECOMES A PASSION – A PASSION THAT IS ALL-CONSUMING AND UTTERLY INCLUSIVE.

Participating fully in the process of life, the true warrior no longer has any desire to avoid any challenge or any aspect of life. Therefore, tears and laughter, happiness and sorrow, good health and bad health, wealth and poverty, light and darkness, man and beast, plant and insect, all are embraced by the warrior with equal joy and in complete humility, for in his heart of hearts he knows from experience that *within the mystery of beingness all are equal.* Yet, realise that in having learned what it is to be free the Warriors of Freedom also do not balk at fighting ferociously everything that is inducive to slavery and any being that tries to entice either them or their fellow creatures into bondage. Such is the joy of the warrior and such is his passion for freedom. In that sense of freedom the warrior's life is one of constant change, constant innovation and is therefore forever new, and each act takes him or her on yet another exciting adventure in the unknown regions of the mystery of beingness.

CHAPTER SIX

SHIFTING THE FOCUS

TO SHIFT THE FOCUS FROM FIXATION TO ABANDONMENT
IS A WARRIOR'S GREATEST ACHIEVEMENT.

Shifting the focus is a concept we have so far simply touched upon, but we now need to look at it in somewhat more detail because, as the aphorism above points out, the ability to shift the focus is in many ways perhaps the greatest art of the warrior. Yet, as with all acts of true *power,* when a warrior does shift the focus the implications and the full impact of what he has done tend to go unnoticed, or if noticed, they receive at best mild interest.

In order to come to grips with this all-important concept we must put it into its proper context, for this concept is so totally opposed to social conditioning, and most especially Western thought, that most apprentices find that putting this aspect of the teachings into practice is incredibly challenging. Yet the only reason why this appears so difficult is because all too often it is taken completely out of context, and anything which is taken out of context tends either to be inaccurate, or else well-nigh impossible to accomplish. Shifting the focus, if taken out of context, is like taking the photograph of just one door and then trying to work out to which of a hundred houses it belongs, without having a complete photograph of all those houses and their doors. Clearly such a task will always appear impossible.

The principal reason why apprentices always tend to get the ability to shift the focus out of context is because of the separative nature of the rational mind. In other words, such apprentices forget that all of the teachings are one hundred percent interdependent, interactive, and therefore thoroughly interrelated. If this is not kept in mind, then time and time again the apprentice will make the mistake of trying to shift the focus only once everything else has failed. To do so, however, is to end up with such a muddle that confusion and chaos must reign, and then the apprentice wonders why shifting the focus did not work.

Shifting the focus is the very first thing an apprentice is taught, in one way or another, but because it pertains to the left side teachings a nagal can never really speak about this to the apprentice until a much later date. Nevertheless, if the apprentice is serious about wanting to walk the Warrior's Path he or she will have noticed at that first session that something extraordinary did take place. The apprentice might not be able to define precisely what transpired, but he or she will have noticed enough to know beyond any shadow of a doubt that they have no option other than to learn to tread the Warrior's Path. The reason for this is that, in each and every case, the nagal would have helped the apprentice shift the focus sufficiently, so as to come into contact with the heart. Once this has been done, no matter how brief the encounter may have been, the apprentice is left with no doubt, for deep down inside we all know that the heart does not lie.

From the above it should now be clear that shifting the focus cannot be grasped with the rational mind, for this is an act of the heart, and the impact of that act can only be grasped within the context of a path with a heart. Perhaps the best way of clarifying this point is to say that shifting the focus means *to think with the heart*, as opposed to thinking with the rational mind. In other words, shifting the focus concerns the deeper implications inherent within the technique of not-doing. Although it is not the ultimate in stalking one's own perception, shifting the focus is nonetheless central to even Dragon Lore. Without the ability to shift the focus correctly and at will the warrior would be just as weak and defenceless as any average man or woman.

> IF YOU WISH TO WIN, EVEN THOUGH YOU MAY HAVE LOST, YOU
> MUST SHIFT THE FOCUS BY APPLYING THE FOURTH ASPECT OF
> THE STALKER'S RULE WITHIN THE CONTEXT OF THE FIRST
> POSTULATE OF STALKING.

The aphorism above defines the formula for shifting the focus, so let us consider what is entailed in this formula. First of all, the fourth aspect of the stalker's rule tells us that *once he has entered into battle, a warrior abandons himself to his actions by allowing his spirit to flow free and clear, for only then do the powers of destiny guide us by paving the way.*

From everything we have learned so far it should not be difficult to understand that to enter into battle, even if it is with another person, does not mean that the warrior is fighting that person as such, but is instead fighting a battle to solve the mystery of his beingness. This is an important point for two reasons. Firstly, whoever, or whatever, the warrior is doing battle with is not an oppressor as such for the warrior, but merely a mirror of his own inner unknown. Secondly, because the warrior already knows from the second postulate of stalking that he is never going to solve this mystery, he is not obsessed with the idea of winning and can therefore relax fully into the battle. These two points, however, cannot be taken at face value, and we will therefore now consider them in greater depth.

Regarding the first point, realise that in choosing his battle a warrior will never choose a battle from which he has nothing to learn, for to do so would be a stupid waste of time and *personal power*. Therefore the only battles a warrior will fight are those that will lead him into a greater understanding of the mystery of his beingness. The reason why this point is so very important is because there is a vast difference between a real battle, and what is termed *discrimination*. Once again this is a concept which apprentices so often get into a complete muddle, and as a result they will turn a challenge which should have been a simple act of discrimination into something of a battle or, more precisely, a scuffle in the dark; and what should have been a battle they will shrug off as if it is merely a mild irritant.

This point brings us back to the concept of mirrors and the fact that every person, every event in our lives and even inanimate objects, for that matter, reflect for us some aspect of our own inner unknown. For example, if you are trying to dig out a rock in your garden and it simply refuses to budge, take it for granted that you are facing your own stubbornness, which might well be as persistent as the Rock of Gibraltar itself. Likewise, if you are driving along in your car and it suddenly starts to jerk in fits and starts, know that your own state of awareness is totally erratic at that moment in time. Similarly, if you have just had a fight with your boss, and you walk out of the office and a gust of wind slams the door behind you, you must take heed of the fact that your own intellectualism is likely to get you fired.

Therefore, when a warrior is being challenged in some way by a mirror from which he knows for a fact he has nothing to learn, then the challenge for the warrior does not lie in going into battle, but in exercising his discrimination. For example, say that you are trying to dig out a rock in your garden, but no matter how deep you dig, or how much leverage you apply, that rock just will not budge. If, in this particular case, you are totally confident that although you have indeed always been very stubborn, you have now honestly transmuted that stubbornness one hundred percent, then you can be fairly certain that the challenge posed for you by this immovable rock lies in the act of discrimination. Perhaps for some reason that you have overlooked, it is not such a good idea to move the rock. Or perhaps there is something else in your life, symbolised by that rock, which you should likewise not try to move or change in any way. But in all such cases, realise that this boils down to making a decision based upon discrimination, and as such does not involve a battle in the real sense of the word. Therefore it would be a complete waste of time and *personal power* to attack that rock with everything you've got.

As far as the people in our lives are concerned, discrimination will often entail having to choose between compromising ourselves for the sake of keeping an old mirror in our lives, or removing ourselves from that person's influence in some way. When we are faced with such a challenge a battle can indeed sometimes be encountered, in the sense that it can prove to be difficult to extricate ourselves from the life of such a person. However, the point to be grasped is that even if such a battle does arise, it will still not be with that particular mirror, but will instead be in the nature of a struggle to discriminate wisely.

In relation to the above, it is wise to remember that one cannot really do battle with oneself, even though it can sometimes be a real battle to put into practice something which we know we should be doing. We can only really enter into battle with an opponent, irrespective of whether such an opponent is another person, an animal, an inanimate object or *power*. Further, as we already know, the only legitimate reason for entering into battle with an opponent is because by doing battle with that opponent we can learn something about ourselves that is as yet unknown to us. Therefore the criterion for ascertaining whether we have a battle on our hands, or whether it is merely a case of having to exercise discrimination, is the simple question: "What is this mirror reflecting for me?" If it is an old mirror, then discrimination is called for. If it is a mirror reflecting present behaviour, then a battle is called for. If it is a mirror of the future reflecting potential behaviour, then it is a warning of a battle to come.

The second point that was mentioned earlier, that is, not being obsessed with winning, is another that causes so many apprentices unnecessary grief. The main reason for this is social conditioning, and therefore even if an apprentice has fought an impeccable battle, but loses, he or she is inevitably overcome by a sense of failure and, worse still, embarrassment or even shame at having failed. Such indulgence, however, is one of the worst forms of self-importance, for it smacks of sheer arrogance. There is absolutely nothing shameful about losing, for the simple reason that even failure is an experience, and experience is knowledge. What can possibly be shameful about knowledge? Even if the person concerned has lost as a result of having been thoroughly unimpeccable, that experience is still knowledge which has been acquired at some cost and thus cannot possibly be any cause for shame or embarrassment. It is for this reason that Toltecs state that there is no failure in the true sense of the word. The worst thing that can happen in all cases of so-called failure is that the apprentice's self-importance gets a huge knock on the head – something a nagal normally finds highly entertaining and to be applauded, rather than bemoaned! Consequently, apprentices who try to elicit sympathy from a nagal for having failed, normally go away seething at the fact that the only thing they did manage to extract from the nagal was raucous laughter.

It is worthwhile here to digress for a moment in order to point out what for the warrior constitutes genuine shame. The only time a warrior has any reason to feel real shame is when he wilfully and deliberately indulges in what he knows to be unimpeccable behaviour. However, although there are millions of acts that can be unimpeccable, the only ones that are considered to be absolutely taboo upon the Path of Freedom are firstly, the abuse of *power;* secondly, spurning the interrelationship of life for selfish gain; and thirdly, insulting the Standing Mother by ignoring intelligent co-operation. These are the three cardinal transgressions looked upon by the Warriors of Freedom as the total antithesis of freedom, and any warrior who at any point in his or her life is found guilty of any one of these infringements will find him or herself at the sharp end of the true warrior's sword, and in addition is normally ostracised by the brotherhood. Furthermore, if the erring warrior has access to the mind-link, the mind-link will be severed without question, and such a warrior then, to all intents and purposes, becomes an outcast, the implications of which are severe to say the least.

Returning now to the point under consideration, realise that it is the deeper implication of this second point upon which we will be concentrating in this particular section of the teachings. This implication concerns the fact that in not being obsessed with winning the warrior can abandon himself to the battle at hand.

The first point to be covered here is the true meaning of the word "abandon". The normal meaning of the word is *to give up one's control,* a definition which is most apt by Toltec standards. However, it is important to note that from a Toltec perspective, to abandon oneself does not mean that one becomes careless or reckless, or that one loses or gives up one's control in the sense of becoming powerless. On the contrary, the control of a warrior is always impeccable. Therefore let us look at what is really meant by a warrior abandoning him or herself.

The meaning Toltecs attach to the term "abandonment" is that the warrior immerses himself fully in the battle at hand. Taking into consideration all of the teachings imparted so far, not a great deal of thought is required to come to the realisation that such immersion cannot be in the sense of becoming preoccupied with, or obsessed with, or fixated by. To immerse himself fully in the battle at hand, and yet remaining wide awake, fearful, respectful and absolutely assured, is an act which requires that the warrior enters fully into a state of awareness in which he is at-one with everything. Clearly, from what we have learned so far, this is not a state of awareness to be found within normal awareness, for within the confines of normal awareness there is always the perception of *me and the world out there*, irrespective of how inclusive the warrior's awareness may be. Therefore, such a state of awareness must belong to the left side.

Something that is often overlooked by the careless apprentice, is the fact that whilst in left side awareness, normal awareness is suspended, and to all intents and purposes the warrior is temporarily not "normal". Although there are huge benefits to being able to access left side awareness at will, this is not a type of awareness which is conducive to the practicalities involved within life upon the physical plane, and certainly not for something as practical as a battle. Consequently, even though the true warrior can enter and exit left side awareness at will, he or she chooses to operate principally from the level of normal awareness, for the simple reason that the warrior is first and foremost a practical being. In this respect the only time a warrior will enter left side awareness is when he engages in the act of dreaming, or entering into battle. It therefore becomes clear that we must look very carefully at what is entailed when the warrior enters into the left side upon entering into battle, for to do battle is a highly practical affair, and thus very different to the private affair of dreaming.

The most important points to be remembered are that left side awareness pertains to the unknown, and that the unknown is a vastness in which we can quite easily "get out of our depth", in the sense of becoming helpless, by having to handle challenges which are completely unfamiliar to us, and about which we know absolutely nothing. This is both the advantage and the pitfall of the unknown, and therefore also of left side awareness. In other words, simply to jump into the unknown in a higgledy-piggledy manner is foolish to say the least, and since the warrior's control must be impeccable at all times, this is not something he will ever consider doing.

Therefore when the warrior enters into left side awareness upon immersing himself in battle, it stands to reason that he will choose to which location within the unknown he transports his awareness, for he cannot afford to end up somewhere in which he might well find himself to be out of his depth as it were. Needless to say, for the fully trained and experienced warrior there are a great many locations within the unknown with which he or she will be completely familiar, but in the case of having to do battle there is one specific position of the assemblage point which is favoured by all true warriors. This particular position is termed *the point of no pity*, and the reason why it is favoured is because it has characteristics which are most suitable for doing battle.

The point of no pity is not really anything like what one would expect it to be judging by its name, although in a way the name is a very apt description for this particular alignment of perception. The principal reason why it is favoured for doing battle is because at this particular alignment the sense of inclusiveness is so immanent and pressing that one becomes completely immersed in the total interdependence, interaction and interrelationship of all. Furthermore, because it is an alignment which is quite far into the left side, there is a total lack of thought, and therefore instead of perceiving things in a linear and sequential fashion, everything appears to be happening all at once in such a way that it is well-nigh impossible to ascertain what is past, present or future.

The best way in which I can explain what from the angle of normal awareness, always appears to be a state of utter chaos, is to use the age-old analogy of likening the point of no pity to a kind of void. The reason Toltecs liken the point of no pity to a void is because it has the peculiarity of apparently isolating whatever it is the warrior is concentrating on, and in such a way that one is aware of nothing else except every minute detail pertaining to that particular event. Because of the complete lack of thought, the point of no pity has the quality of an utter silence, in which time has no meaning whatsoever, and it is therefore as if one has become suspended within a void of silence and timelessness in which there is nothing but the details of the battle at hand.

Because there is no awareness of time in the linear sense, the warrior perceives everything in terms of interrelationship only, and therefore the sense of time is purely dependent upon the speed of the warrior's perception. In other words, if the warrior is quick in assimilating the interrelationship of all, things seem to happen quickly, but if he is slow in his perception, everything seems to happen in slow motion. The advantage in this strange effect upon the sense of time is that the warrior can choose to make things happen as quickly or as slowly as he wishes. For example, if an opponent is physically attacking the warrior, the warrior can choose to perceive his opponents actions in slow motion, and he therefore has plenty of time to counteract. This same tactic can also be used to assess the mental or, for that matter, the emotional activities of an opponent. Realise, though, that all of this applies only to the point of no pity, which it must be remembered is a particular state of awareness, and therefore from the angle of someone witnessing the warrior in battle all actions, as well as the sense of time, will appear completely normal.

The greatest benefit derived from operating from the point of no pity is that although normal awareness is suspended whilst in the left side, the warrior is nonetheless exposed to such an intense vibration of inclusiveness that it is as if he has achieved an enormously high level of sobriety, even though at that particular alignment he could not be further away from true sobriety. Furthermore, in being quite literally exposed to the inter-relationship of all, but in the absence of the rational mind, the warrior does not perceive himself as being separate from anything around him. Instead he becomes one with everything, including his opponent and, as a result, feels his opponent's every move as if it is his own, so that if the warrior's opponent is fighting him from the level of normal awareness, the warrior will even be one with his opponent's thoughts, feelings and emotions.

The advantage in all of this is that the warrior is oblivious to anything other than the battle at hand. Consequently, he himself is not subject to any thoughts or emotions and thus merely flows with the movements of his opponent with the express purpose of overcoming the opponent. All in all there is no doubt that a warrior who is doing battle from the point of no pity is an utterly ruthless being, and yet, in having no thought and no emotion, never once will the warrior react with anger, or hatred, or vengeance, or spite, or any other form of emotion or ill intent as a result of prejudice or wrong thinking. It is for this reason that it was pointed out that the point of no pity, although utterly ruthless, is not really what social conditioning would lead one to believe it is.

In what we have looked at so far, it should now be somewhat clearer what is meant by the warrior abandoning himself. Being at the point of no pity and having no thought and no emotion, but being completely at-one with everything pertaining to his battle, there is in the warrior no sense of having to, or of wanting to, control anything because of that sense of oneness. Yet, even though the warrior experiences a sense of being suspended within a void, the deep sense of inclusiveness found at the point of no pity keeps the warrior very much in touch not only with the minute details within the void, but also with the broader implications of his battle beyond the confines of the void. In other words, although the warrior has immersed himself fully in the battle at hand, in having become one with it, he is nonetheless still wide awake in the deepest possible sense of the word.

The real implications of the word "abandon" lies in not feeling the need to control anything, and it is also herein that lies the meaning of the phrase "allows his spirit to flow free and clear", that is, free from the need to control and clear in the sense of not being cluttered by the influences of both thought and emotion. Moreover, because of the deep sense of inclusiveness, the warrior is very much in touch with his fate and therefore also with the purpose of his dreamer, for at that level of awareness the warrior perceives everything in terms of the progressive unfoldment of his fate. As a result of this, the warrior automatically perceives and experiences his battle only in terms of what it is helping him to achieve in terms of the unfoldment of his fate. Therefore, irrespective of the outcome of that battle, the warrior will always come away having learned a great deal about both himself and his fate, and as such will have won the real battle, that is, to solve an aspect of the mystery of his beingness, even though from the angle of the battle itself he may well have lost, in the sense of not having been able to overcome his opponent. This is what is meant by saying that the warrior can win in spite of having lost the battle.

Another point to be grasped here is the fact that because the warrior is so very much in touch with the purpose of his dreamer at this point, it stands to reason that the *power* guiding the warrior in his battle are in fact the powers of destiny, for whilst he is operating at the point of no pity, the warrior has no thoughts or emotions that can get in the way, if I may use such an expression.

In everything we have looked at here, realise that we have been considering the point of no pity very much from the angle of physical action, but if the truth be told, the true warrior very rarely indeed has any need to fight physical battles. I have described the point of no pity from a physical point of view simply because it is a lot easier to grasp its nature and uses within the physical context. In the majority of cases, the warrior has to fight battles which are non-physical, but even in these battles the warrior uses the point of no pity in exactly the same way as he would for a physical battle. The only difference being that in using the point of no pity for a non-physical battle the warrior only needs to operate at the point of no pity for as long as it takes to ascertain the moves of his opponent and what his opponent's intentions are. In this respect, the warrior can of course re-access the point of no pity whenever the need should arise and, generally speaking, because of its sense of timelessness, even just a few seconds at this point is sufficient to glean whatever needs to be known.

The fact that the warrior does not need to stay at the point of no pity in fighting non-physical battles is just as well, for there is one serious drawback in being at this point. This disadvantage arises because the left side, and most especially the point of no pity, has no linear sense of time, and therefore the logic of sequence which is required for coherent speech is most difficult to access. As a result, the point of no pity is not conducive to verbalisation. Obviously this drawback is not serious when fighting a physical battle, in which it is action that is important and not speech, but when fighting a non-physical battle it can be a real problem if the warrior is forced to remain at the point of no pity for an extended period of time.

In order to overcome this disadvantage Toltecs have, over time, learned that it is possible to access the point of no pity at varying levels of intensity. The experienced warrior can therefore either identify fully with the alignment which marks the point of no pity, or he can merely "touch" that alignment ever so lightly. Naturally, these are the two polarities, but in between these two there are a whole range of possible interactions that can be engaged. If the warrior is merely "touching" the point of no pity lightly, he can draw upon the nature of that alignment whilst still retaining enough normal awareness so that his speech does not become impaired, but the benefits of not having thought or emotion of course fall away. If, on the other hand, the warrior absorbs himself fully in that alignment, his ability to verbalise is temporarily impaired in the sense that, although he can still speak, his speech is best suited to short commands or short statements only. The speech of a warrior who is immersed in the left side tends to become extremely incoherent if an involved conversation is attempted because, as we have already noted, the left side lacks both the logic and sequence derived from the linear sense of time. In this respect, even the sound of the warrior's voice will change quite dramatically, normally becoming deeper and harsher, and if he is fully at the point of no pity, his voice will sound quite flat and emotionless.

It is necessary to point out that there are in fact two points of no pity, namely, the one we have been considering here, and which pertains to the left side, and another one which is situated within the realm of normal awareness. I personally prefer to term this second point *the point of cruelty*. This is not an alignment which the true warrior will ever indulge in, for it is exactly what I have termed it – cruelty. In total contrast to its counterpart, this second point is not by any means devoid of thought or emotion but, on the contrary, can only be accessed by a complete lack of respect for life, or by any intense emotion such as hatred, the sense of revenge, or a malicious intent born of the desire to make others suffer. It is not a point I have any desire to dwell upon for, from the angle of the Warriors of Freedom, it is a most despicable act to align this point wilfully so as deliberately to inflict suffering upon others. I merely mention it here so that the reader may be very clear about the huge difference between the point of no pity, as opposed to the point of cruelty.

The reader will find it interesting to note that the point of no pity is an alignment that a great many average men and women have experienced spontaneously at least once in their lives. It happens quite often that in dire emergencies men and women will unconsciously shift their assemblage points to the point of no pity, with the result that they act with a breathtaking speed and normally end up being the heroes of the day. However, when questioned, such people will become quite sheepish and admit that they do not really know what happened, except that they suddenly perceived everything as if in slow motion, and then acted without any thought or emotion.

Finally, it is also worthwhile to point out that although there is no real substitute for *seeing*, the ability to access the point of no pity is a fairly good substitute if one does not yet have the ability to *see*. This is not a point we need to belabour, for if the reader carefully considers everything we have noted with respect to the point of no pity, this fact will speak for itself.

Having looked at what the fourth aspect of the stalker's rule entails, we now need to consider what it means to apply it within the context of the first postulate of stalking. Here I must point out to the reader that the art of the master stalker lies in his or her ability to apply any aspect of the stalker's rule within the context of any one of the four postulates of stalking. As can be expected, the effect of doing this is that each of the aspects of the stalker's rule will bring forth different results depending upon the context within which it is being applied.

In relation to this, the reader may find it interesting, although not particularly useful at this point, if I digress here for a moment in order briefly to explain what are known as the *five elements of the One Power*. Traditionally, these five elements are known as *earth, fire, water, air* and *spirit*, and it is today a well-known fact in both esoteric as well as science fantasy works, that the so-called magician works his or her magic through a manipulation of any one, or a combination, of these five elements. This is typical of how a lack of knowledge leads to old wives' tales, and how old wives' tales lead to superstition.

The four basic elements are only a symbolic form of the four attributes of warriorship – a type of shorthand that speaks volumes to the fully trained warrior, and which eliminates the need for hours of lofty verbalisation between a nagal and an apprentice who has been trained in and is therefore familiar with the use of such symbols. *Air* is the symbol for *sobriety; earth* is the symbol for *strength; water* for *warmth; fire* for *feeling;* and *spirit* for *pure intent.* (Figure 5). For most actions one only needs one of the elements, but there are actions that require a combination of elements. For example, if an act of discrimination is called for, then only *air* is needed. If, however, an athlete needs to compete in a race, then both *earth* and *spirit* are called for. Likewise, if the warrior is going to heal a person then, depending upon the nature of the illness, he will require either a combination of *air, water* and *spirit* or, in some cases, a combination of all five.

THE FIVE ELEMENTS OF THE ONE POWER & THE FOUR ATTRIBUTES OF WARRIORSHIP

ELEMENT	ATTRIBUTE	LOCATION
AIR	Sobriety	East
EARTH	Strength	North
FIRE	Feeling	West
WATER	Warmth	South
SPIRIT	Intent	All-Pervasive

FIGURE 5

These five elements also have four different qualities that pertain to the four major dimensions of MEST, which were explained in *Cry of the Eagle*, and it is these four different qualities which are revealed by the four postulates of stalking. (Figure 6). For example, *sobriety* has a very different quality within the dimension of *time*, than it has within the dimension of *energy*.

Therefore although we have only five elements, each one of these five has a somewhat different quality depending upon the dimension, or the postulate of stalking in which it is operative. Exactly the same is true of the seven aspects of the stalker's rule, for these seven aspects only serve as the necessary detail to reveal the deeper implications of each of the four attributes of warriorship. In other words, the stalker's rule can be applied to each one of the four attributes of warriorship, in which case the seven aspects of the rule will reveal seven distinct characteristics for each of the attributes. In this respect it must be remembered that it was stated already at the outset that there is only *one* rule which has seven aspects to it.

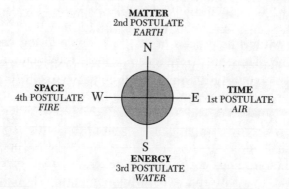

THE FOUR POSTULATES
OF STALKING AND MEST

MATTER
2nd POSTULATE
EARTH

N

SPACE   TIME
4th POSTULATE   W————————E   1st POSTULATE
FIRE   *AIR*

S

ENERGY
3rd POSTULATE
WATER

FIGURE 6

From the above it should be clear why it was stated that we cannot possibly cover everything pertaining to the four postulates of stalking and the stalker's rule in this one book. What I am attempting to impart to the reader in this particular volume are the basic fundamentals that are required in order to come to grips with the intermediate teachings on the art of stalking. Consequently we are here very much looking only at the general overall picture, and leaving out the details until a later stage. In relation to this, I am only making reference to those particular details that are today either causing so much unnecessary confusion, or attracting so much attention, and are therefore all too often central to the growth of superstition, because of humanity's lack of the necessary information.

To return now to our point under consideration. The first postulate of stalking pertains to sobriety within the context of the dimension of *time,* and therefore when we look at the aphorism given on page 158, it is clear that what we have to do is to apply the fourth aspect of the stalker's rule within the context of that quality of sobriety that is expressed within the dimension of time. Therefore let us take a look at what this entails.

First of all, we need to know that sobriety within the context of time implies that level of sobriety at which everything is seen in its logical progression through the linear sequence engendered by time. In other words, some event takes place in our lives, and that event then brings forth a whole series of ripples within the process of life, each ripple giving rise to the next one. Thus, in the aphorism under consideration, we are being warned of the need, even whilst engaged in battle, to take into consideration the whole train of events leading up to the moment of battle, and also the fact that yet another train of events is already transpiring as a result of the battle. To put it in a nutshell, every battle should be an act based upon sober deliberation, and not a helter-skelter *reaction* based upon emotions that have run wild, or upon impulsive thought.

This brings us to a concept which Toltecs refer to as *forebearance.* The meaning which Toltecs attach to this word is very different to average man's normal understanding for, by forebearance, Toltecs are not inferring that the warrior should become a doormat. On the contrary, forebearance requires a considerable amount of true *patience* and *strength*, and nothing builds *intent* more quickly or efficiently than exercising forebearance. This reveals the definition Toltecs give to this word, namely, *forebearance is an act of strength in which the warrior harnesses patience until it has become like a finely strung bow which is lightness itself, but possessing an inherent tension which is deadly.*

What average men and women term patience is not looked upon as patience by the warrior, because the so-called patience of most people is simply a passive acceptance of having to wait, forced upon them either by another person, or by the circumstances in their life. The patience of the warrior, on the other hand, is not a passive acceptance of having to wait, but is instead a conscious and deliberate act of biding his time, and is a decision taken by the warrior himself, rather than having it forced upon him.

The reason why the warrior will exercise forebearance is always for the purposes of stalking, not only his prey, but also his own perception of the situation. By exercising forebearance the warrior has the opportunity and, above all, the necessary detachment to assess the situation at hand completely and thoroughly even in the midst of action and battle. This is a point of such huge import that the apprentice cannot afford to take it at face value, nor for that matter, can the reader. In this respect the reader should reread the example given in *Return of the Warriors* of the soldier fleeing for his life through a field of landmines, for all the teachings given in that example pertain to what we are discussing here.

By not being obsessed with winning or losing the battle, the warrior does not go about his battle with the normal frenzy of the average man who just wants to win as quickly as possible. The warrior who is exercising forebearance feels no need to rush, for whilst he is engaged in battle, time has become of no consequence. Instead, the warrior savours every instant, and in that full appraisal of fractions of a second he perceives such a vast amount of detail, as well as the implications of the detail, that each instant seems to have become an eternity – an eternity which has a sense of timelessness about it, even though the warrior is operating from within the context of time. As a result, such a warrior simply flows with the movements and the intentions of his opponent in an act which is paradoxically not so much like a battle, but rather like the superb movements of two dancers performing a *pas de deux* that contains all the elements of intelligent co-operation. The warrior has, after all, not entered into battle because of his sense of vengeance, or because of his desire to annihilate his opponent, but because he wants to extract from his opponent the *gift of power* the opponent can give him. Herein lies the deeper meaning of the following two aphorisms.

> *THE HUNTER IS INTIMATELY FAMILIAR WITH HIS WORLD, YET REMAINS DETACHED FROM IT.*

> *THE HUNTER DOES NOT PLUNDER HIS WORLD – HE TAKES FROM IT ONLY WHAT HE TRULY NEEDS.*

In exercising forebearance and therefore being in no rush to end the battle, the warrior uses his patience to build his *intent* which, of course, is necessary for extracting from out of his battle the *gift of power* he seeks. As a result of the restraints the warrior deliberately imposes upon his actions in order to hold his patience, his *intent* begins to gather strength, and as it gains in strength so that *intent* begins to move and shift the warrior's assemblage point. This is turn brings about the necessary alignments of perception that enable the warrior to perceive with utter clarity, not only what has transpired in the process of getting to this battle, but also what the *gift of power* it brings him actually is. In this respect, we see once again how the warrior, instead of being fixated upon winning or losing, can abandon himself to the battle and thus allow the powers of destiny to guide him. This is the true meaning of what is meant by *shifting the focus*.

Through the detachment he has acquired by exercising forebearance the warrior's actions have about them a "lightness" that can only be achieved in the absence of intensity. Yet, because the *intent* of the warrior is steadily gaining strength as the battle progresses, the actions of the warrior are also becoming ever more deadly, not only because of that *intent*, but also because the clarity he is gaining from second to second is enhancing his precision with every move.

From all of the above it is clear that if we apply the fourth aspect of the stalker's rule within the context of the first postulate, then it is necessary just to touch the point of no pity ever so lightly. As we have already noted, a full identification with the point of no pity will cancel out the element of time, but in order to do battle in this way the element of time is necessary. We can therefore see how very important it is, not only to be able to access the point of no pity, but also to be able to control our interaction with it.

One point that needs to be clarified here concerning forebearance is the fact that forebearance is not only used within a battle, but is also very often put into practice prior to entering a battle. However, the effect of exercising forebearance is always the same, irrespective of whether we exercise it prior to a battle, or during a battle. The main advantage of exercising forebearance prior to a battle is that it enables the warrior to work out his strategy for battle much more swiftly and efficiently than he would be able to do without forebearance. This is especially true of having to deal with a petty tyrant.

In the final analysis, the warrior who exercises forebearance by applying the fourth aspect of the stalker's rule within the context of the first postulate of stalking will always come out of battle having achieved his objective, namely to claim from his opponent the *gift of power* he had set out to win in the first place. Such a warrior cannot possibly lose in the true sense of the word, even though to all outer appearances he may have lost the battle. This is clear to see in the example of Sean and Willis, for although from an outer appearance Sean lost the battle to Willis, the *gift of power* Sean won in terms of knowledge gained about himself and, most especially, in terms of the self-confidence and self-respect he gained, can never possibly be measured in terms of financial benefits. This is a *gift of power* which Sean could never have bought for all the money in the world, nor would he have been able to acquire it without having gone into this battle, for which he has Willis to thank.

CHAPTER SEVEN

COMBING THE SHADOWS

TO THE EXPERIENCED WARRIOR SHADOWS ARE THE LINK
BETWEEN THE KNOWN AND THE UNKNOWN – A KIND OF
DOORWAY THROUGH WHICH THE UNKNOWN MAY BE VIEWED
WITHIN THE CONTEXT OF THE KNOWN.

We come now to a consideration of the fifth aspect of the stalker's rule. In looking at the deeper implications of this particular aspect, which is all too often taken at face value, we encounter one of those peculiar mystical concepts of the Warrior's Path that is seldom grasped properly by those who are not dedicated to the Path of Freedom. The concept in question is referred to by sorcerers as *shadow gazing*, a technique employed for learning to access alternate states of perception. Warriors of Freedom use this technique somewhat differently and term it *combing the shadows*.

The warrior, just like any other man or woman, will come across situations in his life in which the odds against him seem to be overwhelming, in that it would seem that the warrior cannot move forward, and is therefore to all intents and purposes caught between the devil and the deep blue sea. However, all such situations are purely the effect of illusion, and such illusion is invariably the result of being caught within the confines of one particular view of the world. This may at first appear to sound strange, for if one remembers that a warrior does not have a fixed view of the world, how then can he be caught within any one particular view of the world? Yet it is important to remember that, although the warrior himself does not have a fixed view of the world, those around him are more often than not inextricably caught within their own specific views of the world, and in his interaction with them the warrior is therefore forced to take his fellow man's view of the world into account.

Consequently, although the warrior has the freedom to choose any view of the world which suits his strategy, there are some battles which require the warrior to use the same view of the world as his opponent. However, any view of the world has its limitations, and it is these limitations which will often hamper even the warrior, for if he is forced to operate within the confines of that particular view of the world only, then obviously the warrior is likewise forced to operate within the parameters defined by the limitations imposed by that view of the world. Therefore, in spite of the fact that the warrior is well aware that he is up against the illusions inherent within any one particular view of the world, those illusions are not always all that easy or simple to overcome within the context of the view of the world to which they belong.

In order to make all of this somewhat clearer, think again of the example of Sean and his brother Willis. In fighting this battle with Willis, Sean has no option other than to take Willis' view of the world into account, for there is no way in which Sean can fight this battle other than by meeting Willis within the confines of Willis' view of the world. This automatically means that Sean must communicate with Willis, and tailor his outer actions towards Willis, according to the dictates of Willis' view of the world. Any other approach would simply cause Willis to feel still more threatened by Sean, in which case he would become even more nervous, suspicious, belligerent and unco-operative than he already is. Clearly, if Sean is to "win" this battle against his brother, then it is imperative for him to stalk Willis into a state of co-operation. The only way Sean can really do this is to make Willis believe that he has the upper hand over Sean, and so Sean must play his role according to the parameters defining Willis' view of the world.

From the above it is apparent that although a warrior does not have a fixed view of the world, whilst engaged in battle he or she can nonetheless become temporarily ensnared within the narrow confines of someone else's view of the world. For the experienced warrior, any such trap can only ever be a temporary nuisance, but one which it is not always expedient to avoid. Thus the warrior will often purposely and deliberately walk into such a trap if, by doing so, it enhances his strategy, especially if part of his strategy is to lull his opponent into a false sense of security. However, should the warrior find himself in such a trap, he or she will immediately resort to putting into practice the fifth aspect of the stalker's rule, namely, *whenever faced with impossible odds, a warrior opens himself to the world around him by allowing his mind to become occupied with the little details of life.*

Putting the fifth aspect of the stalker's rule into practice is in itself an utterly misleading tactic, in that it will always give the warrior's opponent the impression that he has outwitted the warrior. In order to grasp how this works, realise that once the warrior is "trapped", he or she will immediately do the unexpected, by apparently ceasing all further resistance. This, of course, is just an illusion, for what the warrior is in effect doing, is temporarily suspending fighting, so as to gain the opportunity in which to survey the situation thoroughly. In other words, by temporarily withdrawing from direct confrontation, the warrior is re-assessing both the situation, as well as his tactics, so as to gain the advantage over his opponent. Consequently, far from having been defeated, the warrior, by withdrawing from the fight, is merely gaining in strength, and will suddenly come back into the attack at any given moment with even more force and *power* than before.

In order to gain some more clarity in all of this, let us look at this synopsis closely and in detail. Firstly, realise that when the warrior temporarily retreats from battle as a result of having come face to face with what appear to be impossible odds, the warrior is using discrimination in order to detach from the situation. However, remembering everything we have learned so far, it should not be difficult to grasp that in detaching himself from the situation, the warrior is in no way relinquishing his control, but on the contrary is tightening up on his control. Therefore, by Toltec definition, the word "retreat" does not mean running away, but means exactly what the word implies, namely, *to treat again*, that is, to treat again using another tactic. Thus, although it may appear as if the warrior has stepped back and lowered his sword, he is actually only adopting another course of action, and in this respect the reader would do well to bear in mind that to retreat is very much an action.

This automatically brings us to a deeper consideration of the terms *action*, *reaction* and *response*. These three terms are not synonymous in the warrior's vocabulary, for they all have very different implications, even though these implications are nonetheless fully interactive. Rather than once again defining these three words, we will instead consider their implications from the angle of the following aphorism.

> ACTION IS THE WARRIOR'S RESPONSE TO THE PURPOSE OF HIS
> DREAMER, WHEREAS REACTION IS THE PRINCIPAL MEANS BY
> WHICH AVERAGE MAN HOOKS HIMSELF TO THE FOLLY OF HIS
> FELLOW MEN.

Action implies implementing something that is new and original, no matter whether it is a new level of perception, a new way of feeling, a new kind of emotion, a new way of thinking, or a new way of speaking, eating, conducting business, or a new way of relating to others. Action implies *living in the now*, and therefore also implies *dancing the edge*. Consequently action is only possible once one has broken out of one's fixed view of the world, which boils down to the same thing as having to wake up in the dream and take control of the contents of that dream. The implications here are that the warrior, in having taken control of the contents of his dream, has also taken *ownership* of his life, and this in turn means that he is impeccably at-one with the purpose of his dreamer. What all of this amounts to is that the warrior is *responding* impeccably to the purpose of his dreamer, by constantly taking action upon the physical plane, and because each of his actions is for ever new, each one takes him into new areas of experience, every new experience yielding new dimensions of *power*.

Reaction, on the other hand, as we have already seen in Chapter Two, is simply a re-enacting of one's folly – something which from the warrior's point of view is not only a stupid waste of time and *personal power*, but also the surest way to remain firmly hooked to the folly of others. Therefore, when the warrior temporarily retreats from the battle, he is not reacting to the situation, but is instead taking an action which will lead him to new knowledge. Although it may appear as if I am belabouring this, it constitutes a point of such huge import that I cannot stress it enough.

So as to grasp the significance of this point fully, realise that whenever average men or women come up against what they perceive to be impossible odds, they will immediately cast aside their swords and either try to escape the situation in some way, or meekly surrender on the terms of their opponent. In other words, the average man always makes the mistake of assuming that impossible odds against him means that he has failed in some way and must therefore submit to the will of his opponent, no matter whether that opponent is another person or a set of circumstances in his life. However, to keep on making the same mistake is to re-enact one's folly.

The warrior, knowing that being up against impossible odds is simply a challenge to explore the unknown, will not submit to defeat, even if by all outer appearances it may seem as if the warrior has been defeated. Consequently the warrior uses the opportunity offered by his apparent defeat to reassess the entire situation in terms of what is known as *combing the shadows*.

Combing the shadows is an action which is in itself an exercise in forebearance, the importance of which was clearly defined in the previous chapter. Since combing the shadows is a technique which is derived from the act of forebearance, in order to understand this concept properly we first need to grasp fully what is meant by the words contained within this mystical phrase. Let us therefore explore the meaning of the term "shadow".

Those of our brothers who tread the Path of High Adventure take the term "shadow" literally, and therefore employ the technique of *gazing* to work directly with the rather bizarre qualities of physical shadows. The rationale behind the technique of *shadow gazing* lies in the fact that physical shadows are but the result of objects blocking the natural flow and distribution of light. The Toltecs of old looked upon this phenomenon in terms of *resistance*. In other words, an object casts a shadow because it *reflects, absorbs* or *resists* the light beams which strike upon its surface. But irrespective of whether the light is reflected, absorbed or resisted, the fact remains that the light cannot pass through the object, and it is this blocking of the free passage of light which Toltecs looked upon as being resistance.

Now bearing in mind that Toltecs regard everything as being an expression of life, and also bearing in mind that all life-forms need the life-enhancing properties of physical sunlight in one form or another, it should not be so strange that already very early on in their pursuit of knowledge Toltec seers became deeply interested in why *physical* life-forms either reflect or absorb, or else completely resist light. Using their ability to *see* the process of life, Toltecs quickly came to realise that the phenomenon termed *resistance* is not so much the result of *density*, but is rather a state of awareness which exists at all possible levels of existence, and includes even those levels that, from a scientific point of view, are looked upon as being non-corporeal, and which give rise to *density*, and *clustering*.

Once this discovery had been made, it did not take Toltecs long to figure out that shadows actually have specific qualities that are directly related to awareness. In other words, *resistance*, being the expression of a particular state of awareness, has differing degrees of *intensity*, and it is these degrees of the intensity of resistance that determine the quality of shadow. Therefore although to the physical eye all shadows look exactly the same, the trained *seer* can nonetheless distinguish different characteristics between one shadow and another, and it is this feature which led Toltecs to the practice of *shadow gazing*, for in the final analysis, shadows are not merely shadows. Shadows, if correctly interpreted by the trained inner vision, reveal a wealth of information about the prevailing state of awareness to be found within the object casting the shadow, irrespective of whether such an object is human, animal, plant or mineral.

Consequently, by employing the technique of *shadow gazing*, a sorcerer can move and shift his or her assemblage point by using the qualities of shadows as a guide. However, this whole technique is based upon *identification*, something which the Warriors of Freedom avoid like the plague, for identification most certainly does not lead to freedom. Nevertheless, I am forced to explain this technique here, not because apprentices to the Path of Freedom are ever encouraged to identify, but simply because there is no way in which to understand *combing the shadows* if we do not understand the technique of *shadow gazing*.

In *shadow gazing* the practitioner will choose any shadow to his liking, and then "open himself up" to the vibrational quality of that particular shadow. Opening oneself up to anything presupposes complete inner silence, and this is of course only possible in the absence of internal dialogue, which it will be remembered, acts as a shield between us and the world "out there". Once such a state of inner silence has been achieved, and there is therefore no shield to block one off from the outside world, it is relatively easy to enter into a state of complete identification with whatever it is one is focusing upon. Therefore, if one is focusing upon, for example, the shadow of a particular tree, then after a while one will begin to identify with the quality *inherent* within that shadow. Prolonged identification with that quality will eventually cause the assemblage point either to move or shift, in order to bring that particular quality into total alignment. Such an alignment will constitute an alternate state of perception in which it is possible to experience that part of the tree's awareness which gives rise to its resistance.

The wise reader will observe most carefully what I have explained so far in relation to aligning the tree's awareness. Note that such alignment is based entirely upon *identification*, which lacks objectivity, for all identification is void of sobriety and is therefore the complete antithesis of *detachment*. Note further that it is also not an alignment of the tree's total awareness, but only an alignment of that portion of its awareness which gives rise to its *resistance*.

In order to grasp the full significance of what we have learned so far, remember that existing between, and interconnecting the *ten points of man*, are twenty-two aspects of awareness termed *jewels*. However, apart from these twenty-two jewels, which are termed *jewels of light*, or simply *light jewels*, there are a further eleven jewels known as the *dark jewels*, in that they all have a property that reflects, absorbs or resists light. Now although all the dark jewels have about them the property of resistance, the one that concerns us here is actually termed *resistance* because, of all the dark jewels, this particular jewel is in a peculiar sense the very embodiment of resistance.

It is well-nigh impossible to explain the dark jewels before we have even tackled and gained some understanding of the light jewels. Therefore let it suffice for now to state that the dark jewels are inherent characteristics of awareness and, as such, should not be confused with concepts such as evil, or what might be termed the *forces of darkness*. Dark jewels are very much part of the *unknown*, but constitute those aspects of the *unknown* which are so deceptive and elusive that they seem to resist being absorbed into the light of the *known*. We therefore refer to the dark jewels as belonging to the *dark side* of awareness, but the dark side of awareness has absolutely nothing to do with what are termed the *forces of darkness*.

It may be fruitful at this point to digress slightly in order to gain some insight into what many people look at as *evil*, the *devil* and *Satan*. From a Toltec perspective, such concepts make no sense at all, for Toltecs know only too well that everything within the manifested universe has a definite purpose, and since all purposes must and do culminate in the evolution of awareness, how can any purpose be looked upon as being evil? Yet, as the old proverb states so beautifully, *there is a devil in anything we do not understand*.

The only reason why the ignorant often look upon the actions of another as evil, or having been inspired by the devil or even by Satan himself, is because all actions seen as evil can invariably be traced back to the inept use of any one of the eleven dark jewels. When these jewels are not understood for what they really are they are never handled with impeccability, and consequently the effects of such inept handling will inevitably manifest in some sort of destructive, or devilish manner. However; since it is the average man's habit to play the blame game, rather than taking responsibility for his actions, Satan, or the devil, has become a very convenient scapegoat, and as a result, men and women are only too eager to give the devil, or Satan, the blame. There is in fact no such being as Satan for, in the final analysis, the devil is only a personification of average man's lack of impeccability, stemming from an ignorance of his own dark side.

What is really most ironic within the whole concept of Satan is the fact that average men and women do not look upon the actions of their fellow men as being but a mirror reflection of their own behaviour. As a result, most people are so busy identifying others as Satanists that they do not even realise that what they are perceiving as being so evil, or devilish, in another person is but the reflection of their own past or present behaviour, or alternatively, the reflection of some hidden potential within themselves! However, by playing the blame game so ardently, and by being so quick to judge a fellow man as being evil, average men and women are for ever trying to separate themselves from those whom they look upon as being evil and, in the process, are constantly plotting the demise, the downfall, or the eradication of Satan and his followers. But the real irony in all of this lies in the fact that the term "Satan" actually means *plotter*, or *to plot against*. Therefore the real Satanists of this world are all those misguided souls who are so separative in their false sense of holiness that they are always wanting to persecute anyone who does not conform to their own sense of separative values. This rather ludicrous state of affairs is the ultimate demonstration of what is meant by *shooting oneself in the foot*, for all those who believe in a devil, or in Satan, are without fail the truly devout Satanists!

The question that invariably comes up here is, "Does this imply that there is no evil?" The answer is really quite simple, and yet, rather difficult to express in just a few short words. Therefore let it suffice for now to say that the only real evil in this world is the *sin of separativeness*, and therefore any action or reaction which is based upon an ignorance of the interrelationship of the one life must of necessity be seen as being potentially evil. Note that I say "potentially" evil, for not all acts of separativeness are necessarily evil. For example, the act of *discrimination* is undeniably an act of separativeness, and yet without discrimination the evolution of awareness would cease. That which makes the act of discrimination "good" or "evil", is the *motive* for discrimination. In other words, if we exercise discrimination so as to get clarity on any issue, then it is "good". If, on the other hand, we discriminate *against* another person on the grounds of that person's race, colour, culture, religion or whatever, and do so purely because of wanting to be separative, then such discrimination can rightfully be termed "evil".

Another question which is also often asked, concerns what the Christian Church has termed *Lucifer, the fallen angel.* Although such a question is honest enough at this point in the teachings, it is nevertheless almost impossible to answer satisfactorily unless the questioner has a profound grasp of cosmology. It is very much like asking a mathematician to explain calculus when one does not yet understand basic algebra. Therefore, the best I can do here is to point out that Lucifer is not a being as such, but rather the *collective consciousness* of a whole host of ancient beings belonging to the inorganic life-stream. Furthermore, the apprentice to the Warrior's Path should not make the mistake of believing Lucifer to be the embodiment of evil. Although in a certain sense this is correct, Toltecs themselves do not regard Lucifer as being any more evil than our own undeveloped potential. Once again it is very much the case of there being a devil in everything we do not understand. The name Lucifer, means *the lightbringer*, the implications of which can hardly be termed evil. More than this it is not possible to say at this point, other than perhaps to give the following aphorism, which, for those with the eyes to see, will hold a hint or two as to the true nature and purpose of Lucifer.

AT THE BEGINNING OF THIS PRESENT SOLAR SYSTEM THE SPIRIT OF ATL EMBODIED WITHIN HIS PHYSICAL EXPRESSION THE FULL EXTENT OF THE SOLAR DEBRIS. THIS SOLAR DEBRIS IS AN UNRESOLVED SOLAR CHALLENGE LEFT OVER FROM THE PREVIOUS SOLAR SYSTEM, AND IS IN THE NATURE OF A TYPE OF RADIOACTIVITY THAT HAS THE POTENTIAL EITHER TO EXPLODE INTO SHEER RADIANCE OR TO IMPLODE INTO UNMITIGATED DARKNESS. IT IS THIS SOLAR DEBRIS, EMBODIED WITHIN THE LUMINOUS COCOON OF THE PLANET EARTH, THAT GIVES ALL

*LIFE-FORMS UPON THIS PLANET THEIR PECULIAR TENDENCY
TOWARDS INERTIA, BUT AT THE SAME TIME ALSO GIVES THEM
THEIR POTENTIAL TO BECOME A RADIANT SOURCE OF RADIO-
ACTIVE LIGHT. THE SUM TOTAL OF THIS DEBRIS IS THEREFORE
LOOKED UPON AS LUCIFER, THE LIGHTBRINGER.*

In returning now to our consideration of *resistance*, it should be
clear that although the dark jewels in themselves are not evil, or
bad, yet all forms of resistance are essentially an expression of
separativeness and thus, if they are handled ineptly, the results
will inevitably be in the nature of some kind of evil. This is an
important point to understand in our consideration of *shadow
gazing*, for clearly, if we identify with resistance alone, it stands
to reason that any such resistance will be misplaced, in that it is
not seen in context with the greater whole of which it should be
an integral part. In order to make this clear, let us once again
look at the example of discrimination.

If we were not able to discriminate *between* day and night, or
light and dark, or summer and winter, or male and female,
positive and negative, credit and debit, etcetera, humanity would
never have been able to develop the rational mind, for one thing,
and without the separative qualities of the rational mind there
would be no mathematics, no science and no technology, nor for
that matter would there be religion, education or even politics.
Consequently, the world would have been a chaotic mess and
human beings would still be nothing more than animals living by
instinct alone. Yet, as we can see so clearly in the world around
us, although the faculty of discrimination is vital to the evolution
of awareness, we cannot afford to take it out of context, for if we
do, then instead of discriminating between what, for the sake of
clarity, might be termed "right" and "wrong", we start to discriminate *against* on the grounds of separativeness.

It is precisely because men and women have never understood discrimination for what it really is that they have taken it

out of context. As a result, people want it to be summer all the year round, they wish that the wind would never blow, they want the sun to shine always, without clouds and rain to spoil the fun and, above all, they want everyone to have the same colour, the same culture, the same language and the same religion. In short, people in general, through having learned to discriminate *against*, rather than *between*, profess to strive for equality, but in actual fact have become so highly separative in discriminating *against*, that there is absolutely no true equality anywhere in the world. Instead, there is only division and hatred, suspicion and fear and, in general, a steadily developing tendency towards a sterile uniformity in which it is becoming increasingly difficult to figure out what is male or female, what is of true value and what is of no value, what is "right" and what is "wrong" and, above all, what is universal law and what is man-made law.

As is clear from the above, resistance, like discrimination, must be seen and practised within its proper context if we are going to avoid using it destructively. Anyone who simply aligns himself with resistance willy-nilly, inevitably becomes an anti-social rebel who does not even understand why he is wanting to rebel, and neither for that matter is he ever clear on exactly what it is he is rebelling against. It therefore stands to reason that to identify oneself with the resistance of a tree is utterly foolish, no matter what one's motive for doing so may be, for in the final analysis, all people are human beings and not trees, and so, what is the point in trying to resist life in terms of a tree?

Although all of this may appear to be quite simple and very understandable when viewed in this light, realise that so strong is the glamour of the *power* offered upon the Path of High Adventure that those who tread this path gladly become ever more separative, and will identify with anything and anybody, as long as they can gain access to abilities that will elevate them above their fellow men and creatures. Just as the path with a heart is the keynote to the Path of Freedom, so is the greed for *power* the keynote to the Path of High Adventure. Consequently the Path of Freedom yields the qualities of *inclusiveness* and *humility* through the right use of discrimination, whereas the Path of High Adventure yields the qualities of *separativeness* and *egotism* through the abuse of discrimination. In this respect it is useful to note that egotism is another of the dark jewels, and greed is a most common manifestation of this jewel. Discrimination, on the other hand, is a light jewel, but as it is clear to see that even a light jewel can be abused, it should not be difficult to understand how truly dangerous the dark jewels can be, for by their very nature they tempt and encourage the practitioner into abuse.

This brings us to a due consideration of the true nature and purpose of resistance, for without understanding this aspect of awareness properly we cannot come to grips with what is truly entailed in *combing the shadows*. The easiest way to grasp the real meaning of resistance is to look at an example of one of its most common manifestations, namely the *force of friction*. Realise that if there was no friction, we would not be able to walk, drive a car, or sail a boat, neither for that matter would we be able to keep a piece of furniture anchored in one spot without having to secure it to the floor in some way. Man tends to take the force of friction so much for granted that he does not even begin to acknowledge how invaluable this force really is. Technically speaking, the force of friction is only one of a great many manifestations of resistance, whilst resistance in itself, as we have already seen, is but one of eleven different expressions of that one universal force known as inertia – a most ancient aspect of solar awareness.

Resistance exists at all levels within the manifested universe and without resistance the evolution of awareness would not be possible, for the simple reason that even the unfoldment of awareness is entirely dependent upon friction of sorts. For example, if we did not have challenges in our lives we would never be able to claim our *power*. Likewise, if we were never faced with conflict we would never learn to discriminate. Therefore central to the whole process of resistance is that universal law known as *Harmony through Conflict*, because where there is no conflict there can be no resistance, no friction, and in the absence of resistance there would be no need to discriminate, and thus harmony could never be achieved, since the manifested universe would remain in an undifferentiated state of chaos.

Now, as we have already noted, resistance has three principal characteristics, that is, resistance can cause an object, irrespective of whether such an object is animate or inanimate, to *reflect*, *absorb* or *resist* light, or to behave in such a way as to demonstrate any combination of either two or even all three of these characteristics. However, for the sake of clarity, we will not concern ourselves here with any life-form other than the human being, and to keep this concept as simple as possible we will also confine our consideration of resistance to human awareness only. In this respect the thoughtful reader will remember that Toltecs define all of the manifested universe in terms of *intelligence*, which presupposes awareness and the evolution of that awareness. Therefore even plants and minerals utilise resistance in order to evolve their awareness, but for the purposes of this book it is impossible to digress into the evolution of awareness as it occurs within kingdoms of nature other than the human. It is mentioned here merely to remind the reader that he or she must cultivate the habit of thinking in terms of inclusiveness and the interrelationship of life if he or she hopes to master the more advanced teachings on the Warrior's Path.

Technically speaking, all the jewels of awareness, that is, the *light jewels*, the *dark jewels*, which are also sometimes referred to as the *hidden jewels*, as well as those peculiar jewels referred to as the *forbidden jewels*, behave very much like atoms, in that just as atoms are essentially unstable ions that will combine with other atoms to form molecules, so too are all aspects of awareness unstable ions that are for ever combining with other atoms to form molecules of awareness. Furthermore, it is these molecules of awareness that can either be *crystallised* into rigid thought patterns, or be maintained in their naturally *fluid* state of being, in which case atoms of awareness are continuously "touching sides" with other atoms in a most fantastic and breathtakingly kaleidoscopic manner.

The important point to grasp here is that each time an atom of awareness touches sides with another atom, the two atoms concerned bond temporarily to form what can be termed *molecules of perception*, and which in the mind of the *seer* create the visual impact of *bubbles of perception*. Therefore, in the case of the person who has a crystalline structure of awareness, these bubbles of perception are so suppressed that there is hardly any movement at all within that person's awareness, and every bit of movement there is, is so inordinately slow as to be practically imperceptible. On the other hand, the more fluid the person becomes, the more freely and rapidly do these bubbles of perception form and move around, so that eventually in the truly fluid warrior, awareness looks very much like a fountain of effervescence, as opposed to the almost "solid" crystal of the average man's awareness.

Having seen this background, we are now better equipped to understand what is meant by *reflection, absorption* and *resistance.* However, realise that when we are speaking in terms of awareness, *light* is synonymous with *perception,* and therefore when a person *reflects* light, it means that he or she is *reflecting perception.* Now from a purely logical point of view, this seems to make a great deal of sense, except that we still do not really know what it means to reflect, to absorb or to resist perception.

In order to grasp all of this clearly, let us look at a few simple examples. First of all, let us consider a man who quickly feels threatened by the words or actions of another. Normally, people who quickly feel threatened are also quick to feel the need to protect themselves, either by becoming very talkative in an endeavour to justify their actions verbally, or else by becoming aggressive to the point of wanting physically to accost the person whom they perceive to be a threat. What should be understood here is that the bottom line of all such behaviour is inevitably the result of some form of insecurity.

Now when such a man, call him John, who feels insecure about himself in one way or another, interacts with another person, whom we will call Peter, John's sense of insecurity will either be reflected, absorbed or resisted by Peter, depending upon Peter's own level of perception. If Peter is also insecure about himself in some way, he will *reflect* John's insecurity, meaning that he will behave towards John in such a way as immediately to set about justifying his actions, or alternatively becoming aggressive towards John. In both instances, though, John will start to become angry, either because Peter's justifications will irritate him in some way, and he will feel that

Peter is making him wrong, or else because Peter is becoming aggressive towards him for no apparent rhyme or reason. In this case, both John and Peter are merely *reflecting* each other's perception and, of course, herein lies the concept of mirrors.

However, if Peter happens to be one of those people who is always right, no matter what, then he will immediately set about to prove his superiority to John, again either verbally, or physically, or in combination. Now, depending upon how convincing Peter is in his forcefulness, John will either once again become angry, or alternatively will end up feeling even more insecure about himself, the normal result of which is that he will slink away quietly like a chastised animal. In this particular case, Peter has obviously *resisted* John's perception.

If, on the other hand, Peter is not so rigidly fixed in his view of the world, he will also have a much more fluid level of perception and he will not be so quick to react in his interaction with John, but will instead carefully assess the interaction in terms of his own knowledge. In this case Peter will be *absorbing* John's perception, so as to assimilate and digest it fully according to his own level of perception.

From these few simple examples it should now be quite clear what is meant by reflecting, resisting or absorbing perception, but realise that in all three instances it is resistance we are considering here, for even absorption is still merely a characteristic of resistance. Generally speaking, most apprentices do not find it difficult to understand why both reflecting and resisting perception should be classified as resistance, but they find it somewhat more difficult to understand how absorption can be a characteristic of resistance.

The key to understanding this lies in the fact that whenever absorption takes place the jewel *discrimination* is activated, but because discrimination is separative by nature, the act of absorption always has about it the quality of separativeness. In other words, even if Peter is a thoroughly fluid warrior who does not practise any form of separativeness, he still cannot just absorb his interaction with John indiscriminately. Peter still has to discriminate between his own knowledge and what he knows for a fact is John's knowledge. Therefore irrespective of how impeccable Peter may be, and even if in his heart of hearts he knows himself to be but a unit of the one life, just like John is also a unit of that same life, he cannot possibly avoid the act of discrimination. The only thing Peter can avoid is to abuse discrimination by discriminating *against* John in some way. At the end of the day, no matter how very vital discrimination is, it still remains separative. This is the way in which *power* has set it up, and therefore even the most impeccably inclusive warrior cannot avoid employing resistance if he is to discriminate wisely in the act of absorption.

In what we have noted here with respect to resistance I have deliberately kept everything as simple as possible, but the reader must realise that if he or she is going to succeed upon the Warrior's Path it is of paramount importance to take every bit of teaching imparted and to explore its every implication, as well as every nuance of every implication. No nagal can ever impart the teachings in their entirety, for the simple reason that a lifetime is just too short to verbalise everything. Consequently, a nagal imparts only enough of any one particular concept to enable the apprentice to put that aspect of the teachings into practice, and thus through his or her own personal experience to fill in detail which would otherwise take an inordinate amount of time to verbalise. Here the reader would be wise to bear in mind at all times the following aphorism.

HAVING RECEIVED GUIDANCE IN ANY ONE PARTICULAR PURSUIT OF KNOWLEDGE, AN APPRENTICE CAN GAIN MORE KNOWLEDGE FROM A FEW SHORT MINUTES OF PERSONAL EXPERIENCE WITHIN THAT PARTICULAR REALM OF KNOWLEDGE THAN IS POSSIBLE TO GAIN FROM A MOUNTAIN OF INFORMATION IMPARTED OVER MANY WEEKS.

Notwithstanding the above, the readers of these books do not have to become worried that I am now suddenly going to start taking short-cuts in the teachings. I will continue to impart as much as is humanly possible to do in each and every book, but in this respect I would be doing the reader a great injustice if I do not point out that the onus lies fairly and squarely upon the shoulders of each and every apprentice to put all teachings imparted into practice diligently, for only through personal experience is it possible to learn the full extent of the teachings. Realise that no matter how old I become, and no matter if I were to write books until the day I drop dead, I would still not be able to exhaust the full scope of the Toltec teachings. If this seems like an exaggeration, then pause for a moment to consider what we have learned so far about only the dark jewel *resistance*. Remember that we have considered resistance only in terms of human awareness, and even in this I have deliberately only skimmed the surface for the sake of clarity. Now what about all the other jewels, of which there are a further thirty-nine? And what about the interaction between one jewel and another? Yet in all of this, we still have not even mentioned the ten dimensions, nor have we mentioned the interaction between the dimensions and the jewels, let alone considered all of this in terms of MEST. I hope this example demonstrates clearly the extent of the Toltec teachings, and why it is so very important that every apprentice should, through personal experience, learn as much as possible by him or herself.

Not only should all of the above clarify the meaning of resistance, but it should also point out very clearly how fundamentally interactive, interdependent and interrelated is every aspect of awareness. Moreover, in having got to this point, it is now far more understandable why Toltecs define *shadow* as the product of resistance.

> *RESISTANCE IS AS FUNDAMENTAL TO THE ACT OF PERCEPTION AS FRICTION IS TO MOVEMENT. WITHOUT RESISTANCE PERCEPTION WOULD BE A MEANINGLESS EXERCISE AND EXPERIENCE WOULD BE VOID OF KNOWLEDGE.*

In the final analysis, all shadows are what, up until now, we have been referring to as *shortcomings*, for no matter what our short-comings may be, each and every one is the result of resistance having come into play in one form or another. In other words, our shortcomings come into being whenever we reflect, resist or absorb perception. Furthermore, it is important to remember that our shortcomings are defined as our unrealised potential, which of course implies that our shadows have inherent within them a potential which it is our duty to explore, for not only are they our passage to *power*, but also our ticket to freedom.

However, it is not only our own shadows that have within them potential, but also the shadows of every other person and being, and the trained warrior, even if he or she is not a seer, can read these shadows like any other person reads an open book. Therefore from everything we have learned so far, it is not difficult to see that combing the shadows means "reading" the shortcomings of either ourselves or another person. Realise, though, that any such "reading" implies perception, and since all meaningful perception is dependent upon the correct use of resistance, *combing the shadows* is technically defined as *a state of detachment brought about by positive resistance*.

It should now be very clear why at the beginning of this chapter I tried to impress upon the mind of the reader the fact that when a warrior retreats, he or she is not running away, nor sub-mitting to defeat. Any such retreat is merely the outer appearance of the warrior having adopted *a state of detachment brought about by positive resistance*. The term "positive resistance" is used to denote the *absorption* aspect of resistance, as opposed to negative resistance which refers to the *resistance* aspect, and neutral resistance which refers to the *reflection* aspect. Therefore, although the warrior has detached from the situation at hand, he or she is fully absorbent, which means that he or she is acutely aware of even the tiniest little detail of everything that is taking place.

An important point to be understood here is that although the impeccable warrior is always fully aware, the act of combing the shadows is nonetheless a level of awareness which transcends normal awareness, and thus the warrior's level of perception is heightened, and therefore even more acute than in normal awareness. This is a most important point for, generally speaking, the average man will only ever shift into this type of awareness when his physical survival is being seriously threatened, and even then it is seldom that he is able to detach from the situation in such a way that he does not become enmeshed in either fear or panic. The warrior, on the other hand, can and does detach so completely from every aspect of the situation, including his own emotions, that he is able to view the situation as a totally objective witness, and as a result is capable of perceiving minutiae which would otherwise have been imperceptible.

All of this is somewhat easier to grasp if we look at a typical example in the life of the average man or woman. Let us take as an example a man called Allan who is being confronted by his employer on the grounds that Allan is incompetent in his work. Whenever they are faced with such a situation, most people will resort to either one of two basic reactions. Either Allan will have been caught totally off guard, in which case he is likely to start panicking. However, in his sense of panic, Allan will not be listening to his employer properly, for he will either be interrupting his employer all the time in his desire to justify his actions, or else he will be so caught up in thinking of justifications, that he still will not be listening properly. Alternatively, upon being summoned to his employer's office, Allan could have suspected that he is going to be fired, in which case he would have walked into the confrontation with his mind filled with all sorts of assumptions, together with a whole mixture of uncontrolled emotions, bringing up suspicion and confusion. Being in such a state, Allan will also not listen to his employer properly, for his preconceived ideas and uncontrolled emotions will colour the confrontation in such a way that Allan is highly unlikely to perceive the confrontation with any real degree of sobriety.

However, the bottom line in both instances is that Allan is *reacting* to the confrontation in such a way that his ability to listen has become impaired and, as a result, he will hear only what he wants to hear or, more accurately, he will perceive everything in terms of what his view of the world is telling him, rather than what his employer is actually saying to him. In this respect, the reader should take careful note of the manner in which the word "listen" is being used in this particular context. Toltecs do not limit the *act of listening* to just the sense of hearing, but instead define it as *the ability to perceive with every fibre of the luminous being*. In other words, the warrior is more concerned with *sound* than he is with the physicalness of either words or other audio impacts, for *sound* is the very basis of *feeling*, and in following his heart, the warrior chooses to *feel* the world with every part of his being, including all of his physical senses.

By not truly hearing his employer, Allan will also not be paying any attention to his *feelings* on the situation, but will instead become completely caught up either in trying to convince his employer that he is in fact a competent employee, or else he will already be thinking of what he is going to do once he is fired. Nevertheless, irrespective of what Allan's reaction amounts to, the fact remains that he has allowed himself to *submit* fully to the situation, and in this has already admitted defeat. If he is trying to convince his employer not to fire him, Allan is in effect pleading to be given another chance, which amounts to the same thing as admitting that maybe he has not been doing his best, but will now try even harder. If, on the other hand, he has already accepted that he is going to be fired, the chances are that Allan is no longer really listening, but is instead busy figuring out where he could find another job, which is tantamount to working out how quickly he can run away from his present challenge.

However, had Allan been a warrior he would have approached the whole confrontation with his employer from the angle of a challenge in which, at face value, the odds against him appear to be impossible. In other words, being an impeccable warrior, Allan knows for a fact that he is not incompetent in his job, but if he is being accused of this, then it means that he is up against his employer's perception and his employer's view of the world. Clearly, in any such situation it will not benefit the warrior to tackle the challenge at hand in any way that is not compatible with his opponent's view of the world for, at least temporarily, his opponent is calling the shots from his supposed advantage.

In any such situation the warrior will immediately relax into combing the shadows. Note that I say *relax into*, implying that the warrior is entering into a course of action which he knows for a fact will enable him to gain the advantage over his opponent, and therefore there is no need for him to fret. Naturally, this is a far cry from relaxing in the sense of having nothing to do. By relaxing into combing the shadows, the warrior becomes completely absorbed in what is a truly superb manoeuvre of stalking – a manoeuvre that is so extraordinarily powerful, and yet so subtle, that no opponent is ever aware of what the warrior is actually doing until he finds himself suddenly, and apparently miraculously, at the sharp end of the warrior's sword.

Having been caught off guard in such a bewildering swing of *power*, any opponent will either capitulate in total confusion, or else will enter into a mad scramble of justifications that inevitably reveal the weaknesses in his or her own reasoning. However, in both instances it is always the warrior's opponent who ends up delivering the death blow to himself either by admitting defeat, or by digging his hole deeper and deeper in his frantic attempts at justification. And yet, the only thing the warrior actually does in combing the shadows is to open himself up to those little details which reveal the potential inherent within his opponent's shortcomings. Here it is important to remember that until we have transmuted our shortcomings, they constitute weaknesses that make us exceedingly vulnerable to the outside world. This is especially noticeable when another person either deliberately or inadvertently triggers our shortcomings in some way, something that is commonly known as *having one's buttons pushed*.

Therefore in combing the shadows, the warrior is taking the most careful note of his opponent's behaviour, for such behaviour will always reveal that person's shortcomings, and also every nuance of these shortcomings. Furthermore, as the warrior is completely objective in his sense of detachment, he perceives his opponent's shortcomings against the backdrop of what is for his opponent the *unknown* within himself. As a result, the warrior can always see very clearly how to manipulate his opponent's shortcomings in such a way that will throw his opponent completely off guard and off balance. This is what is implied in the aphorism given at the beginning of this chapter, namely, *to the experienced warrior, shadows are the link between the known and the unknown – a kind of doorway through which the unknown may be viewed within the context of the known.*

In other words, by comparing his opponent's shortcomings against the backdrop of what his opponent actually knows and understands about himself, the warrior can immediately see his opponent's weaknesses in terms of his unrealised potential. By having assessed the *unknown* against the *known* within his opponent, the warrior now only has to confront his opponent with his own weaknesses, and his opponent is forced either to capitulate immediately, or to dig himself in deeper. Furthermore, since the *unknown* always inspires a sense of fear in the person concerned, the warrior's opponent will become highly insecure in being confronted in this way. As a result, the warrior's opponent swings from being very confident in his apparent defeat of the warrior, to looking around frantically for some form of escape. Let us look at the example of Allan in order to clarify this.

Allan's employer, Errol, who runs a large wholesale clothing company, starts the confrontation by complaining about the fact that Allan seems to spend a lot of time laughing and joking with the clients who come to him for assistance, instead of just assisting them quietly, quickly and politely. In his opening statement, Errol has already revealed the nature of his complaint, but instead of counteracting immediately, Allan relaxes into combing the shadows by admitting that he does indeed like to laugh and joke, but would appreciate it if Errol would be so kind as to clarify his point further. Having been lulled into a sense of security by Allan's response, Errol now feels confident to lay all of his grievances about Allan on the table, even those which he himself secretly regards as being childish and petty. Nonetheless, throughout all of Errol's complaints, Allan merely listens intently, nodding his head from time to time, as if agreeing with everything Errol is saying. In having Allan's full attention, and what appears to be a complete lack of resistance, Errol starts to relax and, in doing so, opens up more and more to Allan, allowing Allan to see a side of him which he normally keeps carefully concealed.

Through listening intently to every implication of Errol's words, the sound of his voice, and noting his body language in talking to Allan, it does not take Allan long to work out that the real issue here lies in Errol's envy of his own openness and lack of inhibition in dealing with even difficult clients. Having ascertained this much, Allan now starts to comb the shadows for anything to do with Errol's sense of envy, and once again it does not take him long to see that, in spite of his outer display of nonchalant bravado, Errol is actually a very shy and withdrawn man who prefers the relative safety of his private office. However, it is also clear to Allan that Errol himself is not aware of his envy of Allan, but has instead chosen to see Allan's friendliness as wasting time in unnecessary banter.

It will therefore not help Allan to confront Errol directly with the real issue, for Errol will simply deny it and, in addition, will more than likely become exceedingly angry and self-righteous by being confronted with the truth. Instead, Allan now assesses Errol in terms of what Errol does not know about himself as opposed to what he does know. In order to grasp how this is done, remember that Allan, through having ascertained what the real issue is, can see how Errol hides his shyness even from himself, by behaving in a nonchalant manner. However, the implications of such behaviour are that Errol is not only easily embarrassed, but because of being introverted, is also easily frightened by any sense of exposure. This is as much as Errol knows about himself, but what he does not know is that all of this stems from the fact that he does not believe that he in himself has anything of real value to offer. As a result of this suppressed fear, Errol is seldom open and friendly with others, preferring instead to remain aloof, and by keeping people at a distance, he hopes that no-one will ever get close enough to notice that he is perhaps not the man he would like himself to be. Therefore by giving the impression of being a very strong man, Errol manages to hide even from himself his deepest fear, but in doing so, also renders himself vulnerable.

Having seen where Errol's vulnerability lies, Allan only has to bring Errol face to face with that fear in order to throw him completely off balance. In this respect, Allan had in the past often wondered why Errol seems to be so keen to avoid any real contact with customers, by being so quick to refer them to Allan, but invariably with a huge display of charm and gracious concern that they should get the best possible service. Because of the way Errol does this, customers are always given the impression that they are being placed in the most capable pair of hands in the business, and that Errol is therefore ensuring that they are getting the personal attention they deserve. Now, however, it is suddenly so clear to Allan that this show of charm and concern is only Errol's way of escaping what he perceives as possible exposure.

Once Errol has finished speaking, Allan merely smiles at him, and then ever so "naively" brings Errol face to face with his fear by asking Errol to work with him on the showroom floor for the next few days so that he can learn from Errol's example. Suddenly terrified, Errol starts to make all sorts of excuses to the effect that he simply does not have the time, and that Allan is just going to have to find his own way the best he can. However, pretending to be completely at a loss, Allan replies that he is now very bewildered, for he has always respected the fact that Errol is extremely busy, and has therefore indeed always tried his best to find his own way without being a nuisance.

Caught off guard in this way, Errol has no option other than to agree with Allan and, in having gained his gap, Allan pushes home his sword by asking Errol if he is dissatisfied with his performance in terms of sales figures. Again caught off guard, Errol is forced to admit that Allan's performance is good, but that he is only concerned about the fact that his business might be getting a reputation because of Allan's bantering with the clients. This time Allan simply holds Errol's gaze until Errol becomes embarrassed and is forced to look away, then asks Errol if he has received any complaints from the customers. Openly admitting to Allan that there have been no complaints, but secretly having to admit that clients have always remarked upon the joys of doing business with Allan, Errol finally has to face the truth within himself.

Blushing furiously, he orders Allan out of his office, muttering under his breath that Allan must think about what he has said to him, but deep down inside already knowing that Allan has defeated him by revealing his envy of the man's open friendliness. Allan suppresses a knowing smile, and politely acknowledges Errol's "guidance" before leaving the office.

Throughout the confrontation with Errol, Allan stood firm in his own knowledge, and yet by doing so he did not jeopardise his career in any way. Instead, as a result of meeting Errol in the midst of his folly, he has earned Errol's respect by not openly proving him wrong, although he clearly pointed out to him his pettiness born of envy. In all of this Allan has given Errol a lot to think about, and as a result Errol's envy of Allan is already beginning to become admiration for Allan's courage and brilliance. Yet, realise that the only thing Allan has actually done is to bring Errol face to face with his own fear, and that if Errol is going to be honest enough to acknowledge fully what has really transpired, then he will not only acknowledge Allan for having outwitted him, but will also thank Allan for having made him aware of his own hidden fear.

If Errol is willing to face his fear, he will gain a deeper understanding of himself, and through that will come to grips with the potential inherent within his shyness and consequent introversion. However, in dealing with warriors, it is the rare man indeed who is capable of seeing what a service the warrior has rendered him by having stalked him in this manner. Mostly, the average man and woman, having encountered the *power* of a warrior in this fashion, will simply try to put the whole incident behind them as quickly as possible, and will continue life as if nothing untoward has ever happened.

Following on from our consideration of what is entailed in combing the shadows, one final word of caution is called for. In the example we have looked at here, the reader must take care not to assume that combing the shadows is quite as simple or as easy as this particular example may indicate. The simplicity of examples is only for the sake of clarity, for if the truth be told, there is nothing simple about the convoluted way in which the human mind operates. It takes time, patience and considerable practice to acquire skill in combing the shadows. In this respect it must never be forgotten that no two people are alike, and that no two incidents are ever identical, no matter how similar the face value may be. Therefore, at the end of the day, the art of stalking ever remains a matter of having skill in the ability to improvise efficiently and professionally in the moment, and this is obviously not a skill which is acquired overnight.

In the hands of the experienced stalker, combing the shadows is a most powerful tool which is so inconspicuous and subtle that the warrior's opponent will often be left with the uncanny feeling that the warrior has at his or her disposal some sort of supernatural power, whatever the implications of this truly nonsensical word may be. Yet, there is nothing "supernatural" about combing the shadows, nor does the warrior have any power which is not within the grasp of anyone who is willing to put in the required amount of time and effort needed to master the art of stalking.

In conclusion, the perceptive reader will have noticed that unlike with the first four aspects of the stalker's rule, I have not dealt with this fifth aspect in relation to the four postulates of stalking. The reason for this is twofold. Firstly, as has already been explained earlier in this book, all seven aspects of the stalker's rule can be applied within the context of any one or more of the four postulates of stalking. In this respect there are no hard and fast rules as to which particular aspect of the stalker's rule must be applied within the context of a certain postulate. Knowing which aspect of the stalker's rule is relevant in any given situation, and applying it within context of the correct postulate, is a skill in discrimination that can only be acquired through constant practice. Therefore by working through the examples pertaining to the first four aspects of the stalker's rule, I merely attempted to give the reader enough insight into how all of this works, so that he or she can at least make a start in trying to use the stalker's rule effectively. More than this it is not possible to do, for it is only practice that will truly give the reader any real understanding of how to use the stalker's rule within the context of the four postulates of stalking.

The second reason why I omitted to explain the fifth aspect of stalking within the context of any particular postulate was for the sake of simplicity. It is important to know that the implications inherent within the fifth, sixth and seventh aspects of the stalker's rule are so vast that, depending upon the context in which they are to be applied, they invariably stretch across two or even all four of the postulates. With respect to the fifth aspect of the stalker's rule, this is clearly evident if one looks at the fact that this particular aspect is concerned almost entirely with *action*, as opposed to *reaction*. Action belongs to the North, just as not reacting in one's accustomed manner is a *not-doing*, which also belongs to the North. Therefore there is no doubt that this particular aspect must be viewed in the context of the second postulate of stalking. However, in considering that the whole purpose of combing the shadows is to achieve a level of sobriety which would normally not be possible, it is immediately clear that we must also look at combing the shadows in terms of the first postulate of stalking.

Therefore, in looking at the example of Allan and Errol, we see that Allan is at a disadvantage in being up against his employer's view of the world, and because of this must strive to utilise the fifth aspect of the stalker's rule. This, as we already know, means having to practise *not-doing* in the sense of, firstly, not reacting to the situation by taking things at face value; and secondly, taking that action termed combing the shadows. It therefore stands to reason that if Allan is going to succeed in not reacting, then he must approach the confrontation with Errol in terms of the first postulate, for only then will he not get caught up in the face value of the situation. But in doing so, Allan is also required to take action in terms of combing the shadows – an act which immediately brings into operation the second postulate. However, realise that although in combing the shadows Allan does achieve a clarity on that confrontation which enables him to gain the advantage over Errol, that clarity is nevertheless applicable only to that particular confrontation. Tomorrow, or the day after, Allan will find himself once again facing a similar challenge with another person; hence the necessity for him to acknowledge the folly of hoping that he will ever be able to solve the mystery of beingness, which of course, plunges him headlong into the fourth postulate.

CHAPTER EIGHT

BEYOND THE VEIL OF TIME

TIME IS THAT WHICH EXPRESSES THE INTELLIGENCE FACTOR WITHIN THE FOURFOLD PURPOSE OF THE UNSPEAKABLE. THEREFORE WHAT IS PERCEIVED AS TIME IS IN REALITY THE MOVEMENT OF INHERENT AWARENESS – THE TRUE EXPRESSION OF BOTH THE INTENT AND THE MIND OF THE UNSPEAKABLE. WE CAN THEREFORE RIGHTFULLY LOOK UPON TIME AS BEING THE ESSENCE OF ALL CREATION, AND UPON THE OTHER THREE EXPRESSIONS OF THE FOURFOLD PURPOSE, MATTER, ENERGY AND SPACE, AS BEING THE REFLECTION OF THE UNSPEAKABLE WITHIN THE ESSENCE OF CREATION, TIME. CONSEQUENTLY WE HAVE NO POINT OF REFERENCE IF WE DO NOT ACKNOWLEDGE TIME AS BEING THE PRIMORDIAL ESSENCE OF THE MANIFESTED UNIVERSE – AN ESSENCE WHICH IS SACRED TO ALL BUT THE PROFANE.

Before we can consider what is entailed in the sixth aspect of the stalker's rule, namely, *a warrior always compresses time*, we first need to gain a better understanding of the true nature of time. In the first two volumes time was defined as the *product of perceiving the process of life*; a perfectly good definition from the angle of the layman and for those with the eyes to see. However, in our present consideration of time it is important that we try to come to grips, at least partly, with the technical definition of time given in the aphorism at the opening of this chapter.

The true nature of MEST is far from easy to understand with the rational mind, and of these four expressions of the fourfold purpose of the Unspeakable time is the most abstract and difficult one to grasp. Likewise, to try to verbalise the nature of

MEST is quite the most frustratingly futile undertaking for any nagal, but since man is as yet forced to use the spoken and written word, we have no choice other than to attempt the impossible. I therefore ask the reader not to take the words which follow here at face value, but instead to try his or her utmost to *get the feel* of what is being imparted. In attempting to explain time I am forced to use words which are so ridiculously limiting and inadequate that I can at best try to impart a *feeling* to the reader, and then hope that the reader will make the necessary effort to flow with that feeling until such time as that feeling translates into experience, for it is only when the nature of time is experienced that there can be at least some measure of understanding of the real meaning of time.

Time is nothing, and yet it is everything, just as space is empty, and yet filled to capacity. What man measures with a clock is not time, just as what man perceives as being the emptiness between two atoms, or the emptiness between two planets, is not space. Time and space are the two polarities that make possible the manifestation of the universe, and consequently they are both expressions of inherent awareness; that is, the inherent awareness of the Unspeakable. Therefore time and space are specific states of awareness, each being the opposite polarity of the other, and in this respect are inseparable and interdependent, for without that awareness termed time there could be no awareness *of* space, and without that awareness termed space there could be no awareness *of* time.

Mathematically the term "awareness *of* time" means "awareness multiplied by time", and the term "awareness *of* space" means "awareness multiplied by space". And yet, both time and space are in themselves states of inherent awareness, and therefore irrespective of whether we are referring to "awareness *of* time" or to "awareness *of* space", both terms amount to the same thing as saying "awareness *of* awareness", "awareness multiplied by awareness" or, more precisely, "awareness multiplied by inherent awareness".

However, what is this awareness that we are multiplying by inherent awareness? From our brief overview of cosmology in *Cry of the Eagle*, we learned that there are not only two types of awareness, that is, inherent awareness and evolving awareness, but also that both types of awareness have two polarities, the one pole being *separative*, and the other being *inclusive*. That pole which separates, is *mind, the thinking principle*; whereas that pole which unites, is *intent, the feeling principle*. Clearly, as we are here primarily concerned with inherent awareness, it stands to reason that this 'other' awareness we are referring to is merely the one polarity of inherent awareness, which implies that what we have been referring to as inherent awareness is in fact the other polarity of inherent awareness. Therefore time and space are the two polarities of inherent awareness, and within this context space is *that* which is the expression of *mind, the thinking principle*, which separates and thus brings about the element we term space; whilst time, being the expression of *intent, the feeling principle*, is *that* which unites and thus brings about the element of *progression*, that is, the *sequential* or *progressive inclusion* of the unknown within the known, and is therefore *that* which gives rise to what is termed time. Yet with both time and space, realise tht we are referring to *that* of the Unspeakable termed *It Moves*.

From what we have learned so far, we see that the term "awareness multiplied by time", in effect means "space multiplied by time", and "awareness multiplied by space" means "time multiplied by space", which of course is one and the same thing, showing that time and space are not only the two polarities of inherent awareness, but also that the product of both is identical; namely, It Moves, that is, active intelligence as defined in *Cry of the Eagle*. Yet, remember that in layman's terms space is defined as being *the product of perceiving the purpose of life*, whereas time is defined as being *the product of perceiving the process of life*. In other words, space has to do with the *purpose* of life, whereas time has to do with the *process* of life. This means that space is an awareness of the purpose of the Unspeakable, and time is an awareness of the process through which that purpose can and must be fulfilled. From this it stands to reason that time is not only an expression of the *will-to-manifest*, but is therefore also an expression of *intent*, and since *intent* is the one and only force present throughout all of the manifested universe, and since the manifested universe itself is but the product of *intent*, (Volume Two), it is clear to see why Toltecs look upon time as being the primordial essence of the manifested universe.

Therefore, although time and space are the polarities of inherent awareness, time nonetheless precedes space. This is something which is not at all easy to grasp, but it will help to think of it in this way. Realise that until *Some-Thing* within the void that marks the Unspeakable stirs, or moves, there is *No-Thing* marking the void, but once or when there is movement, that which marks the void becomes perceptible. However, *once* or *when* both imply the element of *time*, which of course immediately makes the void perceptible as *space* or, more precisely, *a space*. We see therefore not only the interdependence of time and space, but also their interrelationship. Furthermore, as we have already learned in *Cry of the Eagle*, it is because of the intelligent co-operation between these two polarities of inherent awareness that both the manifestation and the evolution of awareness can and does take place. In fact, it is only because of the *constant* interaction between these two polarities that the manifested universe can exist, for the moment these two polarities are merged, interaction ceases, and therefore *It Moves No More*, meaning that the Unspeakable has once again become a motionless void.

It is this constant interaction between the two polarities of inherent awareness, between time and space, that is the true *constant* that eluded Dr. Albert Einstein in his theories on relativity, and which he tried to define in terms of the speed of light. Consequently in Dr. Einstein's equation $e = mc^2$, it is clear to see that $e \div m = c^2$, that is, *energy* divided by *matter* is the product of *time* multiplied by *space* (c^2), meaning that when the two poles of inherent awareness start to interact, the product is the division of *undifferentiated consciousness by differentiated consciousness*, (*Cry of the Eagle*), and it is this division of undifferentiated consciousness that is termed *clustering*. But remember that energy is *the product of power*, and since *power is the product of perception*, we see that the equation $e = mc^2$ reads as energy (e, the product of *power*) = *differentiated consciousness* (m) multiplied by *space* multiplied by *time* (c^2, the constant interaction between the two polarities of inherent awareness).

In all of the above I have tried to give the reader some *feeling* for what is meant by time, and also of its relationship to space, energy, matter, and *power*. However, as I have already mentioned, what I have given here is merely a *feeling for*, and should therefore not be taken at face value, for if this explanation is taken at face value, the reader will come up with nothing but total garbage which makes little or no sense. If, on the other hand, the information imparted here is taken as an aid to generating a feeling on what is meant not only by time, but also MEST and *power*, then that feeling will guide the reader into some form of experience. Needless to say, experience is not only very real knowledge, but even more importantly, also firsthand knowledge.

As we have progressed, the reader will have noted how far we have moved into the unknown in our consideration of time and, as in all cases of having to deal with the unknown, the rational mind is of absolutely no use at all. We can only ever deal directly with the unknown within the context of left side awareness, but until such time as the reader can enter and exit left side awareness at will, the best method by which to proceed is to look for and to note any feelings which come up as a result of experience. Information can never replace direct personal experience, but information, if wisely used, can and does allow one to gain at least some inkling of what type of feeling one is looking for within any experience. Once one has some idea of what it is one is looking for, then one can grasp the relevant feeling that arises from out of an experience, and it is this feeling which is the manifestation of left side awareness. At first all such feelings do not amount to any great deal of enlightenment, but if more similar feelings are also noted and added to the first, then gradually but surely a very real picture does begin to form; a picture which is at first nebulous, but which ultimately begins to solidify into substance that can be grasped by the rational mind. In this respect it is hoped that the information imparted here will give the reader at least some inkling of what type of feelings arising within his or her daily life experiences will lead to a better understanding of what is meant not only by time, but also MEST in general, and how *power* fits into this greater scheme.

Having seen that time is the primordial essence of the manifested universe, and that in this context it is also an expression of *intent*, it should not be too difficult to understand why Toltecs look upon time as being sacred. Realise that, in the final analysis, nothing can be created in the absence of the primordial essence, and it is only because of the presence of the primordial essence that creation becomes an option. In other words, all of creation is dependent upon both the existence and the use of time. But realise also that what man understands as time is merely man's understanding of how time manifests upon the physical plane. Once man has come to grasp the deeper implications within calculus, and has come to realise that these implications can only be grasped through the forgotten science of numerology, we will see a completely new type of mathematics coming into existence – a form of mathematics that will have peculiarly psychological connotations, and that will therefore take into account not only the interrelationship of life, but will also acknowledge the necessity to include the element of time within all mathematical equations.

Because of the element of time, we do not live in an absolute universe. The whole universe is relative to time, relative to the *intent* of the Unspeakable, and once this has been grasped for what it really means, science will come to realise that the manifested universe itself has an *emotional* quality which cannot be ignored. Just as emotion is the expression of *intent* upon the physical plane, so too is time the universal expression of *intent* within the manifested universe, of which the actual physical and visible universe is only a small part. Therefore, strange as it may sound, time is the primordial expression of what can be termed *universal emotion*. Time is quite literally the emotions of the Unspeakable, whatever that may mean or imply, for from our human point of view we simply do not know enough about ourselves to even begin to hazard a guess as to the emotions of the Unspeakable.

However, Toltecs today know enough about time to know that it is not only part of the fourth dimension, but that it is also in the nature of pure emotion. Yet that emotion spans eternity, and is therefore so utterly incomprehensible in its vastness that we can only ever get some inkling of it through millennia of history. As a result Toltec scholars have laboured assiduously over an untold number of centuries, each generation adding their life's work to that of their predecessors, so that slowly, ever so slowly, universal cycles of time have become visible – each cycle being unmistakably the expression of a specific emotional vibration. Consequently we today know that there are no co-incidents or accidents, but that everything within history is but the result of what may rightfully be referred to as the *times* or, more precisely, the result of universal *intent* manifesting first as *power*, and then as *energy* charged with *emotional impetus*.

Therefore, to the Toltec warrior, the impeccable management of time is of paramount importance. No true warrior can look upon time as something which can be frittered away carelessly on all manner of non-essential trivialities or pettiness. To waste time, in whatever way, is unthinkable for the warrior, for to do so is quite literally to waste his allotted opportunity for participating within the act of universal creation. Consequently, for the true warrior, life upon earth has no real meaning if it is merely spent on acquiring a good job, a car, a home, a family and lots of money in the bank. For the warrior, life on earth can only have real meaning when he has spent it in *making his mark* within the universe, of which he or she is a creature. Obviously the only way in which the warrior can do so, is within the context of time, and the only way in which he can manage time efficiently, is by taking full control of his awareness, for as we already know from the equation of time given in both Volumes One and Two, time is inversely proportional to awareness.

Because time is the expression of universal *intent*, we cannot possibly manipulate it in any way whatsoever. However, because it is inversely proportional to awareness, we can, in a manner of speaking, manipulate it by manipulating our awareness. In other words, although we can never affect time in the true sense of the word, we can nevertheless vary our perception of time, either by speeding it up, or by slowing it down. Realise, however, that any such alteration in speed is merely within the realm of perception and not within the realm of physical manifestation as such. Nonetheless, by being able to adjust the speed of time within the realm of perception the warrior is capable of performing the most astounding feats, which from the angle of the average man will often appear to be quite miraculous.

By way of an explanation as to what is meant by speeding up or slowing down time let us look very briefly at the example of the Toltec seer. The art of the seer lies in his ability to align his own perception so accurately with that of, let us say, the person he is *seeing*, that the awareness of the seer temporarily merges with the awareness of the other person. Such a merging of awareness is in the nature of a complete *identification with* the subject, so that to all intents and purposes the seer temporarily becomes the other person. The moment that identification takes place, the seer rapidly adjusts his own perception of time in such a way that he either speeds it up or slows it down, depending upon his purpose for *seeing*.

If the seer is wanting to *see*, let us say, the reason for a particular behaviour pattern in the other person, the seer will speed up time. Realise, however, that it is not physical time that has been speeded up, but only the seer's perception of time. What in effect this means is that through his complete identification with that person, the seer can look back along the whole train of perceptions within that person that culminated in the present behaviour pattern. In other words, it is as if the seer has gone back in time in the space of a few split seconds, whereas in actual fact he has gone nowhere, but has instead brought the past into the present by *compressing* time within the realm of perception, which is not bound by either space or time as such, for all perception, past, present and future, is but the result of alignment, and all alignment is forever present within the luminous cocoon.

Alternatively, if the seer wishes to ascertain, let us say, the motives of a person, then after having aligned that person he will slow down time within his perception. This slowing down of time is much like drawing the present moment out in such a way that even the smallest little detail, and every nuance of that detail, becomes perceptible. It is in fact very similar to slowing down a cinematograph film to such an extent that one can view each frame individually. The effect of being able to see so much detail is that every piece of detail has its own tale to tell, and by putting together these tiny tales the seer is able to *see* whatever the other person may well be trying to conceal. In other words, by slowing down time the seer *expands time* within the realm of perception so that he can view the intentions of the other person as if through a microscope.

What we have noted here as far as the Toltec seer is concerned is of course only one aspect of his art, for the seer's abilities are not confined to only animate objects, but encompass also inanimate objects and, for that matter, also MEST itself. However, because the art of the seer entails a complete identification, it should also be clear why the true seer is not a person who is in any way tempted to use his or her abilities for spying on other people. Complete identification is seldom pleasant, for to identify with someone else's fear, or doubt, or worry, or perverse thought patterns, or chaotic emotions, and to experience them as being one's own, even if only temporarily, is most of the time a thoroughly unpleasant experience, to say the least.

Having considered what it means to adjust the speed of time, realise that even the warrior who is not a seer can still work with time in this manner, although, until he can align his own awareness accurately with that of another person, such a warrior will not gain access to nearly as much knowledge as is available to the seer. Nevertheless, by having learned to take control of his or her awareness the warrior can adjust the speed of time, and can thereby work miracles. Let us therefore take a closer look at what this actually entails in the life of the warrior who is not a seer.

The sixth aspect of the stalker's rule tells us that *a warrior always compresses time. Any battle, no matter how big or small it may be, is a battle for one's life, and in a battle for one's life an instant becomes an eternity – an eternity which determines the outcome of the battle.*

The first point to be noted here is that a warrior always *compresses* time. However, this statement should not be taken purely at face value, for the term 'compress' is used here in its broadest possible connotation, and not in the sense defined earlier when we looked at adjusting the speed of time. What this statement really means is that irrespective of whether the warrior is *compressing* time or *expanding* time, he is not *wasting* time.

Not wasting time does not mean that the warrior rushes around frenetically, working his fingers to the bone twenty-four hours a day, but means instead that the warrior uses his time sparingly and efficiently in whatever he happens to be engaged. In other words, if the warrior is at work, then he is completely absorbed in his work. If he is sleeping, the warrior is completely at rest. If he is relaxing, the warrior is enjoying his relaxation fully. But regardless of what activity the warrior is engaged in, he is always, but always, fully aware of every little detail concerning that activity, his overall response to that activity, as well as everything surrounding, or involving, that activity. This means that the warrior is *wide awake* to his own purpose, even during the hours of sleep, for to the fully trained warrior, sleep is merely an altered state of perception in which normal physical activity is temporarily suspended. Exactly the same can be said about the relaxation of the warrior, because to the warrior relaxation does not mean parking off somewhere like a couch potato that has slipped into a state of semi-consciousness. Relaxation to the warrior is the opportunity to reassess his sense of purpose in relation to the present moment, but within the context of *feeling*, rather than being engaged in mental, emotional or physical activity.

By always being fully aware of his every move, and of every move of the world around him, the warrior is constantly in touch with how his sense of purpose is unfolding, as well as how best it may be materialised within the context of the greater life of which he is a unit. In this respect the warrior is fully aware of the fact that there are no accidents and no co-incidents, and that every occurrence and every act within his life all add up to form a tiny fragment within the purpose of the Unspeakable. Therefore it is only by fulfilling his own fate, his own sense of purpose, that the warrior can truly make his mark within the universe and can thereby claim to be living an impeccable life.

Yet, to live the impeccable life of the warrior is the struggle of a lifetime or, more precisely, a continuous struggle to remain fully alert and perceptive at all times throughout one's entire lifetime. Such a struggle amounts to much the same thing as a battle, for in the final analysis, it is a very real battle continuously to fight off the tendency towards inertia. However, to succumb to inertia is to become caught in a downward spiral – a spiral that tends towards the complete cessation of movement, ultimately ending in decay and eventual death. In this respect it is important to remember that there are more subtle forms of death than simply the death of the physical body. Therefore when it is stated that any battle is a battle for one's life, it is implied that the warrior is not only fighting to keep himself alive upon the physical plane, but is also fighting to remain alive in the sense of *living* an impeccable life. Only by living an impeccable life can the warrior make his mark within the universe, and it is within that mark that lies his future, and thus also his immortality.

In relation to the above it is important to know that we lose what we do not use, and in this respect there are today a great many discarnate beings who can no longer incarnate by virtue of the fact that they have not kept abreast with *the times*. Having lagged behind in the development of their awareness, such people can no longer play a meaningful part in helping to fulfil the purpose of the Unspeakable, and thus have become redundant within the process of life.

Therefore the phrase "a battle for one's life" has implications which by far transcend the face value of this phrase, and of this the warrior is fully aware. The actions of one small instant in time, in whatever lifetime, can and do have their impact upon the warrior for much longer than average men and women are willing to accept or to believe, and the ripple effects of that one instant in time travel across the boundaries of one incarnation into the next, where even more ripples are set up that once again transgress into the following incarnation, and so forth. Consequently, the statement that "an instant becomes an eternity", is no mere metaphor, and the statement that it is "eternity which determines the outcome of the battle", is likewise no metaphor, for any action today forms the basis for the future, just like any challenge today is but the accumulated effects of the past.

Generally speaking men and women are so conditioned into believing that there is just this one life, isolated within the context of time, that they have also come to believe that every day of their lives is somehow an isolated occurrence within their total lifespan. As a result, men and women behave as if time is of no consequence and that their actions can be shrugged off as if they have little to no relevance to the present or, for that matter, the future. Clearly, from what we have learned so far, such an approach to life is not only the mark of insanity, but is also the surest path to self-destruction. Yet, in spite of this, humanity in general has so little respect for life, or for time, that by far the greater majority of people continue to *spend* their lives in pursuit of self-destruction and self-sabotage.

The true warrior, on the other hand, does not waste even an instant of his or her time on earth. Looking upon time as being not only precious, but also sacred, the warrior sets about learning how best to compress time. In this respect there is no technique as such that can be utilised, for in the final analysis it is only by *living* the teachings as a whole that the warrior learns how to compress time. Yet, realise that to compress time is not a matter of occasionally being more economical with one's time. To compress time means that one is fully awake at all times, but in the sense of, firstly, knowing what one's fate in this lifetime encompasses; and secondly, being constantly alert so as to be able to *seize the fleeting moment of chance*.

No matter in how many different ways a nagal tries to explain what it means to compress time, apprentices, like anyone else, always find that in practice it is not easy to come to grips with what is really entailed in doing so. The reason for this is that compressing time is not so much an *action*, but is rather more in the nature of something like a *mood*. This fact is expressed in the following aphorism.

COMPRESSING TIME IS AN OUTWARD EXPANSION INTO THAT VASTNESS TERMED THE PROCESS OF LIFE, SO THAT ONE'S OWN FATE BECOMES VISIBLE. HAVING WITNESSED FATE IN TERMS OF THE

GREATER WHOLE ONE IS LEFT WITH AN OVERRIDING SENSE OF
PURPOSE, WHICH QUICKLY BECOMES AN ALL-ABSORBING MOOD –
A MOOD WHICH GRADUALLY TRANSMUTES INTO INTENT.

In considering everything we have learned so far it should be clear that because time is the expression of universal emotion, it is hardly surprising that either in trying to work with time, or by coming in touch with our fate, both should spark off emotions of sorts. However, because universal emotion by far exceeds the scope of humanness, any contact with it leaves one with only a rather vague, but nonetheless compelling sense that there is something "missing" in one's life. Of course, that something which seems to be missing is our unfulfilled fate, and it is only once we know what our fate is and have begun to fulfil it, that the sense of something being missing begins to change.

The point to be grasped here is that until we do know what our fate is, the element of time will work in our life in such a way as to bring about within us a peculiar type of mood that continues to grow with the passage of time. This is true irrespective of whether we are attempting to tread the Warrior's Path or not. Furthermore, even after one has recognised one's fate, and is consciously trying to fulfil it, that mood will still persist, even though it does change from the feeling that there is something missing, to the feeling that something is incomplete.

In order to understand fully what all of this really means, it is important to remember that all of us are units of life that have our part to play within the evolution of the greater whole. This is what is termed destiny, and in order to fulfil our destiny we periodically incarnate upon the physical plane to enable us to gain the necessary knowledge with which to fulfil that destiny. Now, the knowledge we are seeking can at present only be acquired through experience upon the physical plane, and to this end we need specific challenges that will enable us to learn whatever it is we need to learn. Therefore what is termed fate, is quite literally the knowledge we are seeking in order to fulfil our destiny. How we acquire that knowledge, and how the challenges that are going to lead us to that knowledge will materialise, is entirely up to us once we are in physical incarnation, but throughout our lives upon earth our dreamers are constantly trying to guide us in the right direction, and it is this *guidance* which man tends to look upon as being fate, rather than the *knowledge* which it is his fate to gain. As a result, people all too often feel victimised by the circumstances in their lives, instead of seeing the true *gifts of power* that come their way because of these challenges.

The reason why man generally speaking finds it so difficult to see his fate for what it really is, is mainly due to the eclipse of consciousness that happens at the moment of birth. Because of this eclipse, none of us can ever remember why we came into incarnation, or what knowledge we are seeking. As a result, our dreamers have no other recourse than to try to impress upon us the fact that we have *no time*, that is, we have *no purpose*, or more precisely, we have no purpose because we are temporarily out of touch with *the purpose* of this incarnation. In this respect, remember that our only real purpose is our destiny, or the part we have to play within the evolution of the greater whole, the expression of which is reflected as a unit within universal *intent*.

How that sense of having *no time* will manifest is different for every individual, but sooner or later every person starts to become aware of running out of time in one way or another and, as a result, starts to re-evaluate not only time, but also the purpose of life. Such a re-evaluation always brings about in the person concerned a very real mood of sorts – a mood which once again will vary from one individual to the next, but which nevertheless instils in everyone the sense that something is missing. From the moment this process has been initiated one of two things will happen: either the person concerned will stay with that mood and do everything possible to find that missing something; or alternatively, the person concerned will begin to indulge more and more in all manner of escapisms in order to alleviate the dull feeling of emptiness that comes from having sensed that something is missing.

If we start to look for what is missing we automatically become more aware of everything than ever before and, as a result, even if we are not on the Warrior's Path, life begins to take on a different meaning, which gradually but surely leads one into a greater understanding of the possibilities of what we should be doing with our *time*. From this moment on the apprentice suddenly begins to grasp the deeper implications inherent within one of the very first aphorisms given to every apprentice as soon as his or her training is started.

> *TIME IS THE ESSENCE OF IMPECCABILITY; IT IS ONLY THE SENSE OF MORTALITY WHICH ENGENDERS IN MAN THE DESIRE TO ACT IMPECCABLY.*

We see therefore that time works in two ways; firstly, it brings us to the point of realising that we cannot afford to fritter away our lives upon earth; and then, once this realisation has been made, we begin to sense that there is a purpose to our lives and that all of us do indeed have *something* specific to accomplish. However, whether we ever become aware of it or not, whenever we become aware of the importance of time we come into contact with universal emotion, which brings about within us an indescribable *mood*. Then, because of that mood, we begin to seek out our fate and then to fulfil that fate. In doing so we are responding to universal *intent*, in that we are starting to cooperate intelligently with our dreamers, and thus we also begin to learn what it is to set our own *intent* in the fulfilment of destiny. Yet, in the final analysis, realise that all of this is both as simple and as profound as the following aphorism.

> *WHEN THE TIME COMES, YOU MUST HAVE SUFFICIENT PERSONAL POWER TO UNFOLD THE WINGS OF PERCEPTION TO TOUCH BOTH THE NAGAL AND THE TONAL, SO THAT YOU MAY KNOW THE MEANING OF ETERNITY. IN THAT FLIGHT THROUGH TIME YOU WILL GRASP THE MEANING OF INTENT, AND THEN TOO WILL YOU KNOW THE PURPOSE OF ALL.*

As is clear from the aphorism above, we have in this chapter only touched ever so briefly upon a very broad overview of time, but for the purposes of this book the information imparted is quite enough for the moment. As I warned at the beginning of this chapter, MEST is a truly vast subject, and until such *time* as the reader has a better grasp of the teachings as a whole there is very little point in expounding upon it any further. In Christian terminology, that *time* can only *come to pass* – can only *come into existence* – once the reader realises that the crux of any battle, irrespective of how big or small it may be, is *the battle to compress time*. To this effect, the reader has already been given the only thing he or she will ever need in order to compress time, namely, the warrior's shield.

If every challenge is seen as a battle for one's life, and if every battle is approached from the angle of time, then we instinctively reach for the warrior's shield. In having that shield, in being *wide awake, fearful, respectful,* and *fully assured*, what more could possibly be needed? All that is really required is action. Therefore in compressing time the warrior takes his stance in the North, the place of action, and by working within the context of the second postulate of stalking, remembers that it is his duty to solve the mystery, irrespective of whether this is the mystery of time or the mystery of his beingness. As a result the warrior strives for sobriety within the dimension of time, and in this respect knows that the sobriety he seeks can only be acquired by compressing time in every possible respect.

If you are still waiting, what are you waiting for? You already have your shield, and *time* is passing you by. The only choice you have to make is whether you are going to continue wasting time, or whether you are going to pick up the warrior's shield and start upon your journey right now. You can either put this book down now and waste some more time, or you can put this book down and start living the impeccable life of the warrior immediately. The choice is yours, but remember that *time* is not yours. You may choose to wait, but *time* will not wait for you.

CHAPTER NINE

THE FOLLY OF IDENTITY

A STALKER NEVER REVEALS HIS IDENTITY, NOT EVEN TO HIMSELF.

In considering the seventh aspect of the stalker's rule we come across what, to the majority of apprentices, is possibly one of the most intriguing concepts upon the Warrior's Path, namely, that the *stalker has many faces*. In the light of what is entailed in the art of stalking this fact should hardly be surprising, and yet, in spite of what appears to be the obvious, this concept at first always inspires in every apprentice a strong sense of awe mixed with no small amount of trepidation and suspicion. Consequently apprentices themselves quite unwittingly play right into the hands of the stalker by giving to the stalker many of his or her faces.

The different faces of a stalker are not so much in the nature of different masks worn by the stalker, but are instead the many different ways in which others tend to look upon him or her. As a result, the stalker, of course, laughs and laughs at the folly of it all, for at the end of the day he or she has done "nothing" except to enjoy the effects of someone else's perception. In this respect stalkers are truly the most co-operative people in the whole world, for they will never disagree to play any game by your rules. A game is after all only a game, and all games are fun, even those that make us cry. Therefore no stalker will ever miss out on the opportunity to have some fun, for even if the tears do come, those tears do not have to be tears of self-pity and misery, but can be tears of rejoicing in the poignancy of life.

To the stalker the whole of life is a game – a game which has the most enormous potential for producing fun, provided, of course, that we handle it with the utmost impeccability. Therefore when the stalker laughs and jokes it is never in the sense of being flippant or disrespectful but, on the contrary, only in the sense of rejoicing in the wondrous gift of life. Always being able to see the innate beauty in everything around him, including his challenges, the stalker can only possibly take his tears, or those of anyone else, seriously, if and when he chooses to see the beauty in them. Yet in being able to see the beauty inherent in tears, the stalker's love of life will always surface in such a way that raucous laughter can quite suddenly interrupt even the most heartfelt tears.

Such is the stalker's sense of fun, and within that sense of fun lies both his art and a *power* which, quite frankly, makes most people feel enormously ill at ease. It is after all not considered normal to laugh at someone's funeral, and it is considered terribly disrespectful to howl with laughter amidst the seriousness of a church sermon. To the stalker, life is an endless adventure of fun, and come hell or high water, laughter or tears, there is always in his or her life so much living to do that there is never much time for feeling miserable or morose, depressed or crestfallen. If such a moment happens, as it does to all people, then it is acknowledged for what it is, and then immediately scrutinised as to its potential for fun, for such is the predilection of the stalker.

Yet, realise that to be able to see and to approach life in this way is not an art that can be acquired overnight, nor is it easily acquired. Like with anything else, be it as a virtuoso on the violin, on the tennis court, or on the gymnastics floor, a great deal of blood, sweat and tears go into the making of the master stalker. Not only do all of the teachings have to be lived impeccably, but most especially does the stalker have to erase his or her personal history with the most meticulous care. It is simply not possible to master the advanced teachings on stalking until after every iota of personal history has been erased, for the true art of the stalker does not lie in being able to pull the wool over the eyes of others, but instead lies in the fact that the stalker has no specific identity to defend or to protect. Having no specific identity, the master stalker is not afraid to play the fool, and in not being frightened of being a fool, the stalker can fool anybody with the greatest of ease.

However, this brings us to what is the very crux of *the mists of Dragon Lore*; namely, that by having no specific identity, not even to him or herself, the master stalker is in reality a *master of controlled folly*. This is a concept we touched upon briefly in Chapter Two, and in that chapter it was also pointed out that controlling our folly is essentially the act of intelligent co-operation. However, the time has come for us now to take a much closer look at this concept, for as we have already learned, controlling folly implies that we take control of the contents of that dream we call life.

So what does it really mean when it is stated that *a stalker has many faces*? To get to grips with this concept it is necessary to remember that we are all caught in a dream and that within the context of that dream everything is sheer folly. It is only once we have woken up in the dream that we can begin to control our folly or, in other words, take control of the contents of the dream by co-operating intelligently with our dreamers.

Until we do wake up in the dream all of us will have some sense of identity, but since that identity will be based upon, firstly, believing the dream to be the only reality there is; and secondly, upon our social conditioning, that identity too will be utter folly. Furthermore, as we know from the fourth postulate of stalking, the real crux of the mystery of life is the mystery of beingness, and therefore any sense of identity we may have can only be the product of personal history. How can we possibly know who and what we are if we are a mystery even to ourselves? Consequently, to the true warrior any form of identity is purely part and parcel of our folly.

In terms of warriorship, the only identity worth cultivating is the *totality of the self*. Yet, as we have already learned earlier, there is only one life, one awareness and therefore in the final analysis also only one self, for although we are all individual units of the one life, at the level of the true self there is only *at-one-ment*.

This is a most abstract point to try and verbalise, but it will help greatly to think of it in the following way.

Realise that it is only upon the physical plane that there is a sense of individuality in terms of separateness. At the level of the dreamer there is only group-consciousness, and therefore all sense of individuality at that level is based entirely upon intelligent co-operation. In other words, at the level of the dreamer the sense of individuality exists only in terms of *relationship*, and as such the sense of *self* is purely a matter of *reflection*. This of course, is the very basis of the mirror concept, for it is simply not possible to see yourself without a mirror, and consequently the group-consciousness of the dreamers is not a matter of ethics or of morality, but is instead a necessity based upon the universal law of Light and Reflection.

However, at the level of the nagal, that is, the spirit of man, there is absolutely no sense of separateness nor, for that matter, of group-consciousness, for even group-consciousness still has about it the implications of separativeness. The only way in which I can express the sense of individuality at this level is to liken it to what might be termed the *group-mind*. Anyone who has ever experienced the effects of the group-mind will know exactly what I am referring to. It is quite uncanny how sometimes a whole mob of people can think and act like a single person, and yet if any one of those individuals are questioned afterwards, he or she will maintain that although a sense of complete one-ness had taken over, there was still somehow a sense of individuality within that single-mindedness. Although this analogy is not completely accurate with respect to the spirit of man, as an approximation it nonetheless does serve to demonstrate the deeper implications of the term "the totality of the self".

In this regard it is extremely important to realise that man is so conditioned into thinking of himself in terms of separativeness that he has great difficulty in trying to imagine an identity based upon *collective consciousness*, as opposed to that type of awareness that brings forth the sense of separativeness. As a result, average men and women cannot as yet conceive of the *self* in terms of the *whole*, or the *totality*. And yet, this is exactly what the term "the totality of the self" does imply. Think of it in the following way.

There is only that *one-ness* termed the spirit of man, the nagal, manifesting as millions upon millions of individual units. At first, the manifestation of this *one-ness* does not know itself (themselves) to be a whole, and as a result, each unit sees itself in isolation to all other units. Consequently, each unit develops an individual identity based upon the sense of separativeness, so that from the angle of the manifestation of the *one-ness*, (not the *one-ness* itself), there is no sense of unified purpose, but only apparent chaos. But then, in the fullness of time, one unit after the other begins to realise that there is only one true purpose which is common to all, and that that purpose is the purpose of the *one-ness*. Eventually, once all units are responding to that one purpose, it can rightfully be said that the manifestation of the *one-ness* now knows itself (themselves) to be *at-one* with that *one-ness* we term man or, more precisely, the spirit of man.

In other words, from our human angle, the manifestation of the *one-ness* is at first so unaware that it does not know that all of its parts belong together to form one whole. This is analogous to someone not knowing that his limbs, or his organs, belong to him. But as the evolution of awareness proceeds, the manifestation of the *one-ness* gradually becomes aware of the fact that its arms and legs, as well as its organs, do actually belong to it as one coherent whole, forming the *totality of the self*. However, this gradual unfoldment of awareness within the manifestation of the *one-ness* can obviously only take place as one unit after the other becomes aware of the *totality of the self*.

Now, the point to be grasped in all of this is that in striving to achieve that identity termed the *totality of the self*, all sense of separativeness must give way to a sense of complete *inclusiveness*, for without that inclusiveness there can be no at-one-ment. It therefore stands to reason that in striving to cultivate the *totality of the self* the warrior must open wide his or her heart, and the only way in which this can be done is by *living* the path with a heart.

It is important to know that the implications inherent within *living* the path with a heart are so vast that, to the best of my knowledge, no nagal has ever attempted to verbalise this section of the teachings. In the past, rather than try to verbalise that which cannot be verbalised, nagals simply gave apprentices certain tasks designed to lead them into an understanding of what it is to *live* the path with a heart. At face value such tasks always appear to be rather non-sensical, and at best extra-ordinarily mundane, but if properly designed, carefully moni-tored by the nagal, and impeccably executed by the apprentice, they inevitably lead the apprentice into a level of awareness he or she would otherwise never have been able to achieve. However, all such tasks must be tailored to suit the personal needs and temperament of the apprentice, and to this end the nagal will normally draw upon the apprentice's experiences within daily life to design the needed task. From the angle of the reader, any such tasks given here would be utterly useless, and since the readers of this book would not be reading this book if they are already working with a nagal, I have no option other than to attempt what has hitherto been the impossible. Therefore let us just jump straight into the deep end by using the following aphorism as our point of departure.

> THERE COMES A POINT IN THE LIFE OF THE WARRIOR WHEN IT IS
> NO LONGER ENOUGH MERELY TO TREAD THE WARRIOR'S PATH.
> WHEN THAT MOMENT COMES, THE WARRIOR KNOWS WITHOUT A
> DOUBT THAT THE WARRIOR'S PATH, LIKE ALL PATHS, LEADS
> ABSOLUTELY NOWHERE, AND THAT THE ONLY ADVANTAGE IN
> TREADING THIS MOST DIFFICULT OF PATHS IS THAT IT IS FOR HIM
> A PATH WITH A HEART, IN THAT IT TEACHES HIM THE MEANING
> OF INCLUSIVENESS.

Time and time again a nagal will remind his apprentices that the Warrior's Path leads nowhere, and that to be a warrior is not a goal. Time and time again the nagal will admonish his apprentices to engage fully in the journey, and to forget about all goals. But human nature is such that apprentices will nod their heads "wisely", agreeing fully with the wisdom of those words, and will then promptly proceed in pursuing their desired goal! As if they have not even heard the nagal's guidance the apprentices will ask questions like: "What must I do to make my life work for me?" "What should I do about my relationship?" "Should I take this new job offer?" "Should I buy this car?" "Should I buy this house?" "What do you think?" "What do you feel?" "What do you advise?" And so the questions go on and on, most of them utterly invalid and completely off the point.

Those who become wise are not those who are forever gathering information, but those who have worked out how to ask the *right* questions. In this respect, realise that the majority of people do not ask questions in the sense of wanting to know. Many people ask questions merely to jabber away like so many idiots. To such people questions are not really questions, but just an interesting way of talking. Many other people ask questions simply so that they can prove their own worth by disagreeing with any answer given. To some others, unanswered questions are their excuse for unimpeccable behaviour, and therefore to the likes of these honest answers are total taboo. But by far the greater majority of people ask questions purely from a sense of not wanting to take responsibility for their own actions and for their own lives. Very few people indeed ever ask what might be termed the *right* questions.

To ask the right question means that you take responsibility for yourself, for your own knowledge or lack thereof, for your own challenges and, above all, for your own life. Any nagal who is dedicated to the Path of Freedom will refuse point blank to take responsibility for the lives of any of his apprentices. A nagal will only step in, or take over as it were, if it is clear to him that the apprentice is about to walk into a trap because of a genuine lack of knowledge, but if the nagal knows that the apprentice does have the required knowledge he will simply step back and wait for that apprentice to shoot him or herself in the foot. The way in which I personally express this fact to my own apprentices is by saying to the apprentice concerned, "I know that you know, and I know that you know that I know. So why are you asking me?"

Therefore when an apprentice asks me what he must do to make his life work for him I do not volunteer any guidance at all, but instead ask him to tell me what he is doing, for it stands to reason that the only reason why his life is not working is because he is doing something wrong. Once the apprentice starts to explain what he is doing, the only thing that is really required of me is to guide the apprentice towards achieving clarity on all grey areas. I will normally do this by simply asking the apprentice a series of questions until the apprentice himself comes up with the right answer. If, on the other hand, I can see that the apprentice is talking himself into clarity, then I will merely listen and confirm to the apprentice that he is correct in his analysis of the situation. By handling the apprentice in this way, he quickly enough begins to learn to ask the right kind of question, which in the final analysis, means that he asks the question in such a way that he *himself* can answer it.

I cannot stress strongly enough how very important it is that the apprentice should learn to ask the right questions, for without that ability the apprentice never learns to think for him or herself, never learns to achieve sobriety, never learns to take responsibility for his or her own knowledge, never learns to believe in him or herself, never gains self-respect or self-confidence and, in short, simply becomes a dependant who has absolutely no freedom whatsoever. In this respect I will very often be utterly ruthless with an apprentice who is deliberately trying to act dumb, or stupid. Stupid questions deserve stupid answers, and if an apprentice wants to play at being stupid I do not hesitate to reflect that stupidity back at the apprentice. If I can see that the apprentice already knows why his life is not working, but he asks me anyway, I will give some ridiculous answer to the effect of, "I think you should have some more sex," or "try being vegetarian," or "buy a new car".

Nevertheless, even though apprentices do at times act dumb in an attempt to cover for their lack of action, learning to ask the right question can be tricky when one has always been conditioned into being as ignorant and dumb as everyone else. Yet, learning to ask the right question is not really difficult, provided that one bears in mind that what makes a question right is that one must be able to answer it for oneself, or alternatively, one must be able to ascertain beyond all doubt that one is for the moment incapable of answering it for oneself. So as to grasp this fully, let us look at the questions mentioned earlier.

The first of these questions, and one which nearly always comes up in one way or another, is "What must I do to make my life work for me?" To make this a valid question, or a *right* question, it would be much better to rephrase it in terms of, "What am I *doing* that keeps me from being happy and successful?" The moment the question is phrased in this way, it is immediately apparent that the question is a question to oneself, for no-one other than you yourself can better judge and assess *what* you are doing.

Therefore the wise apprentice will not choose to waste his time with the nagal by expecting the nagal to point out to him what he is perfectly capable of doing for himself, but will instead immediately set about doing a full appraisal of his life at present. This is where a journal is so very invaluable, for by sitting down to write such an appraisal, or simply by making a list of *doings*, one can achieve an enormous amount of clarity that is normally not possible amidst all the mental and emotional chaos arising out of endless internal dialogue.

Once such an appraisal has been completed, the apprentice finds that new questions arise from that appraisal. For example, the apprentice might notice that he tends to be very aloof in his interactions with other people, but if he asks himself why he is aloof he is likely to draw a blank. Instead, he should ask himself in what way is he aloof, and again by listing all the many different ways in which his aloofness tends to manifest, he will achieve huge clarity on his own.

If this procedure of finding the right questions to ask himself is kept up, and is done on a regular basis, the apprentice will find that his list of questions for the nagal will be fairly short and, even more importantly, extremely concise and to the point. By being absolutely clear on what it is he is wanting in terms of guidance the apprentice will not only be very open to the nagal's guidance, but he will also have no difficulty in understanding that guidance. This is what is really implied by the statement that *the apprentice must call forth the teachings.*

Having considered the above question in depth, we do not

need to belabour the others, for it will be quite enough if we simply look at how to rephrase these questions, so as to turn them into valid questions. How then should we rephrase the question, "What should I do about my relationship?" Just by looking at this question it is quite clear that it would never have been asked in the first place if the two people concerned did have a meaningful relationship. Therefore the real question is, "Do I *have* a relationship with 'whoever', and for that matter, do I even know *what* a relationship really is?"

Likewise, look at the next question, "Should I take this new job offer?" Why would the person ask this question if they were happy with their current employment? Clearly the question should be, "What is this new job *offering* me over and above what I already have?" Now look at, "Should I buy this car?" Because cars are expensive, no person in his right mind would consider buying another car if he has no need to buy a car. Therefore the operative question is, "Do I *need* to buy a car at all and, if so, will this car fulfil my *needs*?"

Consider the question, "Should I buy this house?" If you were asked this question, what would be your answer? My own response to such a question would be, "What are you actually asking me?" "Are you asking me if *you* like the house? Or are you asking me if *I* like the house?" "Are you asking me if *you* can *afford* to buy the house? If so, then *how* in hell's name am I supposed to know if you can afford to buy this house or not, when I am neither your accountant, nor your banker?"

"What do you think?" "What do you feel?" "What do you advise?" These are three questions which are frequently asked, and which in themselves are good valid questions, provided that they are asked with the correct motive. In this respect, realise that people, generally speaking, love to be told what to do, but only in the sense that if the guidance given does not work out the way they want it to work out, then they can stone the one who gave the guidance. If we do ask any one of these three questions, then it should only be in the sense of seeking confirmation for something we already know, or alternatively, in the sense of seeking another perspective which we may have overlooked. In this regard, great care must be taken not to ask for someone else's opinion as a result of not trusting one's own knowledge, for to do so is to undermine one's self-respect and self-confidence. There is essentially nothing wrong in asking for someone else's opinion, provided that we also acknowledge our own knowledge with respect to that particular issue. This does not mean that we must dogmatically adhere to only our own view of the world, but it does mean that in asking for another person's point of view we should compare the guidance given with our own knowledge, for by doing so, we will invariably come up with a completely different perspective to the one we had before.

In all of this, realise that what causes apprentices to blunder into asking the wrong questions is the fact that they are *goal* orientated, instead of contenting themselves with taking every step impeccably. As a result, impatience takes over, the journal goes flying against the wall, the chair is kicked over with a vengeance, the bruised foot is nursed angrily and the household pet gets the verbal abuse that was meant for the nagal. Yet, the only one to blame is the apprentice.

Very few people ever pause to consider that their entire life is based upon their own invalid questions and their unimpeccable motives for asking those questions. Therefore instead of using every situation in their lives to gain knowledge and *power*, people *spend* their lives playing the blame game, and in being thoroughly determined to be more dumb than anyone else. Ignorance may be considered to be blissful by some, but is it not ironic that this very ignorance which is considered to be so blissful should also be the basis for the blame game? Therefore it is always a matter of, "Can't you see that I am struggling? Why don't you help me?" "What is the matter with you? Can't you understand plain English?" "Why do you look at me like that? What have I done wrong?" Whilst such an attitude of ignorance is in force it can never be a matter of, "What is the *gift of power* for me in having to do this on my own?" "If I am not being understood, am I myself clear on what I am trying to express?" "What behaviour of mine is causing that person to look at me so accusingly?"

In a similar fashion apprentices trip themselves up constantly in their endeavour to reach a goal that exists only in their own minds. Determined to become warriors, they continuously frustrate themselves by asking, "Why am I not getting it right?" Every time an apprentice asks himself that question, he only succeeds in confirming to himself that he must be dumb, unworthy and incapable. But, in order to *know* that he is intelligent instead of dumb, to *feel* worthy instead of unworthy, and to *believe* that he is capable instead of incapable, the only thing the apprentice has to do is to ask himself, "What am I *learning* right now?" This is such a simple *shifting of the focus*, an act which is so extraordinarily powerful and empowering, that it should be for any apprentice the easiest part of his or her training. Yet, in practice, every apprentice struggles endlessly to *shift the focus* in this way, and only because it looks too simple to be taken seriously. Being caught up in wanting *to be right*, or in wanting to *do it right*, such apprentices continuously invalidate their own learning in the moment, and consequently never do materialise their idea of what it is to be a warrior.

Time and time again a nagal will ask apprentices what it is they have learned, and whether they have given themselves credit for having accomplished that much, but every time this is done the apprentice concerned will look at the nagal as if he is mad. However, the bottom line in all such behaviour is the fact that in the apprentice's mind he has not yet reached his goal, and therefore how can anything he is doing right now possibly be of any value at all? How can cleaning the potatoes impeccably lead to a knowledge of the Sorcerer's World, and how can an apparent failure be an act of true learning?

The true warrior simply looks at the folly of all such behaviour, recalls his own struggle in learning to *shift the focus*, and quietly goes on peeling the potatoes. Such a warrior knows full well from personal experience that it is only once the apprentice has exhausted himself in striving to reach the goal, that it will finally dawn on him that all that is really required is to start trying to *live* like a warrior, instead of trying to *become* a warrior. And yet, paradoxically, it is exactly here that lies the greatest difficulty encountered upon the Warrior's Path. As mentioned in *Return of the Warriors*, the real difficulty of the Warrior's Path does not lie in its academic complexity, but in its utter simplicity. Although there is more than enough upon the Warrior's Path that can befuddle even the sharpest intellect, any academic difficulty encountered exists only because the rational mind is totally goal orientated and, as a result, is forever striving towards *linear advancement* born of *separativeness*, at the cost of *circular expansion* born of *inclusiveness*.

In striving for *linear advancement* apprentices are for ever at odds with everything and everybody around them, for the simple reason that they are still separative in their thinking and always feel that they should be somewhere else, with someone else, doing something else. Hardly ever do they see the *power* in the moment and, therefore, in their way of thinking, they cannot be in the right place, with the right person and engaged in the right occupation. To such apprentices the *present* is of no consequence, and in their effort to *escape* what is happening right here and now they ask questions like, "Why is this happening to me?" The answer is, of course, quite simple. What is happening here and now is your ticket to freedom and your passage to *power*, but if you are going to benefit from this *gift of power*, then you must claim it, instead of complaining about it.

To claim one's *gift of power* means that one must first of all recognise it as being a gift; and secondly, acknowledge that it is ours for the taking. To have such clarity entails not only *living in the moment*, but also requires the *willingness* to be inclusive, rather than being *exclusive*. In other words, instead of trying to avoid, or to escape what is happening in one's life, by being exclusive, one must be inclusive so as to learn as much as possible from every situation that occurs, for only in this way is it really possible to move beyond the need for such experiences. Apropos this, realise that it stands to reason that once we have gained the necessary knowledge or *power* inherent within any situation in one's life, then there is no need to keep on experiencing the same old thing.

Although this appears to be very logical, it is surprising how long people generally spend in trying to duck and dive their challenges, even if they know all the above to be true. The reason for this in most cases is not so much an unwillingness to learn, but rather an unwillingness to be inclusive – a concept with which some apprentices struggle desperately for an awfully long time, and only because they do not have sufficient sobriety. Lacking in sobriety, such an apprentice cannot discriminate between doing something because of *wanting to*, as opposed to doing it simply because it is for him *a path with a heart*.

> WANTING TO DO SOMETHING IMPLIES HAVING A MOTIVE, AND PROVIDED SUCH A MOTIVE IS PURE, THE ACTION WILL BE GOOD. BUT REALISE THAT ANY MOTIVE IS MERELY A SUBSTITUTE FOR THE HEART. ANY ACT ARISING FROM THE HEART IS UNCONDITIONAL, AND THEREFORE DOES NOT REQUIRE MOTIVE.

All apprentices come to the Warrior's Path with a motive, for such motives form part of one's baggage. Some of these motives are quite pure, whilst some others can be quite nightmarish! Nonetheless, *power* does not discriminate against an apprentice on the grounds of impure motive. Whatever our motives to start with may be, we can all work towards realising our full potential and claiming our *power* on the Warrior's Path. However, for those apprentices who wish to pursue the Path of Freedom, there comes a moment in their training when *power* will challenge them to make the choice between the Path of High Adventure and the Path of Freedom. If the apprentice concerned initially came to the Warrior's Path with the pure motive of wanting to achieve freedom, then such an apprentice will have no difficulty at all in making those choices which automatically place him or her firmly upon the Path of Freedom. If, on the other hand, an apprentice came to the Warrior's Path with an impure motive, and has in the meantime not been able to relinquish that motive, such an apprentice will find him or herself having to face a very grave crisis indeed – a crisis that will end either in release, or alternatively in the termination of his or her apprenticeship.

None of us can ever achieve our freedom simply by wanting to be free. As the aphorism above points out so beautifully, *wanting* anything implies motive, and as paradoxical as it may appear at first glance, any motive, irrespective of how pure it may be, is a handicap. How can we be free if we are handicapped in any way? True freedom must be *unconditional*, otherwise it is not really freedom. But any motive is *conditional*, and it is for this reason that apprentices are taught from day one that their decision to tread the Warrior's Path must ultimately be free from both fear and ambition, for in the final analysis, it is never difficult to see that all motive is based upon either some sort of fear, or some sort of ambition. In this respect it is important to realise that, if we truly look for it, even within the purest of pure motives we can always find some element of either fear or ambition.

Therefore, in order to achieve freedom, it is not good enough simply to have pure motives. To achieve freedom means that we must have no motives at all, and here lies the true difference between the Path of High Adventure and the Path of Freedom. Those of our brothers who have strayed onto the Path of High Adventure all started off with pure motive, but through never having had the ability or the willingness to relinquish those motives, they have instead relinquished their freedom.

To relinquish motive is, on the one hand, exceedingly difficult to do, and on the other hand, simplicity itself. The secret lies in having sufficient sobriety to know the difference between *treading* the Warrior's Path because of motive, as opposed to just *living* the Warrior's Path because it is for us a path with a heart. When we tread the Warrior's Path because of motive that motive will keep us firmly fixed on the *goal* of warriorship, in such a way that the *goal* is always more important than the *journey*, and consequently we are forced into a state of awareness which is separative and exclusive, because nothing but the goal is important.

For such an apprentice *the end always justifies the means* and, as a result, that apprentice will never learn to open his or her heart. Being fixed upon achieving the goal, such an apprentice begins to draw more and more upon his or her own inherent awareness, which by nature is linear. As a result, evolving awareness becomes progressively less important to that apprentice as he or she begins to gain strength within the context of inherent awareness, and as the momentum of inherent awareness starts to take over, that apprentice will become ever more driven by the compelling force of linear advancement. Technically speaking, such an apprentice, irrespective of gender, is slowly but surely elevating *masculinity* above *femininity*, for it must not be forgotten that inherent awareness is masculine in relation to evolving awareness. In other words, in such an apprentice there is no intelligent co-operation between male and female, between inherent awareness and evolving awareness, but instead the masculinity in that apprentice is killing off his or her own femininity.

From *Cry of the Eagle* it will be remembered that it is the force of evolving awareness that curves inherent awareness back upon itself to bring about the element of inclusiveness, which is not only an expression of universal *intent* and therefore also the manifestation of the nagal's purpose, but it is also an expression of what the Christian scriptures refer to as the *Christ principle*, and what Toltecs refer to as the *heart*. From this it stands to reason that the true purpose of the nagal is not to annihilate the female, but to bring about an intelligent co-operation between male and female, between inherent awareness and evolving awareness, so that the evolution of *total awareness* can proceed within the context of inclusiveness, for only in this way can the unknown become incorporated within the known so that the *totality of the self* can be achieved.

However, in order for there to be inclusiveness the apprentice cannot afford to remain goal orientated. Sooner or later the goal must be surrendered in favour of the journey, and the only way in which this can be done is for the apprentice to learn to bring about within him or herself intelligent co-operation between inherent awareness and evolving awareness; between male and female. Only once the apprentice is content to *remain* exactly where he or she is in endeavouring to *assimilate* fully *everything* that is taking place right here and right now, can the force of inclusiveness bring about *liberation through intent*, by *circular expansion*. Therefore rather than ducking and diving the *gifts of power* that our challenges bring us, which is what happens when the apprentice is set upon linear advancement, the apprentice must instead face those challenges fully, *assimilate* all *gifts of power*, and then through the force of *inclusiveness* he or she quite literally *outgrows* those challenges through *circular expansion*. If this is done, then all motives automatically fall away, for motives can only have existence where there is a goal.

In order to grasp all of this clearly, realise that to strive for freedom is already in itself a goal, and this in turn presupposes motive. In other words, to start with every apprentice will have a motive of sorts, but even if that motive is only to achieve freedom, it still remains a motive, and therefore even those apprentices with pure motive will still be goal orientated. This state of affairs can only change once the apprentice comes to see the folly in having motives and in being goal orientated. However, in order to have such sobriety, the apprentice must be brought to a point at which he or she can clearly see the difference between *treading* the Warrior's Path, irrespective of how impeccably this is done, and *living* the path with a heart.

To begin with no apprentice ever has sufficient sobriety to be able to make this differentiation, and therefore everyone starts his or her training *treading* the Warrior's Path with a truly admirable zeal and a determination which can sometimes be rather grim, to say the least. However, sooner or later every apprentice begins to tire from the endless struggle to reach a goal which is always receding with every step taken. This is very much like the misguided soul in the old stories, who tries to follow a will o' the wisp, and it is always at this point, once the apprentice is nearing the point of exhaustion, that he or she will begin to wonder if the Toltec teachings are not perhaps just a myth. This is the crisis point which was mentioned earlier, and which every apprentice has to face sooner or later.

When this crisis point is reached, and provided that the apprentice has enough sobriety to know for a fact that he cannot return to his old way of life, such an apprentice becomes caught up in the myth whether he likes it or not. Yet, realise that it is exactly as a result of having started to look upon the teachings as being perhaps nothing more than a myth that the apprentice is forced into letting go of all sense of achievement. In no longer *expecting* that he is ever going to get anywhere at all, and therefore also no longer expecting any kind of a reward, the apprentice has finally reached the *outer fringes of power*. Standing quite literally on the threshold of a brand new life, such an apprentice will do either one of two things. Either he will yield to the lack of sobriety and give up in one way or another, in which case, if he is being trained by a nagal who is dedicated to the Path of Freedom, that apprentice will have his apprenticeship terminated. Or alternatively, the apprentice comes to the realisation that because he is not likely to be going anywhere at all, he might just as well try, to the best of his ability, to live the path with a heart for whatever it may be worth. In that moment, although the apprentice will only become aware of it in retrospect, and only much further down the line, he not only forfeits his motive for having come to the Warrior's Path, but, paradoxically, is also rewarded with his freedom!

Once the apprentice has come to this point in his or her training there is nothing that will any longer hold the apprentice back in his or her progress. Making every effort to live the impeccable life of a warrior, the apprentice becomes so completely absorbed in constantly and diligently *practising* the teachings, that in time the *practising* becomes second nature, and therefore instead of *trying* to live like a warrior, the apprentice just simply starts to *live* like a warrior without even noticing it. In other words, what started off as a conscious *not-doing* becomes an unconscious *reality*, and in no longer having any expectations, or motive, the apprentice does the only thing he can – he starts to open up to the world around him.

Without realising it, the apprentice has started to open his heart and to bring into being the force of *inclusiveness* and, by doing so, unconsciously becomes the myth – becomes the warrior! Yet the apprentice himself is still wholly unaware of the transformation, and it is only as *power* starts to come to him unbidden that it will suddenly dawn on him that his apprenticeship is over, that he is finally a warrior, and that *power* is at his command.

When this moment arrives in the life of the apprentice he or she is invariably overcome by the most indescribably intense feeling of utter humility – a humility which can only be expressed by opening the heart even further and wider than ever before. It is then that the warrior steps back and lowers his or her head, for in that moment there comes the realisation that none of our endeavours as human beings can ever bring us one step closer to warriorship, but only by having come to *accept* the limitations of our humanness do we find the key to warriorship, namely, the force of *inclusiveness*. There is nothing more devastatingly humbling than that realisation, and in that moment every warrior forfeits for ever any desire to strive for anything other than complete freedom – freedom from everything that keeps him or her from throwing wide open even the most secret and previously jealously-guarded recesses of the heart.

Such is the true nature of the Path of Freedom, and such is the nature of *living* the path with a heart. In order to have our freedom we must be brought to the point of giving up our *idea* of what it is to be free, and it is for this reason that no-one can simply, or fraudulently, claim warriorship. It is simply not possible to pretend to be a warrior. To be a warrior is a true *act of the heart*, and implies *living* the path with a heart. It is the easiest thing in the world to love *conditionally*, but to love *unconditionally* is something only a warrior is capable of doing.

In that unconditional love of and for all of life, the warrior meets his or her fellow men squarely in the midst of their folly, and although the warrior does not support the folly, he or she also knows that there is no blame. Now being able to see the madness of the dream for what it really is, the warrior also knows beyond any shadow of a doubt that his fellow creatures are all part and parcel of the one dream, the one folly, and the one life. As a result, the warrior no longer feels the need to force his will upon others in an effort to elevate himself above them, but instead sets himself to the task of world transformation by continuously striving to uplift himself so that those around him too may be uplifted.

In his efforts to move beyond the confines of that madness demarcating the boundaries of the dream, the warrior gradually but surely *includes* more and more of this madness within himself, and the more madness he includes within himself, the more madness he transforms into *beauty*, *peace* and, ultimately, *harmony*. In layman's terms, the warrior, in his or her *inclusiveness*, is becoming *everything to everyone* and, as a result, no longer has an identity based upon separativeness, but acquires instead the beginnings of what in time will become that state of awareness, that identity, termed the *totality of the self*. But in no longer having a fixed identity and in becoming everything to everyone, the warrior also acquires a great many different faces.

The true warrior quite literally has a face for everyone and for every occasion, for no two people or two occasions are alike, but because all people and all occurrences in the life of the warrior are of equal importance, they each deserve whatever is demanded by their needs. Therefore the different faces of the warrior are not masks behind which he or she hides, but are instead an expression of his or her innermost predilection for humility and unconditional love.

Yet, because of the folly of mankind, those different faces will again and again bring forth the most precious reactions from the warrior's fellow men – reactions that will cause the warrior to burst out in heartfelt laughter. However, such laughter is never at the cost of the other person, but is simply the result of the warrior's unconditional love for all of life. In this respect, remember that the warrior cried so many tears in his own efforts at becoming a warrior, that eventually those spent tears created an emptiness within the warrior, an emptiness of motive, an emptiness of expectation – an emptiness that became filled with the force of *inclusiveness*, with the force of unconditional love. Such a warrior can afford to laugh, for in his or her laughter there is no malice, no ill intent; only camaraderie in the folly of the dream. But in now being able to see the folly of it all, the warrior can also see the folly of having an identity to protect and to defend. Consequently, to the warrior, there is no point in having any form of identity and, as a result, he or she continues to become ever more inclusive in pursuit of the *totality of the self*, not because it is a motive for progress, but simply because it has so much heart that it is the best fun in the whole wide world.

When one is having so much fun, come hell or high water, come laughter or tears, who cares about a destination, a goal? Right here and right now is more than enough fun; besides which, it is after all the journey that is the fun part, for any goal, once reached, always brings a disappointment in one way or another. However, to the warrior, who knows the folly of a fixed identity, the greatest mystery of all is the mystery of his own beingness which, naturally, plunges him straight back into the four postulates of stalking again and again. Thus, in having no other recourse but constantly to stalk his perception of himself, the true warrior finds himself caught in a never-ending game. What fun it is to play the game of life over and over, each time to be left breathless with the sheer joy of being able to witness the wonder of it all!

THE WARRIOR IS A MAN WHO HAS LEARNED TO LOVE LIFE AND ALL THE MANY RICHNESSES IT BRINGS HIM – MOST OF ALL THE PATH WHERE HE WALKS. THERE IS FOR THE WARRIOR NO GREATER JOY THAN TO WALK A PATH WITH A HEART. ON THIS PATH HE WALKS, THRILLED BY THE WONDER OF IT ALL, AND IN HIS JOY HE GIVES THANKS IN HIS HEART FOR THIS MARVELLOUS PRIVILEGE BY EMBRACING EVERYTHING HE ENCOUNTERS WITH LOVE AND GRATITUDE.

PART THREE

THE WORLD OF SORCERERS

THE WORLD OF SORCERERS
(Mixed Media: Tony Butler)

CHAPTER TEN

PREVIEW OF THE FOURTH DIMENSION

THERE IS A MARVELLOUS WORLD BEYOND THIS WORLD, KNOWN AS THE WORLD OF SORCERERS – DAZZLING IN ITS SPLENDOUR AND PERMEATED WITH A POWER THAT IS AWESOME. BUT TO ENTER THAT WORLD IS INSANITY FOR ANYONE WHO DOES NOT HOLD THE KEYS, FOR ALTHOUGH SOUGHT-AFTER BY MANY THROUGHOUT THE AGES, THIS WORLD DERIVES ITS NAME FROM THE FACT THAT ITS MATTER HAS BECOME EMBEDDED WITH THE REMAINS OF WOULD-BE SORCERERS WHO DID NOT HAVE THE REQUIRED KEYS.

For the majority of apprentices there is perhaps nothing within the Toltec tradition that is more fascinating than the concept of alternative worlds. The mere idea that Toltecs are capable of accessing invisible worlds beyond this mundane world is the very stuff fairy tales are made of, and warriors' tales of those worlds never cease to enthral. Yet such tales, although inspiring within apprentices a very real sense of heroic adventure, also more often than not induce a deep sense of melancholy – a sense of adventure sparked off by an intuitive recognition of man's divine nature, and a melancholy that seems to bear an oppressive testimony to humanity's present sense of apathy and powerlessness.

Most apprentices simply cannot conceive that they will ever have enough *personal power* to enable them to perceive alternative worlds, much less to access those worlds. Firmly caught up in the belief that they do not have what it takes to claim their divine heritage, such apprentices will often waste a great deal of precious time in day-dreaming about finding some easy or miraculous way of acquiring *power*. However, in spite of the fact that it is the divine birthright of man to have *power* and to wield the magic of that *power*, there is no easy or miraculous

way in which to acquire *power*. Superstition may have led many
to believe in the existence of so-called supernatural power, and
the use of ritual and hallucinogenic drugs may at times afford the
practitioner a brief glimpse of alternative states of reality, but at
the end of the day there is only one true *power* termed the *One
Power*, but which, far from being supernatural, is as natural as
anything else in nature. Being completely natural, the *One Power*
does not suddenly materialise like lightning amidst a puff of
smoke, but has to be painstakingly cultivated and harnessed like
any other product of nature. Although there are Toltecs who
have so much *power* that they can work miracles, that *power* was
not gained through any so-called supernatural process, but is
instead the product of a great deal of hard work over an untold
number of lifetimes. Anyone who desires it can have *power*,
provided he or she is prepared to work for it, and to pay the price
for having it – a price which very few apprentices ever consider
carefully in their desire to have *power*.

Achieving altered states of perception and accessing alternate
worlds at will are, from a Toltec's perspective, only two of the
minor rewards of having claimed one's *power*. Not enamoured
with the glamour inherent within such acts of *power*, the Warriors of Freedom look upon these acts as nothing more than
useful tools in the acquisition of true freedom. Knowing only
too well from personal experience that *power* for the sake of
having *power* is one of the four natural enemies of mankind,
Toltecs tend to steer cautiously clear of allowing their apprentices to indulge in any fantasy based upon the glamour of show-
manship, and in this respect will often remind apprentices that
the true warrior is not a circus animal, and is therefore also not
expected to behave like one.

Average man's sense of being a victim, his sense of self-pity,
and his sense of self-importance is such that, although the majority of apprentices will hardly ever admit to it, most come to the
Warrior's Path with the hidden motive of wanting to acquire
power over their fellow men. The *One Power* may be an awesome
concept, and casting the *Spear of Destiny* and wielding the *Sword
of Power* may be a glorious ideal, but it is nearly always the rather
naive idea of being able to control others with the practices of

sorcery that really thrills and excites the average apprentice. As a result, it is indeed only ever a handful of apprentices that are honestly prepared to undergo the hardships of learning entailed in the acquisition of true *power*, for by far the greater majority of men and women, although they would dearly love to have the *One Power*, are not prepared to pay the price demanded for that *power*.

Preferring instead the apparent cheapness of, and the easy access to, the practices of sorcery, many men and women throughout the ages have chosen the way of the shaman, believing that this path will liberate them from oppression, and will thereby ensure them success in all areas of their life. And yet, ironically enough, by having made this cheap "purchase", these men and women have ended up relinquishing both the *second* and the *third rings of power*, as well as sacrificing their true free-dom – a price which is utterly exorbitant, and which cannot possibly justify the rather meagre returns offered by the *power* of the shaman. The cost of true knowledge is high indeed, but in comparison to the price paid by the shaman, the cost to those dedicated to the Path of Freedom is negligible, whilst the rewards are so very much more and infinitely greater.

However, realise that any such cost is completely dependent upon where one chooses to place the focus. The price for true *power* is one's life, and depending upon how we view our lives, that cost can be seen as terribly high. Yet for those who have come to the conclusion that their present life holds for them no more value, the cost, although it still remains high, is not nearly as high as for those who are unwilling to sacrifice their present life. It is primarily for this reason that it is stated that *only those who come to the Warrior's Path prepared to die can hope for success*, for to wield the *One Power* requires a total transformation, a transformation that demands the death of the old in the total restructuring of the *island of the tonal*.

Yet it is exactly because the Path of Freedom requires the death of the old that most people find the price too high, even if their old way of life is completely miserable and disempowering. It is only when an apprentice is forced to choose freedom as an act of survival that he or she will be willing to relinquish the only life he or she has ever known. Consequently it is hardly surprising that even to this day there should be so few individuals who can wield the *One Power* effectively, even though thousands upon thousands have tried to acquire *power* the "quick easy" way.

Although I know that many who read these books will still be tempted to try and acquire *power* the "quick" way by attempting to access the World of Sorcerers via the "easy" route, I can do no more than point out and stress the huge dangers involved in dabbling in this kind of activity. The danger in all of this lies in the fact that humanity does not as a rule have any real idea of the potency inherent within the act of perception. Most people simply find it too difficult to believe that the world is quite literally whatever we perceive it to be, and therefore when occasionally they come into contact with a person who experiences the world differently to them, they invariably shun such a person by looking upon him or her as being mad, deranged, or insane. And yet, very few of those who are medically classified as being mentally unstable are truly ill, for although some of these people really are unstable, many are merely the step-children of a society that fears alternate states of perception. The stark truth of the matter is that most people who are genuinely insane are not to be found in the mental clinics and asylums of this world, but are often the very people looked upon by society as being honest, reliable and upstanding citizens, and the very epitome of the deep-thinking leader.

With such a state of affairs it is not at all surprising that so many men and women throughout the world should hold on so dogmatically to their idea of what it is to be sane, sensible and practical. It is even less surprising that so many who seek out *power* should have the utterly demented idea that to sacrifice one's freedom brings *power*. Although such reasoning makes no sense at all, realise that there are, and always have been, thousands upon thousands of people who quite seriously believe that the end justifies the means, and therefore there will always be those who are quite happy to jump at the opportunity to have even just a little *power* at whatever the cost, provided they are promised a quick and easy access to that *power*. The fact that such promises tend hardly ever to materialise into anything at all seems to be quite besides the point.

It is still amazing to see how many otherwise intelligent men and women can be tricked into the practices of sorcery simply because it appears or, more correctly, *promises* to give them *power* over their fellow men. Instead of striving to achieve that type of *power* which will grant them freedom from the dictates of their fellow men, such people desire instead to be able to dominate their fellow men within the context of social conditioning – a phenomenon referred to by Toltecs as *the madness of the dream*.

In the days of Atlantis it was adherence to *the madness of the dream* that caused the split within the ranks of the Toltec brotherhood, and it was ultimately also *the madness* that caused the destruction of that continent. Yet, in spite of the lessons of history, this same madness still persists, and even though humanity has lived through two world wars since the destruction of Atlantis, there are many in the world today who still persist in adhering to the original *madness*. Consequently year after year, generation after generation, and millennium after millennium, thousands try to acquire *power* the "quick" way by attempting to gain access to The World of Sorcerers via the "easy" route, in spite of the fact that most of these wretches end up paying grotesque prices for their insane attempts.

From the above it should be clear that The World of Sorcerers is many things to many people, for it is quite literally *The Other*, even to those who have never heard of The World of Sorcerers. Therefore if you are poor, *The Other* is riches in abundance; if you suffer ill-health, *The Other* is perfect health; if you lack knowledge, *The Other* abounds in huge halls of learning filled with knowledge of every description; if you are a victim, *The Other* is being a victor; if you long for temporal power, *The Other* offers an array of possible powers that makes the mind reel under the impact of so much power; if you seek the vision of the mystic, *The Other* is filled with vast realms of unspeakable religious ecstasy; if you seek the secrets of the shaman, *The Other* is populated with a great many beings of every conceivable type offering the most tantalising secrets. In fact *The Other* is everything one can possibly imagine or hope for, and herein lie the deadly traps of this breathtaking world of fairytale magic.

How does one explain to those who have a fixed view of the

world that fantasy is not fantasy, but that it only appears to be fantasy because of being at odds with a fixed sense of reality? How does one explain to such people that so-called fantasy can be made a reality with the magical *power* inherent within the act of perception? When the Wright brothers first conceived of the aeroplane, they were looked upon by many as fantasizing. Before Armstrong took his first few steps on the moon, space travel was regarded as science fantasy. Yet today, both aeroplanes and space travel are no longer merely a glorious day-dream, or the fantasy of a madman, but are instead as commonplace as automobiles. Nonetheless, even though many people today do have the ability to align The World of Sorcerers correctly and to their benefit, what precludes them from doing so is their lack of belief in themselves. In this respect it is vitally important to realise that had the Wright brothers not believed in their ability to build and to fly a machine that is heavier than air, they would never have been able to do so. Likewise, if scientists had continued to believe that it is impossible to fly and direct a craft beyond the earth's atmosphere, space travel would still be only a fantasy.

> THERE IS NO ACT WHICH IS MORE POWERFUL THAN THE ACT OF BELIEVING. THE WARRIOR IS A BEING WHO BELIEVES IN HIS DIVINE ABILITIES AS A MAGICAL BEING OF THE UNIVERSE. THE SORCERER, ON THE OTHER HAND, DOES NOT BELIEVE IN HIS GODLIKE POTENTIAL, AND THEREFORE FEELS THE NEED TO SEEK OUT THAT WHICH HE CAN USE AS A SUBSTITUTE FOR THE POWER HE THINKS HE LACKS.

The aphorism above so very clearly points out the vast difference between the true warrior and the sorcerer, but even though the Toltec brotherhood has always been exceedingly clear on this point, it is a strange quirk of human reason that it is a great deal easier to believe in the negative rather than the positive. As a result, there have always been those of the brotherhood who, in not being able to believe in the godlike potential of man, also could not believe that it is possible to amass *power* without the aid of sorcery practices. It is this lack of belief which has kept the Toltec brotherhood divided for so long, for all sorcery practices are based upon the principle of *forceful manipulation* – a concept and practice which is abhorrent to the Warriors of Freedom.

Most people, even devout Christians, never come to realise that sorcery, in spite of old wives' tales, is nothing more than a certain set of practices designed to manipulate others into doing one's bidding. This is true, irrespective of whether a so-called shaman is using ritual in his attempts at casting a spell of misfortune upon his adversary, or whether a businessman is trying financially to manipulate a business opponent out of the market; whether a witch doctor is using herbs in attempting to heal a patient, or whether the lawyer of a criminal is relying upon his cunning use of words to pull the wool over the jury's eyes. Forceful manipulation remains the basis of all sorcery practices, no matter if the practitioner looks like a sorcerer or not, and no matter in what guise the practitioner wishes to dress his actions. It is just plain stupidity to believe that it is the dress of a sorcerer that makes him a sorcerer, or the fact that he uses strange sounding words in performing obscure-looking rituals, that gives him his power. What makes a sorcerer a sorcerer is his actions, and his motive for those actions. Therefore realise that a judge in a court of law wears equally strange-looking garb, just as the technical jargon of law can sound strange to the uninitiated, but such dress and such jargon do not mean that all judges are sorcerers. However, should such a judge use his knowledge of law to manipulate a court case to fit his sense of justice, then he is indeed as much a sorcerer as any of those who openly profess to be shamans.

From the example above we see once again how man's ignorance of life breeds superstition in the minds of fools. The World of Sorcerers is far more accessible than most people tend to believe, and there are today far more powerful sorcerers within the orthodox disciplines of humanity than those few who still reserve for themselves the traditional title, paraphernalia, ritual, pomp and ceremony.

What exactly, then, is The World of Sorcerers? As was mentioned earlier, The World of Sorcerers is many things to many people, but in essence it is *the world of completion* – a world in which Every-Thing is possible simply because there is no distinction between what was, what is, and what can be. Consequently in this world the concept of potential has no meaning, for here all potential is a reality by virtue of its non-materiality – a feature which makes it the polar opposite of the dense physical world, and hence its name, *The Other*. However, The World of Sorcerers is not only the polar opposite of the dense physical world, but in being the potential of Every-Thing, it is also the blueprint of the dense physical world. Therefore existing within The World of Sorcerers is quite literally every thing that is currently known, all that was known, and all that will ever be known, but yet all of this existing as a complete reality in the present moment which is also the past and the future, and hence the statement that The World of Sorcerers is an utterly bewildering maze. Every part of the maze being *complete* in itself, in that Every-Thing, in order to be everything, has neither beginning nor end, neither fluidity nor definition, this world is constantly turning in upon itself to become everything else. Therefore the *here* is always right here, but also *there*, and then suddenly *everywhere*, so that irrespective of where in the maze one may be, it is possible to be in many places simultaneously, and yet being *nowhere* but *here*. Likewise is the now always right now, but also *just now, before now*, and then suddenly timeless, with the result that this *completion*, which is the distinguishing characteristic of The World of Sorcerers, is utterly impossible to fathom within the context of its non-materiality.

In order to fathom The World of Sorcerers and to find one's way through the maze of its ever-changing forms, one must be in possession of certain keys, referred to by Toltecs as *the twenty-one jewels of awareness*. These keys, which are as immaterial as is The World of Sorcerers are, because of their amorphous nature, also known as the *twenty-one abstract cores*. However, although Toltecs traditionally only ever refer to twenty-one jewels, there are actually twenty-two, a fact which conceals one of the deepest mysteries concerning awareness and the act of perception. In fact, the mystery surrounding the twenty-one jewels of awareness is very much in the nature of a catch-22 situation, for it is almost impossible to gain any understanding of The World of Sorcerers without an understanding of these keys, and without an understanding of The World of Sorcerers it is exceedingly difficult to grasp the meaning of keys that are not really keys at all. Nevertheless, such is the enigmatic nature of much of the Warrior's Path, and so we learn that the only way to grasp the meaning inherent within any enigma is first of all to understand what constitutes the enigma.

Realise that there are no enigmas as such, in the same way that there are no accidents or co-incidents. Any enigma only appears to be an enigma because of a "gap" in knowledge. Needless to say, any such "gap" constitutes the *relationship* between what appear to be irreconcilable paradigms. In other words, the absurdity or the unfathomability of an enigma is only the illusion that paradigms can be irreconcilable. However, only a little thought is needed to understand that nothing within the universe can really be irreconcilable, for such a concept would imply that the universe is a chaos of unrelated fragments – a concept which would be absurd. Therefore it is never the enigma as such that is unfathomable, but instead it is man's absurd insistence in believing that any paradigm which cannot be reconciled with his one and only rational paradigm must of necessity be nonsense, a fantasy or, at best, an enigma that is unfathomable. In this respect it is quite amazing to see how often average man will trip himself up with his own rational mind, for it hardly ever occurs to him that all catch-22 situations are merely the product of rational thought having entered a loop, and that since it is he himself who has set up the loop, he can also undo the loop if he chooses to do so.

Therefore in working with what appears to be the enigma surrounding The World of Sorcerers and its keys, it is important to understand that if we are not to get caught up in rational loops, it is vital that we strive to gain as much understanding as possible of the *relationship* between The World of Sorcerers and its keys. It is also vital to bear in mind that everything warriors do and understand is based upon relationships in one way or another, for in the final analysis there is only one life, the units of which are all utterly and completely interactive, inter-dependent, and therefore interrelated. There is absolutely nothing in the universe which is not related to something else, which is not interacting with something else, and which therefore is not dependent upon something else for its existence, purpose and meaning. I repeat, there is nothing, that is, there is No-Thing other than the one void containing Every-Thing, and as The World of Sorcerers is the potential of Every-Thing, it stands to reason that it is the potential of the manifested universe, the potential of the cosmic *tonal*.

Remember, though, the vast implications inherent within the nature of The World of Sorcerers. Being the potential of the cosmic *tonal*, The World of Sorcerers is quite literally that portion of the potential of the Unspeakable which is currently in manifestation as the manifested universe. In other words, The World of Sorcerers is *that* which the Unspeakable wishes to unfold within its present incarnation, and therefore reflected within The World of Sorcerers is the *fourfold purpose* of the Unspeakable, and thus also the true purpose and meaning of *man*, the microcosm of the macrocosm.

From the above it should be starting to become clear why out of all possible worlds that can be assembled, sorcerers should be so intent upon concentrating all of their endeavours on trying to master *The Other*. However, as we have already learned from the aphorism at the beginning of this chapter, The World of Sorcerers, contrary to what one may be led to believe, did not derive its name from its popularity amongst sorcerers, but instead from the fact that so many countless would-be sorcerers have throughout the ages nurtured this world with their awareness, their *personal power*, and ultimately with their life-essence.

So great has been this artificial nurturing of The World of Sorcerers that today this world is permeated by an accumulation of chaotic human *power* that seems to have acquired a life of its own independent of the *power* inherent within The World of Sorcerers itself. This chaos of human *power* pervades the whole of The World of Sorcerers and has gathered such strength over the millennia that it has become much like the legendary will o' the wisp, which in itself of course adds to the danger of this already dangerous world. In fact, many of the old wives' tales concerning the will o' the wisp, the sphinx, the harpy, the malevolent beings who guard crossroads, the Lord of the Wild Hunt, and all similar tales, have their basis in the deadly deceptions born of the accumulated human remains that haunt the maze of The World of Sorcerers. In Toltec terms this debris of human remains existing everywhere at once within The World of Sorcerers is known as *the mirror of justice*, to look into which spells insanity or death, or both, to those who do not hold the keys to The World of Sorcerers, or it spells *light through darkness* and *liberation through the power of intent* to those who do have the *power* required to use the keys.

Because The World of Sorcerers reflects the *fourfold purpose* of the Unspeakable, it is also in this world in which the secrets concerning matter, energy, space and time can be more readily solved than in any of the other worlds. In fact, it is only by grasping the meaning and the purpose of MEST that it is possible to survive The World of Sorcerers. However, in order to understand this concept, it is important to bear in mind that MEST is not at all what the average man thinks it is, and as this was already partially explained in *Cry of the Eagle*, the reader would do well to revise that section of the teachings thoroughly, for what follows here is by no means easy to grasp without having arrived at an understanding of the fundamentals of cosmology imparted in that earlier volume.

Although time was explained in somewhat more detail in Chapter Eight, it is still not really possible at this point in the teachings to explain MEST fully, but for our present purposes we must at least attempt to gain a better perspective on the implications of MEST within the context of The World of Sorcerers. In this respect it must be remembered that all of the ten worlds are actually *dimensions of awareness existing in four directions*. In other words, The World of Sorcerers is not a world out there somewhere, but is instead a specific state of awareness that is very much part of this world, and yet at the same time also existing beyond this world. This is a most trying concept to verbalise, but it will help greatly to think of it in terms of the atom, although in doing so the onus will be on the reader to bear in mind that the atom is only an analogy for a reality that defies verbalisation.

Think of the dense physical world, that is, the whole of the manifested universe, as being like a gigantic atom. Now think of *matter* as being like the inert neutrons contained in the nucleus of the atom, and think of *energy* as being the positively charged protons, which are also in the nucleus. Encapsulating this nucleus is the space defined by the negatively charged electrons orbiting the atom, and for the sake of our analogy we will let this space represent *space*, in which case the electrons represent *time*. But realise that unlike in the atom, in which the neutrons buffer the protons, energy surrounds and permeates all of matter, just as space is not an empty nothingness, but is instead a very tangible force which both surrounds and permeates both energy and matter. Likewise is time not merely so many electrons orbiting the nucleus, but is instead one whole force defining the parameters of space, but nevertheless also existing throughout space, energy and matter.

Even though this analogy does vaguely help in trying to explain the fourth dimension, it also distorts the reality in that we still end up with a three-dimensional model. In practical terms it is not possible to verbalise, or even to depict graphically the fourth dimension, for the simple reason that the fourth dimension is a *dynamic* sphere which has no fixed centre. I do not know how else to verbalise this, but if the reader can imagine such a sphere in terms of the analogy above, and then visualise the centre of this sphere as being in constant motion in such a way that, as the centre moves, the sphere redefines itself by being drawn inwards by the movement of the centre. Yet every position of the centre marks a definition of the *sphere of beingness* and as such can never be lost. Therefore all positions of the centre, past, present and future, exist simultaneously within the context of time. It is the constant movement of the centre that constitutes the fourth dimension, for had the centre been fixed, there would only have been three dimensions, in which case the fourth dimension and, for that matter, the evolution of awareness, would not have been possible.

In considering The World of Sorcerers, think of the whole of the dense physical world, that is, the manifested universe, as being merely the neutrons of an even bigger atom. In other words, what is MEST within the manifested universe is in its totality only *matter* in The World of Sorcerers, which is why it is stated that The World of Sorcerers is part of the mundane world, but also existing beyond it. This is true of all the worlds, for as we progress up the Tree of Life each world encapsulates the preceding one in terms of *matter*, until finally the first world, in its turn, is encapsulated by the void marking the *nagal*, that is, the No-Thing marking the Unspeakable. This, of course, is the ultimate *sphere of beingness*, of which the centre is the tenth dimension, that is, the dense physical universe, and which, as we have already noted, is in constant movement because of the evolution of awareness.

Now that we have a better idea of how the four components of MEST co-exist, we are also better equipped to start figuring out why they should be termed the *four directions*, although it should be noted that in this respect we can only make a start. The interrelationship of the Toltec teachings is such that we must still cover quite a lot more of the teachings before it will really become clear why MEST should be termed the four directions and why we should even speak about directions at all.

It will be recalled from *Cry of the Eagle* that *materialisation*, that is, materialisation of the *nagal's* desire to incorporate the unknown within the known, is the overall purpose of manifestation, and since this must of necessity arise through practical experience, it stands to reason that this materialisation can only be accomplished within the context of life within manifestation. If this were not so, then there would be no need for the Unspeakable to manifest in the first place. Materialisation is therefore *central* to the *nagal's* purpose, and can therefore rightfully be termed *the centre* of the sphere of beingness, something which is not at all surprising considering that the manifested universe, as we have already noted, is indeed the innermost core of the cosmic *tonal*.

However, materialisation is assigned to the *North*, a fact

which it is not possible to explain at this point, other than to say that *inherent awareness* has a predilection for linear progression, and that *linear progression* is the magnetic north of the manifested universe. Furthermore, since materialisation constitutes for the Unspeakable Its battle, Toltecs also refer to the North as being the battlefield. Yet, remember that materialisation is the centre of the sphere of beingness, and therefore this means that the North, within the context of the fourth dimension, is actually at the centre of the sphere of beingness – hence statements like *the real battle lies within, and not without,* and *all knowledge comes from within.*

We therefore see that materialisation is not only the centre of the sphere of beingness, but because this centre is also the battlefield, the North must of necessity be the place of *action*, and since all action involves *movement*, it is hardly surprising that the centre of the sphere of beingness should be in constant motion. Realise though, that since all materialisation tends to *inertia*, this constant movement of the centre is the ultimate in the act of not-doing, that is, the not-doing of the Unspeakable and, as a result, the North is also the place assigned to not-doing, which, as we know, is the art of stalking oneself. From this it is not difficult to see that it is as a result of stalking Its own perception of Itself that the Unspeakable can and does materialise its purpose, and since this takes place at the very centre of Its manifested beingness, we term the North *the centre of the world.*

Having gained a better perspective on the meaning of the North, remember that materialisation is merely the transfiguration of *energy*, and therefore in speaking about movement as such, what Toltecs are actually referring to is not so much the movement of the centre of the sphere of beingness, but rather the transfiguration of energy into matter as a result of that movement or, more correctly, that action termed the not-doing of the Unspeakable. Therefore true *movement* is the act of nurturing or, more precisely, the act of *nurturing the dream of the Unspeakable*, which as we know from *Cry of the Eagle*, is assigned to the South. Once again it is not really possible to explain the reasons for this here, other than to say that if the North is the place of action and of materialisation, then its polar opposite, the South, must be the energy required for that action, but since energy is the product of *personal power*, the only way in which to harness energy is to *dream*, that is, to access as many different alignments of perception as possible.

If we now revert to our analogy of the atom, it should be clear from all of the above that, within the context of the fourth dimension, matter and energy form the nucleus, which of course, is *movement*. However, all such movement is encapsulated within the purpose giving rise to that movement. In other words *the purpose of manifested life* is what gives rise to movement: what gives rise to both energy and matter. This purpose can only be sensed, for in the final analysis we can hazard a calculated guess only at the *manifested* purpose of the Unspeakable. What may or may not constitute the real underlying purpose of the Unspeakable as yet lies firmly within the realm of the unknowable. Consequently, in trying to fathom the purpose of life, we can at best *feel our way in the dark*, which of course, is the act of mapping out the unknown and, as such must necessitate erasing personal history.

Erasing personal history is assigned to the West, the place of *feeling*, that is, *feeling our way in the dark*, which is the same thing as opening the heart, but since this entails *listening* as defined by Toltecs, it is immediately clear that the West is what is referred to as *sound*. Furthermore, since erasing personal history gradually reveals the *totality of the self*, it stands to reason that this must give rise to a greater and greater understanding of the purpose of life or, more precisely, a greater and greater *feeling* for the purpose of life. However, we have already learned that space is defined as *the product of witnessing the purpose of life*, implying that space is actually an expression of the *purpose of beingness*, and which is gradually and sequentially revealed as the *totality of the self* begins to emerge. This is about as much as can be imparted here concerning the true nature of space, for more than this it is not yet possible to explain at this point.

Finally we come to the "electrons" of our atom model, which we decided would represent time. From *Cry of the Eagle* we know that time is the first component of MEST that is materialised in the manifestation of the universe, and since time is the universal expression of *intent*, (Chapter Eight), this is not at all surprising. However, what more often than not confuses apprentices at first, is the fact that being the universal expression of *intent*, time is of course the emotions of the Unspeakable, but as time is assigned to the East, which is the place of *sobriety*, a faculty of the mind, it appears as if we are up against a huge contradiction in the teachings. However, there is no contradiction as such if one remembers that *intent* and *mind* are the two polarities of the one awareness, and because awareness itself precedes manifestation, it must follow that the only reason why the Unspeakable would manifest is because It has started to recapitulate, and because of that recapitulation has acquired sufficient sobriety to acknowledge the need for manifestation. Once the necessary sobriety has been achieved, the *intent* of the Unspeakable starts to manifest in terms of *desire*, which as we know from Volumes One and Two is not only what Toltecs refer to as *colour*, but which is also the bedrock of all emotion, and therefore ultimately also of time.

The deeper implications of why emotion should be termed *colour*, and why time should be assigned to the East, are unfortunately far too complex for our present purposes. All we are trying to do at this point is to get some idea of what the fourth dimension actually entails, so that we can at least gain a working knowledge of The World of Sorcerers, the very essence of which is the reflection of Every-Thing, including the fourfold purpose of the Unspeakable, that is, MEST. Therefore once again I must ask the reader to be patient.

To grasp MEST in its entirety is not possible without a thorough foundation in all aspects of the Toltec teachings, and right now we are still very much in the process of trying to cover those fundamentals of cosmology that could not be covered in *Cry of the Eagle*. Nevertheless, we now have a better perspective on the four directions which constitute the fourth dimension, and therefore in the following chapter we are going to start looking at these directions in terms of awareness, for it must not be forgotten that, in the final analysis, the four directions are specific states of awareness, and it is these four prime states of awareness that we need to come to grips with in order to grasp the meaning and the nature of The World of Sorcerers.

CHAPTER ELEVEN

THE TWENTY-ONE JEWELS

THE KEYS TO THE WORLD OF SORCERERS ARE TWENTY-ONE
JEWELS REFLECTING A LIGHT THAT IS LETHAL TO THE
IGNORANT. BUT WHOEVER HAS THE POWER TO HOLD THESE
KEYS IS MASTER OF THE WORLD OF SORCERERS AND MAY ENTER
AND EXIT THAT WORLD SAFELY AND AT WILL.

In considering the four directions in terms of awareness we have several options open to us, depending upon where we choose to place the focus. For our present purposes I am going to adopt the method which is used in explaining to apprentices what their specific role within the Toltec unit encompasses, for although this method leaves many questions unanswered, it is nonetheless also quite the easiest to follow in terms of the four directions. In time all questions will be answered, but for the sake of simplicity let us first of all opt for the simpler method.

The Toltec unit is based upon the laws of evolution, which are not laws that were devised by man, but laws that were discovered by Toltec seers over a great many generations of seers. I make this point here because in the section that follows I am simply going to make one statement after another without any attempt at trying to substantiate these statements at this point, for if we are to achieve clarity on this material, then details must perforce come only later. If I were to try and explain every statement, the reader will become so confused and lost in detail, that he or she will not be able to see the wood for the trees.

If we look at the Toltec unit, we see that the way in which *power* has set it up is quite awesome in its implications. First of all, realise that all units are comprised of both men and women, and that all men and women naturally fall into four very definite groups. In other words, although every individual is unique in his or her own right, in the final analysis there are only four types of men and four types of women corresponding to the fourfold purpose of the Unspeakable. As a result, these four types of men and four types of women are also assigned to the four directions.

In relation to the above, it is important to remember that the *male* is *positive* relative to the *female*, (*Cry of the Eagle*), and that in practice this means that the *male* equates with the *known*, whilst the *female* equates with the *unknown*. Also bear in mind that it is the purpose of the male to anchor all knowledge, meaning that it is the male who has to make knowledge practical within life upon the physical plane. The purpose of the female, on the other hand, is to assist the male in mapping out the unknown by bringing forth fragments of the unknown which she feels is needed within the context of any particular endeavour. As we saw in *Cry of the Eagle*, this necessitates the act of intelligent co-operation between male and female, which of course, both implies and yields the element of *inclusiveness*. Therefore although it is the female who takes the lead in entering into the unknown, it is nevertheless the male who takes the lead upon the physical plane by opening the heart, not only so that intelligent co-operation can take place, but also so that the element of inclusiveness can come into being, for without inclusiveness it is not possible to incorporate the unknown into the known. Consequently each of the four directions within the Toltec unit has a male and a female half, the purpose of which is intelligent co-operation bringing forth inclusiveness.

The way in which the male and female warriors within a Toltec unit are placed is not difficult to grasp once we understand what the four types of men and the four types of women are. I am not at this stage going to explain the four different types, other than to say that the four types come about because all men and women have a natural predilection for any one of the four directions. However, that predilection is not something which is chosen at random by the individual, but is instead determined firstly by destiny, and secondly by fate. Therefore it is not a question of the individual deciding for him or herself in which direction they would like to be; nor for that matter, is it the nagal who decides this. The role of the nagal here is merely to use his seer's ability to point out to the apprentices who will in time become the warriors of his unit, what their respective directions and functions are.

Another point which must be reiterated here is that because the unknown is female relative to the known, and because the female has a dual nature, that is, the *mother* and the *woman*, each of the female directions within the Toltec unit also reflects this duality. As a result, each of the female directions is made up of two women, one channelling the *power* of the *mother*, and the other channelling the *power* of the *woman*.

In order to understand how this works, it is important to know that all men and women also have a natural predilection for either the *art of dreaming*, in which case they are called *dreamers*, or for the *art of stalking*, in which case they are called *stalkers*. The dreamers are those men and women who are naturally intro-spective, and therefore who also tend to be relatively quiet and withdrawn. The stalkers, on the other hand, are those men and women who are naturally extroverted, and therefore who tend to be relatively domineering and outgoing. In the case of women, this predilection manifests in such a way that the dreamer will be the one who quite naturally channels the *power* of the woman, whereas the stalker quite naturally channels the *power* of the mother. Consequently the stalkers are always the bossy ones, whilst the dreamers are the more quiet introverted ones.

Before we look at the actual structure of the Toltec unit, let us first of all list the four types of men and the four types of women. The types of women are traditionally referred to in terms of the *four principal winds*, the characteristics of which are extremely reminiscent of those qualities of awareness that mark the four directions. Consequently we have the Easterly women, referred to simply as *the East*, which are those women who have a natural predilection for *sobriety*. As a result these women have the tendency to be light-hearted and breezy, and so are likened to *the morning breeze*. Next we have *the North*, with their natural predilection for *strength*, and which are therefore likened to *the North wind*, for when the North wind really gets going, which is towards midday, it can be with a strength and a vengeance that takes its toll on most. *The West* is pure *feeling*, for like the haunting afternoon wind coming from the west, the Westerly women tend to be broody and melancholic. Finally we have *the South*, which, having a predilection for warmth and nurturing, are also likened to the warm night wind blowing from the south.

The four types of men are traditionally always referred to by their natural predilection. Consequently in the East we have the *Scholar* who is preoccupied with sobriety and therefore with the Mastery of Awareness. In the North we have the *Man of Action*, for as his name implies, this man is preoccupied with action and therefore also with materialisation. In the West we have the *Man Behind the Scenes*, for this is the man who is predominantly concerned with erasing personal history, and therefore with *feeling* and ultimately with the Mastery of Intent. Next we have the *Courier*, who, in not having a specific direction as such, can be attached to any one of the male or the female directions.

In order to understand what it is entailed in the fourth type of man, that is, the Courier, it must be remembered that the direction to which an individual belongs is a matter of destiny, and therefore never changes. In other words, if it is your destiny to be a Scholar when in a male incarnation, and a Northerly woman when in a female incarnation, then whenever you incarnate as a male you will automatically be a Scholar, and whenever you incarnate as a female, you will be a Northerly woman. However, since the purpose of incarnation is to evolve awareness, it would be exceedingly limiting if you could only ever incarnate either as a Scholar or as a Northerly woman. The way in which *power* has set it up for us to overcome this problem, is that we can also incarnate as a Courier because of the fact that a Courier has no specific direction as such. This means that a Courier is much like a wild card, and because he can be attached to any of the male or the female directions, it is possible for us to gain experience and knowledge in any of the male or female positions in all four directions.

Therefore attendant to each of the male and the female directions is a Courier, and the exact position is once again determined by fate. So if you incarnate as a Courier, then the direction you will become attached to depends upon what it is you have to learn in this lifetime. For example, if you need to learn about feminine *strength*, you will gravitate towards the female North, but if you need to learn about masculine *action*, you will find yourself working with a Man of Action in one way or another. We will presently be looking at this in more detail, but I give this particular example here merely to help clarify the nature of the Courier, and in this respect, one final point needs to be mentioned. Although the Courier is predominantly one of the four types of male, there are very rare cases in which a Courier may also incarnate as a female. Why this should be so is far too involved for our present purposes, but I point out this fact because female couriers do exist.

Having considered the four types of male, the reader will have noticed that because the Courier has no specific direction, the male South seems to be vacant. The reason for this is that the male South, the place of *warmth*, of *nurturing*, and of *power*, is always filled by a nagal; that type of man which, because of his peculiar energy configuration, can fulfil the role of any one of the males and, once fully trained, also the role of any one of the four females. Consequently a nagal is not a type of man as such, for in a most esoteric sense he is a mixture of all the males and the females. As a result it also stands to reason that it should be a nagal who takes the lead in both the purpose as well as the direction of the Toltec unit, for his principal duty is firstly, to train those apprentices who will in time become his unit of warriors; and secondly, to lead that unit to freedom.

In addition to the nagal man, there is also a nagal woman, who has much the same energy configuration as the nagal man, except that she contains within herself the characteristics of only the four types of woman. Because of this one profound diffe-rence in their make-up, the training of a nagal woman differs from that of the male, in that it is not her duty either to teach, or to lead, but instead to aid the nagal in leading the Toltec unit to freedom. In order to make this point clear I always use the following analogy.

Think of the Toltec unit as being like a ship, manned by the warriors that comprise that unit, and the captain of which is the nagal. The aim of the captain, the nagal, is to navigate his ship to freedom through the darkness of the unknown upon the ocean of life. However, being aboard the ship amidst the darkness of the unknown, it is difficult for the captain to see all of the hidden dangers concealed within the unknown, and which we will look upon as being like rocks just beneath the waves in the ocean of life. In order to help him navigate the ship safely, the nagal therefore employs the services of the nagal woman, who is not aboard the ship itself, but is in a tiny one-man boat of her own which she can navigate with ease and skill in between the treacherous rocks unseen from on board the ship. In this way the nagal woman precedes the ship, and in pointing out to the nagal where lies the greatest danger, she assists the nagal in mapping out the best course for the ship to take. From this analogy it is clear to see that the nagal woman is very much part of the nagal's unit of warriors, and yet because of the nature of her duties, she is also apart from the unit, not physically, but in terms of awareness. Consequently the nagal woman also is not fixed to any one particular direction, unlike the other females, but because of her predilection for *power* and freedom, and because of her close association with the nagal, she is very definitely attached to the South.

Having covered this much we are now in a position to consider each of the four directions in terms of awareness, which brings us hard up against the twenty-one jewels of awareness. However, a word of caution is called for here, for although we are now going to be looking at awareness in terms of the twenty-one jewels, realise that in spite of the fact that every individual has his or her predilection for specific aspects of awareness, all of us nonetheless have all twenty-one aspects of awareness within our make-up. Any predilection is merely in the nature of *approach*, and therefore does not imply that other aspects of awareness are ignored, or excluded in any way.

Predilection for any one of the aspects of awareness is technically speaking the individual's *specialised approach to the greater whole* which, of course, is the fourth dimension. Furthermore, in defining the four directions in terms of those aspects of awareness that constitute them, we will adhere to the *flow of power* as it occurs *during* manifestation, rather than *within* manifestation. The reason for this is that the flow of *power* during manifestation is easier to relate to in terms of trying to come to grips with the fourth dimension, whereas the flow of *power* within manifestation pertains to the evolution of awareness within the process of life upon the physical plane.

Only one more point must be covered ever so briefly here if we are to understand what is meant by the twenty-one jewels of awareness. This point concerns what is known as the *science of numerology*. The science of numerology encompasses, amongst other things, the fact that numbers denote specific alignments of perception, but why certain numbers should be assigned to certain alignments is far too complex to explain at this point. Let it suffice for now to point out that although Toltec seers have painstakingly revealed the laws of this science through a great many generations of research, the laws which govern this science have not been formulated by Toltecs, but are instead based upon universal laws and principles which are far more precise than anything man could have invented or calculated.

Therefore, in looking at the structure of the Toltec unit, we see that in the East, the place of the *rising sun*, we find the Scholar, and since this man is predominantly occupied with sobriety, that aspect of awareness, or that jewel of awareness which is central to his approach to the evolution of awareness is the jewel termed *knowledge*, and to which is assigned the number 14. Attached to this man's position within the Toltec unit is a Courier, known simply as the Scholar's Courier, and whose predilection is for that jewel termed *discrimination*, to which is assigned the number 17. Now when these two males work together, that is, if they co-operate intelligently with each other, the effect of their joint endeavour is equal to the sum of their jewels. In other words, if the Scholar and his Courier exercise intelligent co-operation between them, the result will be knowledge plus discrimination, that is, the acquisition of new knowledge through the act of discrimination.

Realise, though, that new knowledge can only arise when there is a willingness, firstly, to build upon our former knowledge; and secondly, to relinquish our former level of perception.

However, to relinquish a level of perception is an act which implies the death of the old, for the simple reason that any new knowledge must of necessity encompass a new level of perception. In this particular case it is clear to see that new knowledge is brought about through the medium of discrimination based upon existing knowledge, and this of course results in the death of the old. In terms of numerology we express this as 17 + 14 = 13.

In order to understand this rather strange-looking mathematics, it should be noted that, according to the laws of numerology, numbers that are to be added are as a rule first reduced to a single digit by addition, and only then are the single digits added together. If the final total after addition is greater than 33, then such totals are again reduced by addition until the number does not exceed 33. Therefore in this particular example, the whole process is as follows:

$$17 + 14 = (1 + 7) + (1 + 4) = 8 + 5 = 13.$$

Had the final total been greater than 33, say for example, 67, then the total would again have been reduced by addition, that is, 67 = 6 + 7 = 13. This is true even if the number had been, for example, 96875, in which case the reduction would read: 96875 = 9 + 6 + 8 + 7 + 5 = 35 = 3 + 5 = 8.

At this point it is appropriate to digress for a brief moment in order to point out that Couriers, like all of the males, can be either dreamers or stalkers, and that it does not matter which of the two they are. In this respect it is only the female directions that must have one dreamer and one stalker in each of the directions, and therefore cannot have two of the same in any one of the directions. The nagal too, like the other males, can be either a dreamer or a stalker, and the nagal woman, by virtue of the fact that she is the only female in her role, and because she is in a sense not part of the unit, can also be either a dreamer or a stalker. Female Couriers too can be either dreamers or stalkers, because the female Courier does not affect the feminine quality of a direction.

Returning now to the Toltec unit, we see that the male East brings forth *new knowledge through the medium of discrimination*, and that this results in *the death of the old*. However, in numerology a double number is the product of the *relationship* between the digits comprising the number. Therefore *knowledge*, that is, jewel 14, is a most specific vibration of awareness that is unique in its configuration, namely, 1 and 4. Note that I state 1 *and* 4, and not 1 *plus* 4 which has a different meaning. There can of course be a great many different types of knowledge, but these other types of knowledge are *not* considered to be *the jewel* termed *knowledge*, for the simple reason that they do not have the same configuration as jewel 14.

In order to grasp this point, realise that jewel 14 is essentially the product of the relationship between 1 and 4, in that 14 is in reality 10 + 4, as opposed to, say, 7 + 7, or 3 + 6 + 5, which also add up to 14. However, 14 from 7 + 7, and 14 from 3 + 6 + 5, both have different energy configurations to 14 from 10 + 4, even though all three can be seen as knowledge. Furthermore, 10 is in itself a double number, meaning that 10 is in reality the product of the relationship between *fluidity* (1) and *absolute freedom* (0). The numerological implication of this is that 10, which is the jewel *impeccability*, can only be achieved through fluidity within the context of absolute freedom. In more precise terms this means that where there is not fluidity of perception within the context of complete freedom from social conditioning, impeccability must perforce be distorted.

From the above it should be clear that although any 14 is the product between *fluidity* and *stability*, yet they are not the same as jewel 14, which has its basis in 10 + 4. The implications inherent within jewel 14 are that when perception is fluid, and yet stable in spite of that fluidity, then true *knowledge* is the result, but the fluidity that is required must be that fluidity acquired through *impeccability* within life upon the physical plane, for it must not be forgotten that the physical plane is the tenth world and the medium through which the jewel *impeccability* must be evolved. In other words, true *knowledge*, or *personal power*, is in reality *impeccability* (10) plus *stability* (4). Furthermore, realise that true knowledge (14), that is, *personal power* acquired through practical experience, will always lead to *freedom and change* (5), for the simple reason that 1 + 4 = 5.

Discrimination, jewel 17, is likewise the product of the relationship between *fluidity* (1) and *guidance* (7), but as with all double numbers, that fluidity must be *grounded* in *impeccability* (10) within the context of life upon the physical plane. In simpler terms this means that *impeccability* (10) plus *guidance* (7) yields *discrimination*. Therefore the jewel *discrimination* implies being fluid enough to receive the guidance inherent within the challenges posed by life upon the physical plane, and in this respect, true *discrimination* will always lead to *harmony and balance* (8), for 1 + 7 = 8, as opposed to, for example, racial discrimination which has its basis in the configuration 1 + 25.

Regarding the above, I would like to use the example of discriminating *against* in order to demonstrate how the aspects of awareness can interact in terms of the four directions to produce not only the positive results we term jewels, but also those negative results such as racial discrimination. Therefore in the case of racial discrimination, which is based upon the separative nature of the rational mind, we see that it properly belongs in the East, by virtue of the fact that it pertains to *sobriety*, albeit the negative side of sobriety.

The reason this negativity comes about is because, firstly, awareness is centred in the East; and secondly, we have pure *fluidity* (1) which, not yet having been grounded in impeccability achieved through life's experience, tends to manifest in terms of the individual not having the necessary *personal power* to think and to decide for himself. Consequently such a person will demonstrate his fluidity in terms of simply "going with the flow" of what appears to be a very logical assumption.

Moreover, in not yet having acquired *impeccability*, that person will not *accept* the challenges of life in terms of receiving *guidance* (7), but will instead be *tempted* to avoid those challenges in such a way as to manifest the dark jewel *temptation* (25). In other words, in discriminating *against*, whether it is racial discrimination or any other form of discriminating *against*, the individual is practising a form of discrimination that has its basis in the *fluidity* of the fool (1) coupled with *temptation* (25).

As a result, although 25 still reduces to 7, that 7, because its origin is in 25, will manifest in its negative form, that is, *the need for guidance*, and therefore the total equation will read, "the product of the relationship between *fluidity* and *the need for guidance*", that is, $1 + (-7) = (-6)$. The negative form of jewel 6 is *the need for choosing between the old and the new*, which will manifest as a form of discrimination, although such discrimination obviously cannot lead *to harmony and balance* (8).

In the example above, we also clearly see that in reducing numbers to a single digit, we should also take care to change the sign should the double number fall into the range of numbers from 22 through to 32, for these particular numbers, which, technically speaking, are known as the *dark jewels*, are numerologically positive only in their double number form. Note that I state "numerologically positive", for in essence the dark jewels never do manifest in a positive sense except within the context of the greater whole of which they are also a part.

In other words, within the process of life as a whole, the dark jewels provide the necessary friction that makes possible the evolution of awareness, and in that sense they are considered positive. Likewise, within the life of the individual, it is because of the relationship between the light jewels and the dark jewels that our *shadow side* comes into being, and since our *shadows* are our shortcomings, and since our shortcomings are our ticket to freedom and our passage to *power*, the dark jewels once again make the evolution of awareness possible.

When we now look at jewel 13, *the death of the old*, it must not be forgotten that we are here referring to that *aspect of awareness* which brings about death of the old, and not to *death* in terms of the universal force. Therefore jewel 13 implies that *death of the old* is the product of the relationship between *fluidity* and *mixed abundance*. However, remember that because this is a double number, we can equally well say that *impeccability* (10) plus *mixed abundance* yields *death of the old*. The implications here are that *death of the old* should be in the nature of judicious "pruning", or judicious elimination of the undesirable within the context of *mixed abundance*. Also, realise that whenever there is such a judicious elimination of the undesirable, which is necessary when dealing with mixed abundance, the result will always be *stability* (4), from $1 + 3 = 4$.

From everything we have learned so far concerning the male

East, it should be a lot clearer how new knowledge is acquired through the medium of discrimination, and what this actually entails. Furthermore, it is also clear that *the death of the old* in the East comes about as a result of intelligent co-operation between the Scholar and his Courier, a co-operation that yields *freedom and change* (5) plus *harmony and balance* (8); two qualities that are in perfect synchronicity with the quality of *the judicious elimination of all that is undesirable.*

From all of this it should now also be easier to grasp how the male warriors within the East use their predilection for their own specific jewels in both the acquisition of *sobriety*, as well as its continual evolution. In this respect it must not be forgotten that it is the duty of a warrior not only to unfold his or her full potential, but also to research and to evolve that potential according to the dictates of his or her fate.

In the female East we have the Easterly Dreamer, the Easterly Stalker and the Courier attached to the East. The predilection of the Easterly Dreamer is jewel 13, *the death of the old*. However, as we have already learned earlier, because this is the East, this lady achieves her full potential by acquiring a *fluidity* grounded within *impeccability*. Then by bringing that *fluidity* to bear upon *mixed abundance* (3), she judiciously eliminates all that is undesirable within *mixed abundance*, so as to bring about the quality of *stability* (4) through *death of the old* (13).

The Easterly Stalker, on the other hand, being predominantly concerned with the evolution of awareness through the medium of life upon the physical plane, has a natural predilection for jewel 12, *forebearance*. True *forebearance* is the product of the relationship between *fluidity* and *destiny*. The implications here are subtle indeed, for 2 is not only the number of *destiny*, but also the number of *humility and understanding*. In other words, it is only through having acquired both *humility* and *understanding* that the force of *destiny* can be unfolded consciously and impeccably. Furthermore, because 12 is a double number, we can equally well say that *forebearance* (12) is the sum of *impeccability* and the force of *destiny*, or alternatively, the sum of *impeccability* and *humility and understanding*. However, realise that true *forebearance* (12), that is, *impeccability* plus the force of *destiny*, will invariably yield *creativity and joy* (3), and where there is creativity and joy, the end result will always be a *mixed abundance* (3).

The Courier to the East has a natural predilection for jewel 2, for to this man the force of *destiny* is of paramount importance, as is the quality of *humility and understanding*. Being a prime number, jewel 2 does not appear to have the complexity of the double numbers, and yet this is merely another example of the fact that the world is not what it appears to be. In order to grasp the implications of jewel 2, realise that inherent within the number 2 is the basic *duality* of *nagal* and *tonal*, implying that the force of *destiny* is inextricably interwoven with this duality. Jewel 2 concerns the relationship between the *nagal* and the *tonal*, and is therefore the very essence of intelligent co-operation.

When these three warriors in the East co-operate intelligently, the result is once again the sum of their jewels, namely:

$$2 + 12 + 13 = 9.$$

The implications here are that when the force of *destiny*, *forebearance* and *the death of the old* combine in the East, *completion* is the result. However, jewel 9, like all the prime numbers, is not as simple as it appears to be, for inherent within this jewel is the reconciliation of two qualities that appear to be diametrically opposed to one another, namely, *stability* (4) plus *freedom and change* (5). Within the scope of this book it is not feasible to explain the prime numbers to any great depth, but let it suffice for now to say that all the prime numbers pertain to the awareness of the *nagal*, that is, to *inherent awareness*, whereas all the double numbers pertain to the awareness of the *dreamer*, that is, to *evolving awareness*. All other numbers are merely complex permutations pertaining to life on the physical plane, that is, to the *dreamed*.

Therefore in considering jewel 9, which is *completion*, it becomes apparent that 9 in some way defines the outer parameters of *inherent awareness*, which in a most peculiar sense it indeed does, for remember that 9 marks that particular clustering of vibrational frequency known as The World of Sorcerers and which, as we have already learned, is in reality an expression of the fourfold purpose of the Unspeakable, and therefore also an expression of Its potential in this present manifestation. It is primarily because of this fact that *materialisation*, which in essence is *stability* (4), always tends to *inertia* and therefore has to be constantly countered by the force of *freedom and change* (5). As a result, jewel 9 is therefore in a most esoteric sense the primal expression of *not-doing*, and as we know from the previous chapter, it is this primal not-doing that gives rise to the fourth dimension.

Therefore, in the final analysis, we see that the sum of the Easterly jewels yields a *resistance* to the force of inertia so that the purpose of the Unspeakable may be fulfilled to *completion*, and not just partially so. As a result, the female East has the overall quality of *the urge to completion through the medium of humility and understanding born of forebearance and the death of the old*.

When the male East co-operates intelligently with the female East, the result is the sum of the respective totals, namely:

$$(14 + 17) + (2 + 12 + 13) = 13 + 9 = 13.$$

In other words, the predominant quality that emerges in the East is *death of the old* brought about by that *death of the old* engineered by the male East in response to the *urge to completion* brought forth by the female East. In a nutshell this amounts to the technique of recapitulation, and it is for this reason that the East always excels in *sobriety*. Moreover, since the East is also the origin of *time*, it is beneficial to point out here that the warriors in the East are constantly working with the deeper implications of *time* in one way or another and, as a result, are traditionally and collectively referred to as *the time stalkers*, irrespective of the fact that some will be stalkers and others will be dreamers. Although it is not possible to explain this point here, it is mentioned merely in the sense of rounding off this section of the teachings.

In following the flow of *power* as it occurs during manifestation, we now come to the West, the place of *death* and of the *setting sun*. Here we find the *Man Behind the Scenes*, who has a natural predilection for working with the force of *intent*, and thus he is most drawn to jewel 16, known as *liberation through the power of intent*. This man's Courier, on the other hand, has much the same disposition as he himself, and therefore feels most at home in the darkness of the unknown. Consequently the Courier of the Man Behind the Scenes loves to work with jewel 15, that is, *light through darkness*. Being on the same axis as the East, and because the West is also the place of *death*, it is hardly surprising that intelligent co-operation between these two men should also yield *death of the old*, that is:

$$15 + 16 = 13.$$

Nonetheless, the implications in the West are quite different to those in the East, as they should be, for the West is after all the polar opposite of the East. First of all, in looking at the jewel of the Man Behind the Scenes, we see that 16 is in reality 10 + 6, meaning that the sum of *impeccability* (10) and the *act of choosing between the old and the new* (6), yields *liberation through the power of intent* (16). Alternatively, we can also see that *liberation through the power of intent* is the product of the relationship between *fluidity* (1) and *the act of choosing between the old and the new* (6), bearing in mind, of course, that the *fluidity* called for here must be *grounded* in *impeccability*.

The implication in all of this is that *choosing between the old and the new* is very closely allied to *discrimination*, in that such choosing must be done judiciously, or impeccably. The reason for this is that 6 is not only an aspect of *inherent awareness*, in that it is a prime number, but it also denotes the *duality* of the female. In other words, 6 is the primal expression of *discrimination*, in that it concerns the vitally important act of *discriminating with divine inspiration between the mother and the woman*, both of whom are needed for the purposes of evolution.

In Toltec terms the *mother* is that aspect of *mind* that lends itself to the force of inertia, in that its tendency is towards preservation, unity and stability. The *woman*, on the other hand, is that aspect of *mind* that lends itself to the force of separativeness, in that it wants to divide and to separate the known from the unknown in support of the male's purpose, that is, in support of the fact that before the unknown can be incorporated into the known in an intelligent and meaningful way, the two must first be separated out into the two polarities.

From the above it should be clear that the Toltec phrase "discriminating with divine inspiration", implies that in choosing between the old, that is, the *mother*, and the *new*, that is, the *woman*, the warrior cannot base such discrimination upon any form of prejudice or haphazard assumption, but instead needs to rely upon *divine inspiration*, a term used for denoting the act of *listening to the heart*. It therefore stands to reason that jewel 16 has inherent within it the quality of *guidance*, for 1 + 6 is indeed equal to 7. Furthermore, from this it is also obvious why it should be *feeling* that is assigned to the West, for in both the male West and the female West, *listening to the heart* is vitally important in *feeling one's way in the darkness of the unknown* – the unknown being marked by the *setting sun*, as opposed to the known marked by the *rising sun*. Consequently the Man Behind the Scenes is the man who works directly with the heart and with *feeling*, as opposed to his polar opposite, the Scholar, who works directly with mind and with *sobriety*.

The Courier to the Man Behind the Scenes is predominantly concerned with mapping out the unknown, and hence his predilection for the jewel called *light through darkness*. Jewel 15 is the product of the relationship between *fluidity* (1) and *freedom and change* (5), or alternatively the sum of *impeccability* (10) and *freedom and change* (5), for it must never be forgotten that in referring to *fluidity* derived from 10, we are implying that type of *fluidity* which is derived through life's experience upon the physical plane, and which, in the final analysis, amounts to the same thing as *impeccability*. Therefore *light through darkness* can only emerge when *freedom and change* is exercised within the context of *impeccability*.

The implication in the above is that there can be no *light* emerging from out of the *darkness* of a challenge if we strive to *free* ourselves from that challenge by trying to avoid it, or if we attempt to *change* our fate in some way. Only by facing our challenges fairly and squarely can there be *light through darkness*. True *freedom and change* is freedom from the debilitating restraints of social conditioning and a consequent change in our self-image. Needless to say, from this it is very easy to see that *light through darkness* (15) must yield the ability to *choose between the old and the new* (6), for 1 + 5 = 6.

We see therefore that the overriding emphasis in the male West is to bring about *stability* (4) within the realm of the irrational unknown by initiating *the death of the old* (13) through the medium of *liberation through the power of intent* (16), coupled with the acquisition of *light through darkness* (15). This is achieved through the medium of that *guidance* (7 from 16) received in listening to the heart, in conjunction with the acquired ability to *receive divine inspiration in choosing between the old and the new* (6 from 15), again through listening to the heart.

The female West, being made up entirely of prime number jewels, does not have the quiet stability to be found in the other three female directions, which all have a majority of double numbers. As a result, the Westerly females, including their Courier, are fondly referred to by their fellow warriors as *mad*. In this respect the men from the male West really do have their hands full most of the time in having to contain the Westerly females, for whenever these women go into one of their "mad" phases, which is rather more often than not, their Courier, whose predilection is for *mixed abundance*, tends to join them, with the result that all hell breaks loose! Yet, demonstrated in this fact, we once again see the need for polarity, for in many ways it is the fiery "madness" of the female West, coupled with the sombre broodiness of the male West, that tends to balance out the rather cool and somewhat clinical collective sobriety of the East.

The Westerly Dreamer is the most "mad" of the two Westerly women, in that not having much patience with logical assumptions, her natural predilection is for pure *fluidity* (1). Being predominantly concerned with the *One Power*, this lady cannot be bothered with all of the nit-picking so prevalent within the world of humanity, and thus has the most amazing ability to cut straight through all pettiness to the very heart of any challenge. Being so very fluid in her natural dislike of human pettiness, the Westerly Dreamer can "bounce" her way through life on her head if need be, for in herself she has no regard for any form of self-importance, and least of all self-pity, both of which tend to get in the way of unfolding and achieving the *One Power* (1). Having such a disposition, the Westerly Dreamer also has no regard for anyone else's sense of self-importance or self-pity. As a result, unless she is contained, this lady can quite literally turn a whole nation upside down when she suddenly gets it into her head to go on a rampage against all that hinders freedom in the acquisition of man's divine heritage. In this respect it is interesting to note that the majority of so-called female martyrs, such as Joan of Arc, were Westerly Dreamers.

In relation to the above, it must be realised that jewel 1, being an aspect of *inherent awareness*, has a natural tendency towards *linear progression*. Therefore unless pure *fluidity* is contained, in the sense of being *grounded* in *impeccability* achieved through practical experience within life upon the physical plane, it will always revert to its natural tendency to forge straight ahead in the face of all odds. This does not imply that the Westerly Dreamer is not impeccable in her actions. On the contrary, when she is caught in the "madness" of her vision, her grasp of the true purpose of the One Life is exceedingly impeccable, in that it is utterly free from all sense of self-importance and self-pity. However, in not having any sense of self-importance at all, this lady also does not care a fig about what others may or may not think of her actions, and therefore unless she is contained and directed when the "madness" overtakes her, she will simply forge ahead with a sense of purpose that often appears to be the actions of the fool, or the clown, by virtue of her total disregard for the opinion of others.

The Westerly Stalker, on the other hand, being much more concerned with the practicalities of life upon the physical plane than the Westerly Dreamer, is somewhat less "mad" than her counterpart, and yet, in having a predilection for jewel 5, this lady also has the tendency to go on a mission with a vengeance. Jewel 5 is, of course, *freedom and change*, and notwithstanding what we have already learned about this jewel, realise that it too is an aspect of *inherent awareness*, and also very closely allied to jewel 1, for inherent within 5 is the *One Power* and its fourfold expression, namely, *sobriety, strength, feeling* and *warmth*. As a result, whenever the Westerly Stalker goes into one of her "mad" phases she is usually a rather weird mixture of all four expressions of the *One Power*, and thus there is always an incredible clarity within the otherwise apparent "madness" of the Westerly Stalker – a clarity that she will deliver with a warmth and a strength that unfortunately all too often comes across like the oddly "benign" actions of a fired-up bulldozer sweeping all before it with the "good" intention of imparting a most treasured, albeit impassioned, feeling.

Any warrior will testify to the fact that if you should ever have difficulty in learning the true meaning of *freedom and change*, then the person whose assistance you should enlist is the Westerly Stalker. This lady will simply bulldoze you most unceremoniously out of your view of the world, and if you still do not know what constitutes *freedom* after that, she will demonstrate *change* by changing your image of yourself in no uncertain terms, and will more than likely do so in such a manner as to leave you with very little room for doubting that she finds you to be an absolutely brainless moron. After such a lesson in the very definite disadvantages of vanity, this lady will without a doubt embrace you with all the love and warmth of the proverbial matron, will pat you on the head like a favourite pet, and if you are not quick enough in making good your escape, will promptly set about stalking you into your next lesson! Whilst it is true that to be stalked by an Easterly Stalker is to know without a doubt that you have been stalked, to be stalked by a Westerly Stalker is to be left wondering if you have not perhaps been seriously manipulated!

Yet, notwithstanding anything we have noted about the two Westerly women so far, these two ladies really are the *heart and the soul* of the Toltec unit in a very literal sense. Although even their fellow warriors within the Toltec unit have to learn through many an arduous trial, and many a painful error, to appreciate the Westerly women fully, once their apparent "madness" is understood for what it really is, these two ladies are the heart personified! Ruthless to the n'th degree in their natural tendency to forge straight ahead, and utterly fearless in their deep sense of uncomplicated simplicity, these two ladies are truly formidable opponents in any battle.

Furthermore, because of their total inability to be swayed, the courage of the two Westerly women is such that their sense of loyalty to the cause, and therefore also their loyalty to their fellow warriors, is something that is not only unsurpassed, but also heartrendingly beautiful to behold. In this respect, neither of these two ladies will bat an eyelid at sacrificing themselves in the defence of a fellow warrior, but, rest assured, they will not do so without giving that warrior an earful of verbal abuse. And yet, although that abuse will be so designed as to tear strips off the ego, it will also always be filled with such profound meaning and deep poignancy that tears invariably come unbidden to the eyes of the witness. Such is the true inner beauty of these two most special ladies – an inner beauty arising out of an intrinsic selfless-ness, and which is by far their most distinguishing characteristic.

Attendant to the two Westerly women is the Courier to the West who, as we have already noted, has a predilection for *mixed abundance*. Inherent within jewel 3 is the fundamental triplicity of the manifested universe. Consequently within 3 we encounter the relationship between *inherent awareness* and *evolving awareness*, but within the context of the purpose of the Unspeak-able. Therefore jewel 3 is primarily concerned with how best to nurture and to keep intact the results of the interaction between the *linear progression* of *inherent awareness* and *the circular inclusion* that comes about as a result of *evolving awareness* being fixed to its centre. The results of this interaction, because they pertain to both *inherent* as well as *evolving awareness* are, of course, what is referred to as *mixed abundance*.

However, jewel 3 is also referred to as *joy and creativity*, for inherent within this jewel is the childlike, as opposed to childish, desire to surround oneself with *mixed abundance* for the sheer *joy* of not only collecting, but also for the *joy* of being able to *create* something out of the bits and pieces collected, irrespective of whether these are material things, or simply titbits of interesting information. In this respect we are all familiar with how any child is quite capable of crying at one moment, and then laughing the next; of building a sand castle with glee, and of destroying it with equal glee once completed; of collecting sea shells with huge enthusiasm, then merely to forget them totally in the equally enthusiastic pursuit of a sudden new interest.

From the above it stands to reason that the Courier to the West, because his jewel is a single digit, and therefore having a natural tendency towards *inherent awareness*, is far more inclined towards forging straight ahead than he is towards trying to create order within *mixed abundance*. The end result is that the Courier to the West is quite the best collector, for in his love of forging ahead within the context of *mixed abundance*, he quite literally collects everything in sight, irrespective of whether it is gossip, objets d'art, musical instruments, poetry, books, photographs and, in short, everything which may or may not be useful. However, although this man's talent for *joyful creativity* never ceases to amaze, his childlike enthusiasm for life does not allow him to linger with any one book long enough to finish reading it, although admittedly, his spontaneous openness of heart does normally enable him to grasp intuitively the contents of the book, even though he has never read it fully. Likewise will he find it far too time-consuming to learn to master any of the musical instruments he may have collected, although once again, his intuitive grasp of anything is such that he will normally have an uncanny ability to improvise superbly on just about any musical instrument.

When these three warriors from the female West co-operate intelligently, we see once again that the result is the sum total of their respective jewels, that is:

$$1 + 5 + 3 = 9.$$

The meaning here is that in the female West *completion* (9) is achieved through the medium of pure *fluidity* (1) coupled with *freedom and change* (5) in the childlike pursuit of that *creativity and joy* (3) that yields *mixed abundance* (3). This type of *completion* cannot possibly be more different to that type of *completion* generated in the East; namely, the urge to *completion* through the medium of *humility and understanding* born of *forebearance* and *the death of the old*. *Completion* in the East, true to the dictates of *sobriety*, means *being finished* in the sense that everything is sorted out and no loose ends remain unattended to. Therefore the East always has the quality of being immaculately neat and tidy, ordered, and everything perfectly accounted for. But *completion* in the West most of the time never does have the quality of *being finished* in the true sense of the word, but is more in the nature of a rather delightful and truly childlike higgledy-piggledy order of sorts amidst what can only be termed inspired chaos!

In relation to the female West the reader will find it interesting if we digress slightly at this point in order to demonstrate the universality of the *One Truth*. The example I would like to use is one recorded in the Christian bible, namely, the well-known episode when Christ returned from a trip to find his disciples fishing from a boat on the Sea of Galilee. Having been informed by his disciples that they had had no luck all through the night, Christ instructed them to lift the fishing net and to cast it to the other side of the boat. Even though such an injunction must have made little sense to the disciples, they nonetheless obeyed, and when the net was pulled up after having been cast to the other side as instructed, they beheld a miracle, for it was filled with one hundred and fifty-three fishes.

This episode is one of the most beautiful examples of irrationality versus rationality, for clearly, if there had been no fish on the one side of the boat, then why in exactly the same spot would there be fish on the other side of the boat? Yet, what Christ taught his disciples on that day was the importance of shifting the focus so as not to become obsessed with rational assumption. Furthermore, by instructing them to cast the net to *the other* (9) side of the boat, Christ was pointing out to his disciples the importance of aligning The World of Sorcerers and, in so doing, becoming capable of performing a miracle.

In this particular example, Christ showed his disciples how to align The World of Sorcerers, firstly, by shifting the focus; and secondly, by being *fluid* (1) enough to *change* (5) their view of the world, as well as their self-image, thereby acquiring the *freedom* (5) necessary to become truly *creative* (3). The result, as we already know, was their *joy* (3) when they again raised the net and found plenty of fish inside – one hundred and fifty three to be exact – 153 – the jewels assigned to the female West, 1, 5 and 3. Later we will again look at how to set about aligning The World of Sorcerers, but I wanted to give this example here merely because it is so very appropriate in demonstrating the fact that where there is true knowledge there is only the *One Truth*. What separates and divides, what causes one person to be suspicious of another, and what causes one religious sect to condemn another, always boils down to a lack of true knowledge and a vision limited by the narrow and all too often inaccurate confines of rational assumption.

To return now to our consideration of the West, we find that when the warriors in the male West co-operate intelligently with the warriors in the female West, the result is, as always, the sum of their respective totals, namely:

$$(15 + 16) + (1 + 5 + 3) = 13 + 9 = 13.$$

The implications here are again very different to those in the East, for although the end result is still *stability* (4) through the medium of *the death of the old* (13), it must be remembered that, according to the laws of numerology, these two types of *stability* are completely different by virtue of their different constituents. Therefore *stability* in the West is based upon pure *feeling*, and is therefore completely irrational, whereas the *stability* in the East is based entirely upon *sobriety*, and is therefore the very epitome of that lovely sober clarity born of the impeccable use of the rational mind.

Consequently we have the East on the one hand, *stable* in having brought about *death of the old* through the medium of *sobriety*, and on the other hand we have the West, also *stable* in having brought about *death of the old* through the medium of *feeling*. This is the horizontal axis marked by man standing with his arms stretched sideways, embracing both the *rising sun* as well as the *setting sun*, the East and the West. In that embrace, man incorporates within his beingness not only the known and the unknown, but also the very meaning and purpose of life upon the horizontal axis, that is, life upon the physical plane. By embracing both the East and the West equally, by embracing both polarities of life upon the physical plane, that is, the *rising sun*, life, and the *setting sun*, death, man achieves true *stability* by bringing about *death of the old*, or death of all that hinders his progress along the Path of Freedom, and this he does with both *sobriety* and *feeling*, with *mind* and *heart*.

Finally, because the warriors in the male West as well as the female West are predominantly preoccupied with *feeling* in one way or another, they are, because of that openness of heart, also acutely aware at all times of the warrior's duty to help fulfil the purpose of the Unspeakable. Because of this fact, and bearing in mind that space is defined as *the product of perceiving the purpose of life,* the Westerly warriors are traditionally and collectively referred to as *the dreamers in space*. Therefore upon the horizontal axis, or within life upon the physical plane, we see the necessity for, firstly, using the *art of stalking* in the Mastery of Awareness, and secondly, the *art of dreaming* in the Mastery of Intent. As was mentioned earlier, this does not imply that all of the Easterly warriors are stalkers, and that all of the Westerly warriors are dreamers, but it does imply that in working with *sobriety* it is vitally important to stalk our own perception constantly; whilst in working with *feeling* we must cultivate an openness of heart that can only really be acquired through dreaming.

Next in line is the South, which, it will be remembered from *Cry of the Eagle* is known as *the gateway to the nagal's world*. Accordingly in the male South we find both the nagal and his Courier. The nagal, because he is not a specific type of man, unlike any of the others, does not have a particular predilection for any one jewel, for his duty as nagal requires of him an equal efficiency with all of the jewels, male and female, as well as with those jewels known as the *dark jewels* and the *forbidden jewels*.

Nevertheless, because of what is required of him in terms of leading others to freedom, the jewel that is normally assigned to the destiny of a nagal is jewel 18, which is primarily centred upon the meaning of *courage*.

Courage means many things to many people, but in essence it is the product of the relationship between *fluidity* (1) and *harmony and balance* (8), which is the same as the sum of *impeccability* (10) and *harmony and balance* (8). However, inherent within jewel 8 is the harmonious balance existing between the tenth and the ninth world, that is, between the dense physical world and The World of Sorcerers. That balance, existing upon and maintained by *harmony*, is by its very nature exceedingly fragile and therefore easily upset. Furthermore, because all *harmony* is dependent upon the interrelationship of life, it is invariably man who tends to upset that balance in one way or another whenever he ignores the interrelationship of life through his actions, physical, emotional or mental. Consequently it stands to reason that there can be no true freedom where there is not *harmony and balance* between the ninth and the tenth worlds, for not only is the ninth world the blueprint of the tenth world, but it is also the mirror in which is reflected the purpose of the Unspeakable. Therefore whenever the balance is disturbed between the ninth and the tenth world, the resultant disharmony reflected in The World of Sorcerers distorts all of life upon the dense physical plane.

From the above it follows that the real meaning of *courage* is to strive to restore and to maintain both *harmony* and *balance*, a task which, because of humanity's general ignorance of the interrelationship of life, is truly formidable at the best of times, and well-nigh impossible most of the time. And yet, in spite of this, that which is required of the nagal at all times, is *hope* in the face of all odds, and *persistence* even amidst constant defeat. To keep on hoping when all seems hopeless, and to keep persisting when there never seems to be any light at the end of the tunnel, takes a type of *courage* that is impossible to verbalise. Yet, realise that if the nagal was to give up hope and to stop trying, what hope would there be for any of those whom it is his duty to lead to freedom?

The only way in which any nagal can ever hope to fulfil his fate is to reconcile the two aspects of awareness which constitute his own jewel. In other words, the nagal strives to reconcile *fluidity* (1) and *harmony and balance* (8) – two aspects which by their very nature are fortunately most compatible. What in effect this boils down to, is that the nagal must make every attempt to be so utterly impeccable in his own perception that he can find ways and means whereby at least some measure of freedom can be achieved amidst the constant turmoil and turbulence brought forth by humanity within both the ninth and the tenth worlds. Whenever any nagal accomplishes even just this little bit, then at least a tiny, a minuscule portion of the Unspeakable's purpose has been materialised through the medium of *completion*, for realise that *courage* does reduce to *completion*, in that

$1 + 8 = 9.$

Assisting the nagal in his herculean task is the nagal woman. I wish to explain the nagal woman's role at this point, for although she is technically-speaking not part of the rest of the unit, nonetheless, because of her exceedingly close association with the nagal, she forms part of the male South, rather than forming part of the female South.

The jewel of the nagal woman is 9, *completion*, a fact which in itself speaks volumes to the perceptive apprentice. Not only do all four of the female directions within the Toltec unit add up to 9, but so too is the jewel of the nagal woman 9 – which is not at all surprising if one remembers that the nagal woman has the characteristics of all four types of women. However, inherent within jewel 9 is one of the greatest paradoxes to be found within the Toltec teachings, namely the reconciliation of jewels 4 and 5, for 9 is, according to the laws of numerology, 4 + 5. Why it should be 4 + 5, as opposed to, say 6 + 3, or 2 + 7, or even 3 + 3 + 3, is not within the scope of this book, but let it suffice for now merely to point out the significance of this fact.

Remember that it is the purpose of the Unspeakable to incorporate the unknown within the known, but that this can only be done through practical experience gained within life upon the physical plane, irrespective of whether this is the dense physical plane or not. Now, as we already know, fulfilment of this purpose is what we term materialisation, but since all materialisation naturally tends to inertia, there is always the danger that the process of evolution can be arrested before true *completion* of the Unspeakable's purpose has been achieved. Furthermore, realise that, in the final analysis, the force of inertia is the negative manifestation of the very same force we look upon as being *stability* (4). This is necessarily so, because for any act to be really meaningful, including the incorporation of the unknown within the known, such an act must be grounded in *stability*, and it is, of course, exactly herein that lies the danger already referred to.

Therefore counteracting the force of inertia (-4), which is inherent within *stability* (+4), is that aspect of awareness termed *freedom and change* (5), and it is this that is the paradox, for clearly (-4) + 5 = 1, and not 9.

This paradox rests upon the question of how *completion* can ever be achieved if everything is kept in a state of perpetual *fluidity* (1). We have in actual fact already partly answered this question in the previous chapter when we took a brief look at the nature of the fourth dimension and, in doing so, saw that the centre of the sphere of beingness is in constant motion, that is, in a state of perpetual *fluidity* (1).

As is clear to see from what we have learned here, this *fluidity* (1) of the centre of the sphere of beingness comes about because of the fact that *freedom and change* (5) counteracts the force of inertia (-4). Yet, realise also that in spite of the natural tendency of materialisation towards inertia, materialisation can only come about because the *stability* (+4) inherent within MEST itself makes it possible for the Unspeakable to fulfil Its purpose.

In other words, on the one hand we have the sum of the *stability* (4) of MEST and the urge towards *freedom and change* (5) bringing about *completion* (9); and on the other hand, we have the sum of the force of inertia (-4) and the urge towards *freedom and change* (5) bringing about the perpetual *fluidity* (1) of materialisation. However, the stunning intelligence in all of this, is the fact that the force of inertia and *stability* are not two separate forces, but are instead one and the same force, manifesting two different aspects of itself simultaneously, but both working together in perfect harmony with *freedom and change.*

The result of this weird paradox is that, although the purpose of the Unspeakable is continuously being materialised, all such materialisation is kept in a state of perpetual *fluidity* so that premature stagnation is never possible. It is for this reason that it is stated that The World of Sorcerers is the world of *completion*, in that it is constantly folding in upon itself to become Every-Thing else. In the final analysis, realise that we are here looking at one of the most breathtaking phenomena of the universe, namely, how it is indeed possible to achieve a *completion* that in reality never ceases to continue *coming to completion.*

It is also within this awesome phenomenon that lies the true nature of the *eternal now*, for in The World of Sorcerers, and therefore inherent within jewel 9, past, present and future co-exist as one *potential*. Every facet of that potential is capable of being materialised, and yet through being kept in a state of perpetual *fluidity* once materialised, it has neither beginning nor end, has neither a past nor a future, for within the realm of potential, what was, is and can be, co-exist as one interrelated whole, the parts of which are not only thoroughly interdependent, but are also constantly interacting in such a way that every moment is now, and within the now every occurrence is a *completion*.

Therefore, from all of the above it can now be seen that, in having a predilection for jewel 9, the nagal woman, in a most esoteric sense, embodies within herself the nature and the purpose of The World of Sorcerers. Also, because all of the female directions add up to 9, it is not so difficult to grasp why the nagal woman should have the characteristics of all four types of women. Furthermore, because the nagal woman embodies within herself the nature and the purpose of The World of Sorcerers, the fully trained nagal has no difficulty at all in being able to "read" in the beingness of the nagal woman the reflections within The World of Sorcerers brought about by the actions of humanity. It is for this reason that it is said that the nagal woman assists the nagal in ascertaining where lies the greatest threat or danger in the moment, and because of her ability to do this, the nagal woman is traditionally referred to as *the beacon light* by which the nagal navigates the ship which is his unit of warriors.

Intelligent co-operation between the nagal and the nagal woman is the sum of their jewels, namely:

$$18 + 9 = 18.$$

The implications here are that the nagal woman is at her most *courageous*, and also truly *complete* when she is fulfilling her fate in working together with a nagal, for 18 reduces to 9. Conversely, as we see from the equation above, the nagal draws double *courage* from the co-operation between him and the nagal woman, and since the *courage* that is demanded of him is more than the average human being is capable of, this added *courage* is something every nagal treasures above anything else in the world. Together these two beings give each other *courage*, and together they strive for *completion*, but in their heart of hearts knowing that neither of them can ever truly win. The nagal woman can at best, like her progenitor The World of Sorcerers, keep turning in upon herself in constantly becoming Every-Thing else in fulfilment of the purpose of the Unspeakable. The nagal can at best keep *hoping* that with every tiny bit of freedom achieved, his efforts at trying to restore and maintain *harmony and balance* are not in vain, even though again and again he faces defeat at every moment of every day. Yet such is the nature of these two beings, and such is their predilection, that neither are ever really happy and fulfilled unless they are fighting to find a way in which to turn an impossible battle into a battle that it is possible to win, even if just in some small way.

This then brings us to the nagal's Courier, a man whose predilection is most aptly for jewel 20, namely, *honour*, for realise that at the end of the day it is *honour* that is to be found at the core of any warrior's heart. Yet, as we have discussed many times before, the warrior's sense of *honour* is very different to that of the average man or woman. True *honour* is the product of the relationship between *humility and understanding* (2) and *absolute freedom* (0).

Although we have already dealt with both of these two jewels, namely, 2 and 0, it will benefit the reader greatly if we expand a bit more here on the deeper implications of that mysterious jewel which has no number, for although we assign the number zero to this jewel, the implications are that it is nothing, that is, No-Thing.

From the above it is immediately clear that to try to do justice to jewel 0 in this book is well-nigh impossible, for if the truth be told, many volumes can be devoted to just this one jewel alone, and still the reader will more than likely feel none the wiser, for how does one explain *that* which by its very nature is *no-thing*? Therefore let it suffice for our presen purposes merely to say that jewel 0, because it is no-thing, is the origin of all the jewels, as well as permeating them all. Like its progenitor, the *spirit of man*, the *nagal*, jewel 0 is the *void* containing every-thing, for as paradoxical as it may sound, the *void* is the ultimate in awareness, for within that *void* the nature, the meaning, and the purpose of all, stands revealed in the *eternal now*. From within the *void*, that is, from within that aspect of awareness to which no number is assigned, there are no questions, for there is no-thing to understand. Likewise, from within the *void*, there is no freedom, for there is no-thing from which to be free, and hence is it referred to as *absolute freedom*. Yet care should be taken not to take these statements at face value, for no-thing does not imply emptiness. The fact that the *void* is no-thing simply implies that it is not *that* which we can verbalise, for in essence it is the ineffable, the Unspeakable.

From what we have learned here, it should be clear that true *honour* is the product of the relationship between *humility and understanding* (2) and the *void* (0). The implications here are so vast that verbalisation is exceedingly difficult, but it will help to think of it in terms of what were probably the most profound words ever spoken by the philosopher Socrates when he said, "I am the wisest man in the whole world, for I alone know that I know nothing".

In this truly brilliant statement, Socrates tried his level best to verbalise the true nature of *honour*, and to the Toltec warrior who is thoroughly versed in the properties of words, those few words do indeed speak volumes. However, it takes a fair amount of explaining in order to qualify the nuances of these words and, in this respect, I personally have always been enormously envious of Socrates, for although those who are fully trained in the properties of words can verbalise anything that needs to be verbalised, the problem is that apprentices never come to the Warrior's Path already literate. However, to judge from the teachings of Socrates, his students were all fully literate when they came to him!

Nevertheless, realise that the overall import of this statement by Socrates is very much a statement of *humility*, in that Socrates *understood* enough about life to know that, relative to the greater life of which we are units, none of us knows much at all. It is only the ignorant fool living in the tiny cocoon of his view of the world who tends to think that his rational mind can provide the answers to everything. Therefore when Socrates said that he knows that he knows nothing, he was in fact stepping back to lower his head in utter humility, for he was fully willing to admit that even all of his wisdom as a philosopher was as nothing in comparison to all that he still did not know. To have such *understanding* that it automatically brings about *humility*, in itself already indicates the truly wise man.

Furthermore, in making reference to himself as "I alone", Socrates was referring to I, *the all-one*, meaning the *totality of the self*, and in saying that "I alone know", he was actually saying "I, the all-one know". It stands to reason that the only real knowledge there can be, is knowledge of the self, that is, knowledge of the *totality of the self* – the *all-one* – and when that knowledge is fully conscious, one can indeed say "I, the all-one know", or alternatively, "I know the all-one (which is me)". However, Socrates is not merely indicating that he knows the *totality of the self*, for he goes on to say "I alone know that", meaning "I, the all-one know *that*". What is *that*? Socrates himself answers this by saying "nothing", meaning *no-thing*, that aspect of awareness termed the *void*. However, he stresses the fact that this knowledge of the *void* is conscious, for he prefaces the answer with "I know (nothing)". In other words, what in effect Socrates is saying here, is "I know myself as the all-one who knows *that* termed no-thing, but I am fully conscious of what I know".

With such a knowledge, and with the *humility* that comes

with the full *understanding* of what it is he does know, Socrates has every right to proclaim himself a wise man. Furthermore, since he places his wisdom firmly in perspective by saying "the whole world", meaning that he grasps full well that there is only one life, and therefore also only one *totality of the self*, he is indeed the wisest man, for only the wisest of the wise have the *honour* necessary not to try claiming knowledge for the personal self.

Therefore in this one brilliant statement, Socrates not only describes the relationship between individual identity, the *totality of the self* and the *void*, but he also very neatly defines the true meaning of *honour* within the context of the interrelationship of the one life. This is about the best I can do to impart at least some *feeling* for what is implied by *honour*. If I were to describe it in a nutshell, I would say that true *honour* is that *humility* which overcomes a warrior in the moment when he or she comes to *understand* the deeper implications of what it is to be *absolutely free*. To know oneself to be one with all selves, good, bad and indifferent, is to *understand* the meaning of what it is to be *humbled*, and to stand free from the need to judge, and to stand free from being judged, is true *freedom*. In that *absolute freedom* there is no-thing other than an utter sense of beingness, and, in the final analysis, what else can *honour* be but *beingness*?

When the nagal and his Courier co-operate intelligently the result is:

$$18 + 20 = 11.$$

In other words, the relationship between the nagal and his Courier brings forth *strength*, a quality which both of them need in the fulfilment of their respective duties. From what we have already learned about numerology, it is clear that the *strength* referred to here is in reality the sum of *impeccability* and pure *fluidity*. The implications here are vast, but let it suffice to say that because, in an esoteric sense, the nagal represents *the nagal*, that is, the *spirit of man*, and because of the nature of his duties, the nagal is often required to act with an utter *fluidity* that has not yet been tried and tested within life upon the physical plane. This, of course, amounts to having to improvise in the moment and, as a result, the nagal often finds himself walking a very fine line indeed between leading others to freedom and being a complete fool. Naturally, in his close association with the nagal, the nagal's Courier runs a very similar risk, as indeed does the nagal woman, for the result of intelligent co-operation between these three beings is still *strength*:

$$18 + 20 + 9 = 11.$$

Bearing in mind that the South is *the gateway to the nagal's world*, it is not at all surprising to find that in the female South we have the three jewels, *impeccability* (10), *vitality* (19), and *guidance* (7). The Southerly Dreamer, being a warrior who is primarily concerned with nurturing the purpose of the Toltec unit, has the natural predilection for jewel 10, for without *impeccability* this lady would not be able to discriminate with any wisdom between what should be nurtured and what should be eliminated.

In order to grasp this fully, remember that 10 is in reality the product of the relationship between pure *fluidity* (1) and *absolute freedom* (0), and that the implication here is that where there is not fluidity of perception within the context of complete freedom from social conditioning, *impeccability* must perforce be distorted. Furthermore, from what we have already learned about *absolute freedom*, we see that the Southerly Dreamer too is deeply concerned with *pure fluidity* in relation to the *void*, but in a much more direct way than any of the other warriors who have double number jewels, for the simple reason that her jewel *is* 10.

Apropos the above, I must point out to the reader that the onus is on him or her to take the information imparted throughout this chapter, and also elsewhere throughout all of the books, and to compile his or her own notes on each of the jewels of awareness. It is not possible for me to keep repeating everything already stated in order to bring all statements together into one whole. Every apprentice is expected to do such correlation by and for him or herself, for only in this way does the apprentice really come to grips with the teachings, and only in this way is it possible for the nagal to keep covering new ground without the unnecessary waste of time in having to nurse the apprentice into doing his or her "homework". Having said this, there is now no need for me to expound any further upon jewel 10.

The Southerly Stalker has a predilection for jewel 19, for it must not be forgotten that the South is the place of *personal power,* and that *vitality* is an aspect of *energy* which is the product of *personal power.* Further, since all stalkers are primarily concerned with life upon the physical plane, this lady is acutely aware of the fact that true *vitality* is the sum of *impeccability* (10) and *completion* (9), for all *vitality* arises from *a job impeccably completed.* In other words, sloppy performances tend to drain one of *vitality,* whereas *impeccability* tends to revitalise one, in that it replenishes *personal power.* As is all too clear to see from this jewel, the product of the relationship between *fluidity* (1) and *completion* (9), is *impeccability* (10), implying that in order to bring anything to *completion impeccably* it is necessary to be *fluid.*

In the last sentence of the previous section I chose my words most specifically so as to demonstrate a point which, for the sake of simplicity, I have not yet mentioned, but one that should be mentioned here, for the careless apprentice all too often tends to overlook this important point. Realise that part of the usefulness of numerology is that, firstly, any numbers in an equation can be dealt with in the same way as in mathematics, in which case they yield useful definitions; and secondly, where numbers are not *equated* but merely *related,* these numbers can be swopped around without affecting the validity of their relationship, in which case we can clearly see the interdependence of the qualities represented by these numbers.

In looking at the example above, we see that jewel 19 is the product of the relationship between *fluidity* (1) and *completion* (9), but, as we already know, care must be taken to bear in mind that the type of *fluidity* we are referring to here is that *fluidity of perception* within the context of complete freedom from social conditioning which, in the final analysis, constitutes *impeccability* (10). Therefore it equally well makes sense to say that jewel 19 is also the sum of *impeccability* (10) and *completion* (9).

Now in working with the actual equation, we see that *impeccability* plus *completion* is equal to *vitality*:

$$10 + 9 = 19.$$

In other words, we immediately have a useful definition of what is meant by *vitality*. However, from this equation it is also clear to see that *impeccability* is equal to *vitality* minus *completion*, ($10 = 19 - 9$), an equation which points out a very subtle, but nonetheless exceedingly important implication, namely, that in order for a warrior to be impeccable he must have enough vitality to complete whatever is required of him. Not to have enough vitality would mean that the warrior runs into a deficit, in which case he will deplete himself and be no good to anyone, least of all to himself, or alternatively, he will just give up without having completed the task. Needless to say, in this equation we also get another definition of *impeccability*.

We can also see that *completion* is equal to *vitality* minus *impeccability*, ($9 = 19 - 10$), meaning that in order to bring anything to completion, the warrior must have sufficient vitality to sustain impeccability, for it stands to reason that if the warrior does not have sufficient vitality, his actions, physical, emotional and mental will be less than impeccable, and therefore the completion would also be less in quality. In this respect, realise that an equation of this type does not allow for anything that is not exact. In other words, this equation can only be true when $9 = 19 - 10$, for if it was, say $9 = 18.999 - 10$, or $9 = 18.999 - 9.25$, it would not be true; and if it was, say $9 = 20 - 11$, it would be true, but then we would not be talking about *completion* relative to *impeccability* and *vitality*. Once again this equation gives us a good definition of the deeper implications inherent within *completion*.

If we now consider the *relationship* existing between the digits of jewel 19, it becomes apparent that *vitality* comes about whenever we are fluid enough in our perception to bring that perception to its natural conclusion, that is, to its completion.

Further, in order to bring anything to a completion we need to be fluid enough in our perception to acquire the necessary vitality. Likewise, in order to be fluid in our perception, it implies that we must have sufficient vitality to bring that perception to completion, in that we are not simply going to take the perception at its face value and then leave it at that.

In relation to all of the above, and as an exercise in learning to work with numerology, the reader should try to work out for him or herself the implications and definitions that can be gleaned from the great many different equations which can be set up using the aspects of awareness. In this respect it is important to know that wherever there is a lack of something it is denoted by a negative sign. For example, what would be the quality of the end product if an individual does not handle a task impeccably?

In this case, where there is a *lack of impeccability*, but where we wish to know the quality of the end product, that is, *completion*, we simply set up the facts as *lack of impeccability* (-10) plus *completion* (9), and then finish the equation by filling in the answer. Therefore the equation would read as:

$$-10 + 9 = -1.$$

The implication here is that where a task is tackled with a *lack of impeccability* but is forced to *completion*, the result will be *negative fluidity*, meaning that the end product will be neither here nor there, in that it will have no clear definition, will serve no definite purpose, and will therefore not have any real value.

Having discussed the two females in the South, we still have to consider the Courier to the South, who has a predilection for jewel 7, namely, *guidance*. In order to grasp the deeper implications inherent within this prime number, it is important to know that 7 concerns the relationship between the *triplicity* of the *dreamer* and the *quaternary* of the *dreamed*. This is in truth a most abstruse subject which goes far beyond the scope of this book, so let it suffice for now simply to say that inherent within 7 is the very essence of intelligent co-operation, in that for any incarnation to have real meaning and purpose, there must be a fully intelligent co-operation between the *dreamer* and the *dreamed*. In fact, the *dreamer* always does co-operate fully and intelligently with the *dreamed*, but the same cannot always be said of the *dreamed*. Therefore what is implied by *guidance* is that the *dreamed* must be willing to *accept* the challenges posed for it within life upon the physical plane by the *dreamer*, for only in this way can there be a fully intelligent co-operation between both the *dreamed* and the *dreamer*. As a result, it would not be incorrect to say that 7 is also the number of intelligent co-operation.

When all three warriors in the female South co-operate intelligently with each other, the result is:

10 + 19 + 7 = 9.

This time we see that although the female South also brings about *completion*, this completion is the sum of *impeccability*, *vitality* and *guidance*; a total which speaks for itself. Where there is *impeccability* and *vitality*, coupled with the willingness to take *guidance* from the dreamer, anything can be resolved, that is, every challenge can be brought to a *completion*. It should therefore now be clear why the South should be termed *the gateway to the nagal's world*, for as we have already noted, the nagal not only needs *strength* (11) within himself, but likewise also demands *strength* from his unit of warriors, in that all challenges must be brought to *completion* (9).

When all of the warriors in both the male South and the female South co-operate intelligently, the result is:

(18 + 20) + (10 + 19 + 7) = 11 + 9 = 11.

Once again the implications are so simple as to speak for themselves, for it is quite evident that where the *strength* (11) of the male South is added to the *completion* (9) of the female South, that is, *impeccability* and *vitality*, coupled with the willingness to take *guidance* from the dreamer, there can only be one possible outcome, namely, a *strength* that has the potential to move mountains. Now add to this *strength* the jewel of the nagal woman, which is *completion*, and we see that *strength* only becomes stronger. Yet, if one looks again at the sum of the jewels in the South, *courage*, *honour*, *impeccability*, *vitality* and *guidance*, it is not difficult to grasp why the quality of *warmth* should be assigned to this quarter, the place of *nurturing*, and if we add to that *warmth* and *nurturing* the *completion* brought forth by the nagal woman, it is also not difficult to grasp why this should be the place of *power*.

Finally we come to the North, the place of materialisation, and that mystical place in which are coalesced the Mists of Dragon Lore. This is the very *centre of the world*, also known as the *pivot of the three rings*, the place of *action*, and the *battlefield* of the warrior.

In the male North, as can be expected, we find The Man of Action, whose natural predilection is for jewel 6, namely, *choosing between the old and the new*. Because we have already covered the significance of this prime number we do not need to dwell upon it again here, other than to point out that all action, in order to be true *action*, rather than *reaction*, must have its basis in the act of *discrimination*. If this were not so, then all *action* would amount to nothing but *folly*. Only where there has been a careful *choosing between* what has served a purpose, and that which is now needed, can *action* be controlled *folly*. Consequently The Man of Action is really very much considered the master of *controlled folly*, and because of the humour inherent within all *folly*, this man can always find something to laugh about, no matter what the situation may be. As a result, The Man of Action is traditionally referred to as *The Clown* amongst his fellow warriors, for even when everything else may have failed, this man's innate sense of humour never fails.

Moreover, because it is the principal duty of the nagal to guide his unit of warriors to freedom, he is obviously constantly on the lookout for what constitutes the *needs* of the unit in the moment and, as a result, there is always a very close bond between the nagal and The Man of Action. That bond is the sum of their jewels, namely:

18 + 6 = 15.

Courage plus the ability to *choose between the old and the new* often sends these two men deep into the unknown, to search there for the *light* which must come *through the darkness* inherent within any challenge. In times like this, it is once again the humour of The Man of Action that will make even the most serious challenge seem hysterically funny, and through that rare ability to see *the lighter side* of life, the *light* can indeed always be found.

Attendant to The Man of Action is his Courier. Because of his close association with The Man of Action, whose predilection is for *choosing between the old and the new,* this man, as can be expected, has a predilection for jewel 8, *harmony and balance.* Once again we do not need to dwell upon this jewel, for we have already covered its significance.

Intelligent co-operation between these two warriors yields *knowledge,* that is, *new knowledge* (14):

6 + 8 = 14.

Since we have already discussed the implications inherent within this concept, we only need to point out how very different from the Scholar's *knowledge* is the *quality* of *knowledge* brought forth here. The reason for this is self-evident, for clearly the constituents are completely different, but presently we will be taking a much closer look at the deeper implications of this fact.

Naturally, because the Courier of The Man of Action has a predilection for jewel 8, this fosters also in him a very close association with the nagal, with the result that not only is there a close bond between the nagal and The Man of Action, but also between their respective Couriers. Once again this bond is the sum of the jewels:

18 + 20 + 6 + 8 = 16.

In other words, where there is *courage, honour,* the ability *to choose between the old and the new,* as well as *harmony and balance, liberation through the power of intent* (16) is the inevitable result.

In our consideration of the female North, we will this time first consider the Northerly Stalker. This lady has a predilection for jewel 4, namely, *stability*. This too is a prime number we have already discussed, but in connection with the Northerly Stalker it is important to know that, apart from everything we have already noted, this number is the one most directly concerned with the fourfold purpose of the Unspeakable, and therefore with The World of Sorcerers. Consequently this lady busies herself with finding out as much as she possibly can about how that purpose tends to manifest itself in terms of *potential* within life upon the physical plane. In other words, the Northerly Stalker is the warrior within the Toltec unit who is eventually the most adept at working with the *tensions* within the web of life.

However, being fully aware of the fact that her jewel has the dual quality of both *stability* and *inertia*, the Northerly Stalker works with *tension* in the sense of keeping those *tensions* as *stable* as possible, for, as paradoxical as it may sound, it is only in this way that *inertia* can be offset. To grasp this fully is not all that easy, but it will help to think of it in terms of *movement*. Realise that all *action* arises out of *tension*. Therefore if we look at something like the pendulum of a clock, we see that the perpetual movement of that pendulum is dependent upon the tension in the spring which drives the pendulum. Clearly, unless the tension within that spring is maintained, the movement of the pendulum will tend towards *inertia*. Although this example is overly simplistic when it comes to the reality of working with the *tensions* within the web of life, it nonetheless serves our present purposes reasonably well. Much later in the teachings, when we again return to the concept of *tension*, we will be able to look at this concept in greater detail.

From the above it is therefore clear to see that the Northerly Stalker, in working so directly with *tensions*, not only tends to direct them with her stalker's ability, but also more often than not tends to fuel them! This is an occupation which has earned for the Northerly Stalker the traditional nickname of *The Spoon*, for she does indeed spend most her time stirring!

The Northerly Dreamer too is highly sensitive to *tension*, but because her predilection is for *strength*, jewel 11, she tends to explore *tensions* much more from the angle of how they may be used in the sense of playing one off against another. In order to grasp this, realise that 11 is in reality the sum of *impeccability* (10) and pure *fluidity* (1). In other words, this lady is primarily concerned with how she can reconcile *impeccability* with the pure *fluidity* of *tensions* existing within the web of life. This is an act which requires considerable skill in being able to negotiate a fine line between remaining *impeccable*, and being an "absolute twit", as the Northerly Dreamer within my own unit often calls herself. In having this predilection for playing a fine line, this lady has a most natural aptitude for politics, and therefore if her counterpart is *The Spoon*, then traditionally this lady is *The Cauldron*. Therefore between the Northerly Stalker's stirring, and the Northerly Dreamer's cooking up of plots, the North, like any battlefield, is treacherous to say the least! Yet realise also that just as it takes *power* to meet *power*, so does it take *treachery* to survive the *trickery of the spirit*.

Attendant to the two Northerly ladies is their Courier; a man whom one would not expect to find in the company of these two ladies, for his predilection is for jewel 21, namely, *peace*. And yet, once again this is a fine example of why it is so important not to take words at their face value. True *peace* is in reality *honour* (20) plus pure *fluidity* (1), and from what we have noted in connection with the Northerly Dreamer, it is clear to see that this man too has a natural love for danger.

To reconcile *honour* and pure *fluidity*, that is, a *fluidity* which has not yet been tried and tested within life upon the physical plane, is likewise to negotiate a very fine line indeed, and yet it is easy to see how every *success* in such a dangerous operation cannot fail to bring *peace* to the individual concerned. There is nothing more satisfying than to know that although you could have ended up in total disgrace, *success* has brought even more *honour*, or at least, for the moment. Next time, who knows? It could be quite different, but for now there is only the sweetness of that *peace* which comes from knowing that one has survived a dangerous job well done.

Intelligent co-operation between the three warriors in the female North is:

$4 + 11 + 21 = 9$.

From what we have already learned from all of the above, it is clear to see that *completion* in the North is once again utterly different in quality to that in any of the other three quarters. Here in the place of *action, completion* is a risky business, for by its very nature it is based upon a most tenuously delicate set-up – a set-up that can perhaps be best described as a *fragile truce*. What with the dual nature of *stability*, the political uncertainties inherent within *strength*, and the dubious future of *peace and success, completion* in the North can at best be looked upon as a *stepping stone* that is in every possible way only *the calm before the storm. Materialisation* must be kept *fluid*, for never can *the centre of the world* become *inert*, because if it did, the fourth dimension would collapse in upon itself and the evolution of awareness would cease. Therefore with every step taken the previous stepping stone becomes undone within the *stream of life*. Such is the way in which *power* has set it up, and therefore to these three warriors in the female North, not only is danger the name of the game they play, but so too is love of danger their deepest predilection. The sheer *daring* of these three warriors is such that they will not hesitate to jump in where angels fear to tread.

Intelligent co-operation between the warriors of the male North and the female North is:

$(6 + 8) + (4 + 11 + 21) = 14$.

The implications here are such that we can choose to make them as complicated or as simple as we wish. My own particular preference is for simplicity, for when one is engaged in fighting for survival upon the battlefield of life, it is invariably the simple things in life that become the most profound, and which convey the most poignant meaning. Therefore, from my perspective, the nicest way in which to enter into battle is with *knowledge*, with *daring* and, of course, with *humour*.

In the face of the incredible odds against one, how can one

not have humour? Not to have humour would mean that we take ourselves seriously, in which case the odds against us are such that the most overpowering sense of apathy would overcome us even before the battle is engaged. On the other hand, to retain one's sense of humour in the face of all the odds against us, means that we do not take ourselves seriously, but instead we *go in there* and we give it our everything. And when we feel as if we have nothing left to give, then we recall that *the only failure in life is the failure to fight*. In that moment the impeccability of the warrior's spirit surfaces to spur us on into renewed effort, and to inspire us with an even greater strength of purpose than ever before. Therefore, to take ourselves seriously is to succumb to our *folly*, whereas not to take ourselves seriously is to know with every fibre of our being that all we can do is to *control our folly*.

WE DO NOT CONTROL LIFE. WE CAN AT BEST CONTROL THE WAY
IN WHICH WE SURF THE WAVES UPON THE OCEAN OF LIFE.

If we *go in there* with *knowledge*, with *daring* and with *humour*, and give it everything we've got, then irrespective of whether we win the battle or not, we will come out the other side having learned a great deal. Therefore once again we will have acquired *new knowledge* through practical experience, and that *power* is ours for the keeping - *personal power* that the warrior uses in order to claim his *freedom*, for remember always that 14 reduces to 5.

In having looked at all twenty-one and, in fact, at all twenty-two aspects of awareness, we have also seen how these interrelate with one another. Thus it should now be relatively clear how the warrior uses the different aspects of awareness in his or her pursuit of *power* and freedom, for although we have been considering the aspects of awareness in relation to the Toltec unit, realise that the Toltec unit is only a physical plane model of true *man* - that magical creature of the universe that is essentially a fourth-dimensional being. Consequently, when we look at the result of intelligent co-operation between all of the warriors within a Toltec unit, we see that this result is, as we can expect, the sum of the totals in each direction, that is:

13 + 13 + 11 + 14 = 15.

The implication here is that through their combined efforts, the Toltec unit of warriors brings forth *light through darkness*, which, in the final analysis, boils down to the ability to *choose between the old and the new*, for realise that 15 reduces to 6.

This is the purpose of true *man*, standing erect along the vertical axis, North-South, and with his arms stretched sideways along the horizontal axis, East-West. By embracing both life and death equally, *man* unites the faculties of *mind* and *heart* to bring about a *stability* acquired through the *death of the old*. Then by "grounding" that *stability* in a *strength* acquired through his predilection for *warmth*, for *nurturing* and for *power*, he triumphs in achieving a *knowledge* through his *daring action* that enables him to transmute *darkness* into *light* - a *knowledge* which is true *power*, and a *knowledge* that places him firmly within the realm of magical creatures.

Such is the nature of true *man*, and such is his divine destiny. By having the ability to wield the *power* inherent within each of the twenty-one aspects of awareness, *man* is the master of The World of Sorcerers – a world in which he is as much at home as he is upon the dense physical plane and as he is in his natural abode termed MEST.

In all of the above we have at least gained some perspective on how *man* is meant to use the twenty-one keys to The World of Sorcerers, and what the results are in making use of those keys. If we look carefully at everything we have learned so far, we see that the four female directions, embodied within the nagal woman, all add up to *completion*, jewel 9. However, when this *completion* is added to any one of the male directions, the *quality* of that particular male direction is not changed in any way; that is, the quality remains *untouched*, although, clearly, it has been enhanced by the addition of *completion*. Such is the nature of true *completion*, and such then is also the nature of The World of Sorcerers, for in essence it is the world of *completion*.

If you are not already a sorcerer, The World of Sorcerers is nothing! And because it is nothing it cannot make you a sorcerer. Yet to become a sorcerer in order to be able to access The World of Sorcerers is a fatal mistake, for to do so is never to learn the use of the twenty-one keys required to enter and exit that world. Those keys can only be mastered upon the Path of Freedom, and to enter The World of Sorcerers without them is a fool's venture - a venture from which you will not return to tell your tale.

Time and time again I am questioned on why it is not possible to access The World of Sorcerers safely without the twenty-one keys, and time and time again am I forced to shake my head in silence, for how does one verbalise the ineffable? The only thing I can do is to stress over and over that The World of Sorcerers is a *fantasy* that is not a fantasy; to stress that it is a *potential* that is more real than reality because of its *non-materiality*; to stress that it is the fourfold purpose of the Unspeakable which has neither beginning nor end, neither definition nor substance in terms of human definition and substance. To enter such a world without the relevant keys that enable one to remain *untouched* by the *power* of that world, is to become lost in a maze of *endlessness* or *beginningness*, depending upon where we should choose to place the focus.

Yet, once the twenty-one aspects of awareness have been mastered, any warrior can safely enter and exit The World of Sorcerers at will, for with those keys he or she is master of the four directions, and with four directions at his or her fingertips, no warrior can ever become lost; not even in the utterly deceptive maze that constitutes The World of Sorcerers. In this respect, remember that The World of Sorcerers, like all of the worlds, exists in four different dimensions, collectively termed MEST; the fourth dimension. However, since each expression of MEST is a particular expression of the fourfold purpose of the Unspeakable, it stands to reason that The World of Sorcerers is a very different place within, say *time*, as opposed to, say *energy*. Although this is true of all ten of the worlds, it is particularly relevant with regard to The World of Sorcerers, for being the *reflection* of the fourfold purpose of the Unspeakable, it is impossible to distinguish in which dimension one finds oneself once one is within this world. Yet, again, it is only by being able to use the twenty-one keys with skill that one can find one's way around and, most importantly, out of The World of Sorcerers.

In time to come, once it becomes possible to give the Sorcerer's Explanation, all of the above should make a great deal more sense than it possibly does right now. And yet, you, as the reader, have already been given more than enough information here to start working at "collecting" the twenty-one keys to The World of Sorcerers, and to start learning how to use these keys with skill, for with every skill mastered, you are in effect beginning to *align* The World of Sorcerers consciously.

In conclusion, remember that in all of what you have learned throughout this book, you have taken your first few steps towards beginning to coalesce the *Mists* of what in time will become *Dragon Lore* – the divine ability of man to conjure, and to work true magic – the magic of life. In this respect, aligning The World of Sorcerers is only one of those steps. Already in this book, and in the previous two books, you have learned many more. Whether you put those steps into practice and begin to walk, is up to you. Whether you turn your steps into sprinting, is also up to you. And whether you will ever gain enough impetus from your steps to fly, is equally much up to you.

That you may find your way, and in finding your way, take flight, is my deepest wish for you all, for at the end of the day, there is no greater *joy* than when you *go in there*, to give it your everything, your all! Remember this always, for in treading the Warrior's Path the odds against are truly astronomical. I say this, not because I wish to dismay you, or to dishearten you, but to point out that so often even a highly-talented apprentice will turn away from the Warrior's Path just because he has succumbed to his folly. In moments like that, should you ever feel it is too much to go on, should you ever feel that you will never make it, then remember my words:

AS WARRIORS WE GO IN THERE AND WE GIVE IT OUR EVERYTHING. AND WHEN WE FEEL AS IF WE HAVE NOTHING LEFT TO GIVE, THEN WE RECALL THAT THE ONLY FAILURE IN LIFE IS THE FAILURE TO FIGHT. IN THAT MOMENT THE IMPECCABILITY OF THE WARRIOR'S SPIRIT SURFACES TO SPUR US ON INTO RENEWED EFFORT, AND TO INSPIRE US WITH AN EVEN GREATER STRENGTH OF PURPOSE THAN EVER BEFORE.

THE TOLTEC UNIT

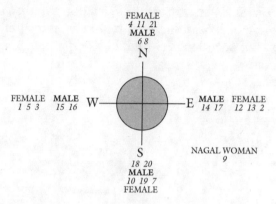

FIGURE 7

TABLE OF JEWELS

DIREC-TION	MALE			FEMALE		
EAST	Scholar Courier	14 17	Knowledge Discrimination	Dreamer Stalker Courier	13 12 2	Death Forebearance Destiny
WEST	Man Behind Scenes Courier	16 15	Intent Light Through Darkness	Dreamer Stalker Courier	1 5 3	Fluidity Freedom and Change Mixed Abundance
SOUTH	Nagal Courier	18 20	Courage Honour	Dreamer Stalker Courier	10 19 7	Impeccability Vitality Guidance
				Nagal Woman	9	Completion
NORTH	Man of Action Courier	6 8	Choosing Between Old and New Harmony and Balance	Dreamer Stalker Courier	11 4 21	Strength Stability Peace and Success

FIGURE 8

APPENDIX

THE VARIOUS RANKS ACCORDED WITHIN THE TOLTEC TRADITION

RANK	DESCRIPTION
APPRENTICE	A newly recruited novice
HUNTER	An apprentice who has achieved a working knowledge of what it is to hunt for *power*
WARRIOR	A hunter who has achieved a working knowledge of the First and Second Attention
WARRIOR OF THE FIRST ATTENTION	A hunter who has mastered the First Attention and who has a working knowledge of the Second Attention
WARRIOR OF THE SECOND ATTENTION	A Warrior of First Attention who has achieved a high level of skill in the three principal techniques
TOLTEC (OF THE FIRST ATTENTION)	A Warrior of the Second Attention who is a seer and who has taken responsibility for leading his/her people

At this point every Toltec has the choice between following the Path of High Adventure or the Path of Freedom. For those who choose to follow the Path of High Adventure the highest rank accorded remains that of Toltec, but for those who choose the Path of Freedom there are a further three ranks as follows:

WARRIOR OF THE THIRD ATTENTION	A Warrior of the Second Attention who has chosen the Path of Freedom and who therefore also has the rank of Atl'aman
TOLTEC OF THE SECOND ATTENTION	A Warrior of the Third Attention who is a seer with enough knowledge of the Second Attention to be able to lead his/her people wisely within the unknown
TOLTEC OF THE THIRD ATTENTION	A Toltec of the Second Attention who has a considerable knowledge of the Second Attention, and who is actively engaged in pioneering work
ATL'AMAN	This rank is accorded to any warrior or Toltec, irrespective of rank, once such a warrior or Toltec has proved him/herself dedicated to the purpose of the Spirit of Atl

Nagals and nagal women who are Toltecs of the Third Attention are given an honorary name by their fellow Toltecs which serves as their official title for all lifetimes thereafter. This name denotes both their training and lineage as from the time of having been accorded the rank of Atl'aman.

INDEX

B

F

G

H

Listening, 196, 261
  defined, 197
  to the heart, 146, 151, 278, 279
    defined, 151
    importance of, 147, 278, 279
    meaning of, 126, 148
    misconceptions regarding,
      147
Love, 154
Lost star, a, 68
Lucifer, 186, 187
Luminous cocoon, the, 147

M

Magic, ii, 41, 44, 308
  defined, 65
  nature of, 18
  the key to, 20, 65
  types of, iii, 42
Male, the,
  East, 269, 270, 273
  nature of, 264
  North, 300, 301
  purpose of, 264
  South, 267, 286, 288, 294,
    295, 301
  West, 277, 279
Man,
  accusations of, 185
  actions of, 109, 184, 287, 290
  band of, 58
  becoming, 20, 141
  beginnings of true, 19
  dark side of, 185
  destiny of, 306
  four groups of men and women,
    264
  heritage of, vi, 12, 81, 247
  horizontal axis of, 285, 286
  hour of power for, 81
  journey of, 46
  life of, 109, 123, 216
  luminous cocoon of, 58
  magic of, 18

  mistakes of, 57, 231, 251
  nature of, iv, vi, 10-16, 18, 19,
    27, 41-43, 46, 57, 58, 63,
    81, 107, 108, 134, 142, 184,
    196, 216, 240, 247, 250,
    253, 256, 264, 286, 306,
    308
  odds against, 181
  potential of, 11, 18, 27, 41, 43
  power of, 42, 43
  predilection of, 306
  questions of, 227
  responsibility of, vi, 81
  ten points of, 183
  the spirit of, 55, 58, 59, 140,
    224, 225, 292
Man Behind the Scenes, the,
  courier of, 277, 278
  predilection of, 277, 278
Manifestation, 259
Man of Action, the,
  courier to, 301
  predilection of, 300, 301
Materialisation,
  defined, 289
  nature of, 259, 260, 276, 289,
    290, 304
  of potential, 69
MEST,
  analogy of, 258
  and the four directions, 259
  and the four postulates of
    stalking, 170
  nature of, 171, 257, 289, 307
  secrets of, 257
Metaphor, 30, 31
Mind,
  caught in the, 61, 63, 68
  centre of the, 149
  defined, 66
  manipulation of the, 67
  nature of the, 39, 43, 58, 66,
    67, 151, 207, 277, 286, 306
  power of the, 67
  the finite (rational), 27
  the group, 224

CRY OF THE EAGLE

The Toltec Teachings – Volume Two

Cry of the Eagle is the sequel to *Return of the Warriors*. In this book Théun expands upon the fundamental concepts contained in Volume I, and also presents the more advanced teachings and techniques of the Warriors Path. Some of the concepts covered in this second book represent the closely-guarded inner teachings of the Toltec tradition, which have never before been openly disclosed: most notably, the teachings given on the mystery of awareness as revealed in the hidden potential of men and women, the dreamer and the dreamed, and dancing with death.

As he continues with his task of revealing all of the Toltec teachings, which he claims are mankinds rightful heritage, Théun, in *Cry of the Eagle*, provides further insights into the value and purpose of practical techniques such as stopping the internal dialogue, stopping the world, handling the four natural enemies of mankind, and Toltec dreaming. Illustrating the various concepts and techniques with examples taken from the daily life of average men and women, the author takes the reader through the teachings step by step in a manner that is designed to be accessible to everyone.

This is a highly valuable handbook for anyone who is serious about wanting to study this powerful and ancient tradition. It is also recommended to students of comparative religious studies, who will benefit from the information imparted on the well-kept secrets of the Qabalah and mystical Christianity.

THIS DARNED ELUSIVE HAPPINESS

The source of nearly all of the world's problems, as well as the problems in our lives, can be traced to a fundamental breakdown in our relationships.

In spite of centuries of progress, as well as thousands of books on this subject, why is it that we still fall down when it comes to handling our relationships?

In this easy-to-read book Théun Mares gives us some answers, and shows how the whole of life exists as a thoroughly interrelated web of relationships. Taking the reader step by step through an understanding of what it is to relate to the self, as well as to one's own gender. Théun reveals the most astounding truths concerning men, women and children, and provides the tools with which to handle any type of relationship, whether a romantic relationship, a business relationship, the relationship with your child, or with yourself.

NEXT IN THE TOLTEC TEACHINGS SERIES

SHADOWS OF WOLF FIRE
By Théun Mares

Freedom is not just a mythical nebulous concept out there. True freedom needs to be fought for, and attained. To understand what freedom really means, we need to go back to its origins.

In this fourth volume Théun lifts the veils of myth as he takes the reader back to the roots of freedom buried within another time, another place – a time when the Wolf People were reared as hounds of war in a place that knew only the sounds of war and not of peace – a time when the hope engendered by the concept of freedom came into being amidst the explosive chaos of the birth of an infant sun – a time when this concept went echoing across the galaxy like the haunting howl of a lone wolf, and only those from the Dog Star dared to answer.

Having gone back to the very beginning Théun goes on to show what freedom means in the world today, and how, in practical terms, we can set about achieving it in our lives.

INSTITUTE FOR THE STUDY OF MAN

Practical courses and workshops based on the
Toltec Teachings.

Elizabeth Schnugh is director and founder of the Institute for the Study of Man, which provides practical courses based on the Toltec approach to life.

Her ten-year experience as financial director of a large multi-national company convinced Elizabeth that a radical change was needed in the ways in which we do things, as well as in the ways in which we relate to each other, and life.

She has been working closely with Théun over the past few years to design and present a series of courses with the emphasis on providing people with tools with which to uplift themselves and to change their lives.

Elizabeth says: *The bottom line for every single person is to believe that they do have the answers for themselves. We teach people to address the issues in their lives from where they originate, rather than treat the symptoms. What this boils down to is handling relationships, for at the end of the day all of life is about relationships. We give people practical tools to transform all types of relationships, and we address them at all levels.*

For further details, as well as information on organising courses in your country, please contact:

INSTITUTE FOR THE STUDY OF MAN

P O Box 2294 Clareinch 7740 Cape Town South Africa
Telephone: 27-21-683 5892
Fax: 27-21-683 0084

COURSES AND FESTIVALS
run by Théun

Apart from his own full-time apprentices, and those who come to him on a consultation basis, Théun also has other people working under his guidance towards the furtherance of the evolution of awareness through the medium of the Toltec tradition.

Théun also runs two residential courses revealing the deeper implications of the Warrior's Path – *A Leap to Freedom*, and *On the Fringes of Power*. In addition, he runs a course specifically designed for men, in which men are brought face to face with the true meaning of masculinity and what it is to be male according to the dictates of the Warrior's Path. The male course – *The Power of the Male* – is supplemented by on-going workshops run by Deon Marais, one of Théun's apprentices.

The female equivalent of this course – *The Mysteries of the Female* – as well as its supplementary workshops, is run by Elizabeth Schnugh, who is also an apprentice of Théun. Both Théun and Marianne, the nagal woman, play an active role in providing guidance at these supplementary workshops.

From 1999 Théun will be reviving the ancient annual festivals in an effort to put men and women back in touch with their innermost core, and the relationship between that core, the planet, the solar system, interstellar activity, and the unseen worlds of both the organic as well as the inorganic life-streams constituting the universe. Due to the demands upon his time, Théun will run just one of these twelve festivals per year, meaning that each festival will occur only once every twelve years. For detailed information on either these courses, or the festivals, visit our website **www.toltec-foundation.org**, or contact Lionheart Publishing directly at the address printed overleaf.

ORDERING OUR BOOKS

Order our books from your favourite bookstore.

Alternatively, detailed ordering information, as well as online purchase options, can be found on our website:
www.toltec-foundation.org

For direct sales in the USA, call toll-free: 1-888-822-6657

For direct Sales in England and neighbouring areas call:
44-1206-255777

Otherwise please contact us directly.

Lionheart Publishing
Private Bag X5
Constantia 7848
Cape
South Africa

Telephone: 27-21-794 4923
Fax: 27-21-794 1487
email: cajmi@iafrica.com
www.toltec-foundation.org

Our website contains more information about the Toltec teachings and courses. We will also be posting regular articles of interest. Come and visit us!